IFIP Advances in Information and Communication Technology   496

Editor-in-Chief

Kai Rannenberg, Goethe University Frankfurt, Germany

Editorial Board

TC 1 – Foundations of Computer Science
  Jacques Sakarovitch, Télécom ParisTech, France
TC 2 – Software: Theory and Practice
  Michael Goedicke, University of Duisburg-Essen, Germany
TC 3 – Education
  Arthur Tatnall, Victoria University, Melbourne, Australia
TC 5 – Information Technology Applications
  Erich J. Neuhold, University of Vienna, Austria
TC 6 – Communication Systems
  Aiko Pras, University of Twente, Enschede, The Netherlands
TC 7 – System Modeling and Optimization
  Fredi Tröltzsch, TU Berlin, Germany
TC 8 – Information Systems
  Jan Pries-Heje, Roskilde University, Denmark
TC 9 – ICT and Society
  Diane Whitehouse, The Castlegate Consultancy, Malton, UK
TC 10 – Computer Systems Technology
  Ricardo Reis, Federal University of Rio Grande do Sul, Porto Alegre, Brazil
TC 11 – Security and Privacy Protection in Information Processing Systems
  Steven Furnell, Plymouth University, UK
TC 12 – Artificial Intelligence
  Ulrich Furbach, University of Koblenz-Landau, Germany
TC 13 – Human-Computer Interaction
  Marco Winckler, University Paul Sabatier, Toulouse, France
TC 14 – Entertainment Computing
  Matthias Rauterberg, Eindhoven University of Technology, The Netherlands

IFIP – The International Federation for Information Processing

IFIP was founded in 1960 under the auspices of UNESCO, following the first World Computer Congress held in Paris the previous year. A federation for societies working in information processing, IFIP's aim is two-fold: to support information processing in the countries of its members and to encourage technology transfer to developing nations. As its mission statement clearly states:

> IFIP is the global non-profit federation of societies of ICT professionals that aims at achieving a worldwide professional and socially responsible development and application of information and communication technologies.

IFIP is a non-profit-making organization, run almost solely by 2500 volunteers. It operates through a number of technical committees and working groups, which organize events and publications. IFIP's events range from large international open conferences to working conferences and local seminars.

The flagship event is the IFIP World Computer Congress, at which both invited and contributed papers are presented. Contributed papers are rigorously refereed and the rejection rate is high.

As with the Congress, participation in the open conferences is open to all and papers may be invited or submitted. Again, submitted papers are stringently refereed.

The working conferences are structured differently. They are usually run by a working group and attendance is generally smaller and occasionally by invitation only. Their purpose is to create an atmosphere conducive to innovation and development. Refereeing is also rigorous and papers are subjected to extensive group discussion.

Publications arising from IFIP events vary. The papers presented at the IFIP World Computer Congress and at open conferences are published as conference proceedings, while the results of the working conferences are often published as collections of selected and edited papers.

IFIP distinguishes three types of institutional membership: Country Representative Members, Members at Large, and Associate Members. The type of organization that can apply for membership is a wide variety and includes national or international societies of individual computer scientists/ICT professionals, associations or federations of such societies, government institutions/government related organizations, national or international research institutes or consortia, universities, academies of sciences, companies, national or international associations or federations of companies.

More information about this series at http://www.springer.com/series/6102

Federico Balaguer · Roberto Di Cosmo
Alejandra Garrido · Fabio Kon
Gregorio Robles · Stefano Zacchiroli (Eds.)

Open Source Systems: Towards Robust Practices

13th IFIP WG 2.13 International Conference, OSS 2017
Buenos Aires, Argentina, May 22–23, 2017
Proceedings

Editors
Federico Balaguer
National University of La Plata
La Plata
Argentina

Roberto Di Cosmo
Inria and Paris Diderot University
Paris
France

Alejandra Garrido
National University of La Plata
La Plata
Argentina

Fabio Kon
University of São Paulo
São Paulo
Brazil

Gregorio Robles
Universidad Rey Juan Carlos
Madrid
Spain

Stefano Zacchiroli
Paris Diderot University and Inria
Paris
France

ISSN 1868-4238   ISSN 1868-422X (electronic)
IFIP Advances in Information and Communication Technology
ISBN 978-3-319-57734-0   ISBN 978-3-319-57735-7 (eBook)
DOI 10.1007/978-3-319-57735-7

Library of Congress Control Number: 2017938159

© The Editor(s) (if applicable) and The Author(s) 2017. This book is an open access publication.
Open Access This book is licensed under the terms of the Creative Commons Attribution 4.0 International License (http://creativecommons.org/licenses/by/4.0/), which permits use, sharing, adaptation, distribution and reproduction in any medium or format, as long as you give appropriate credit to the original author(s) and the source, provide a link to the Creative Commons license and indicate if changes were made.
The images or other third party material in this book are included in the book's Creative Commons license, unless indicated otherwise in a credit line to the material. If material is not included in the book's Creative Commons license and your intended use is not permitted by statutory regulation or exceeds the permitted use, you will need to obtain permission directly from the copyright holder.
The use of general descriptive names, registered names, trademarks, service marks, etc. in this publication does not imply, even in the absence of a specific statement, that such names are exempt from the relevant protective laws and regulations and therefore free for general use.
The publisher, the authors and the editors are safe to assume that the advice and information in this book are believed to be true and accurate at the date of publication. Neither the publisher nor the authors or the editors give a warranty, express or implied, with respect to the material contained herein or for any errors or omissions that may have been made. The publisher remains neutral with regard to jurisdictional claims in published maps and institutional affiliations.

Printed on acid-free paper

This Springer imprint is published by Springer Nature
The registered company is Springer International Publishing AG
The registered company address is: Gewerbestrasse 11, 6330 Cham, Switzerland

General Chair's Message

Free and open source software (FOSS) has gone through a series of phases, from a little-noticed movement, to early industry adoption in the lower levels of the software stack, to inroads in the vertical application market, to merely table stakes in modern software development: In recent years, disruptive applications in the trendy segment of machine learning are natively born as open source. There is no doubt that in just over 20 years FOSS has radically changed the way software is designed, developed, evolved, distributed, marketed, and sold.

One could be tempted to say that since FOSS is now mainstream across all layers of software development, with even its most fierce former opponents turning into fervent adopters, it has reached its maturity phase and there is no longer a need for a specialized forum dedicated to studying it, like the one OSS has being providing for over a decade.

Nothing could be further from the truth: With the huge number of newcomers that now embrace FOSS without having contributed to its evolution, and knowing very little of its values and inner workings, it is now more essential than ever to study, understand, and explain fundamental issues related to the business models, organizational structures, decision-making processes, quality metrics, and the evolution of the free and open source software ecosystems in general.

This effort involves a variety of scientific disciplines, ranging from core computer science, to social sciences and economics, and this work must be performed in close connection with the developer communities that are reshaping our software world daily.

We were, therefore, delighted to see this 13th International Conference on Open Source Systems, OSS 2017, continuing to provide an international forum where a diverse community of professionals from academia, industry, and the public sector, as well as developer communities, come together to share research findings and practical experiences, which form the necessary basis for developing a corpus of good practices that are needed now more than ever.

Organizing a conference always requires dedication and commitment from a motivated core group of people, who deserve the sincere gratitude of all our community. The program chairs, Gregorio Robles and Fabio Kon, spent considerable energy organizing the review process and setting up the conference program. The proceedings, which are for the first time available as Open Access thanks to a generous donation from the IRILL research initiative on free software, have been carefully edited by Stefano Zacchiroli; we do hope that all future conferences will follow this path. Bjorn Lundell, Paulo Meirelles, Diomidis Spinellis, and Megan Squire did a great job of promoting the conference, and Martin Michlmayr took care of the contact with the communities. Imed Hammouda and Greg Madey chaired the Doctoral Consortium, and Alessandra Garrido and Federico Balaguer were great local chairs. Tony Wasserman provided a precious link with IFIP. Cedric Thomas, OW2's CEO, immediately accepted the invitation to come and share his precious experience in an inspiring invited talk.

Finally, special thanks go to Sebastian Uchitel, the general chair of ICSE 2017, with whom I had the pleasure to work in close connection for more than a year in order to make the organization of the conference possible in Argentina: We were enchanted to have brought OSS 2017 and its community to "mi Buenos Aires querido."

March 2017   Roberto Di Cosmo

Program Chairs' Message

It is a great pleasure to welcome you to the proceedings of the 13th International Conference on Open Source Systems (OSS 2017). The range of papers published in *Open Source Systems: Towards Robust Practices* is a valuable addition to the existing body of knowledge in the field. Contributions cover a range of topics related to free, libre, and open source software (FLOSS), including: licensing, strategies, and practices; case studies; projects, communication, and participation; tools; project management, development, and evaluation.

The OSS 2017 conference represents a long-standing international forum for researchers and practitioners involved in a range of organizations and projects, to present and discuss insights, experiences, and results in the field of FLOSS. The maturity of research in our field is also reflected in the range and number of excellent contributions received.

We are very pleased to have received 32 contributions (28 full and four short paper submissions) for the technical program, from which we included 16 full papers and three short papers (representing an acceptance rate of 57% for full papers). Every paper received at least three reviews by members of the Program Committee, and was carefully discussed by Program Committee members until a consensus was reached. Based on the reviews for each paper, one of the two program chairs initiated an online discussion among the reviewers in order to reach consensus. The two program chairs facilitated this process for the different papers. All decisions were based on the quality of the papers, which considered the reviews and the outcome of the discussions. We did not have a minimum or maximum number of papers as a target. Five of the 16 papers were conditionally accepted, subject to the authors addressing the reviewers' comments and suggestions.

The program also included a keynote (by Cedric Thomas), a Posters and Tool Demonstration session, and a doctoral consortium with five PhD students presenting their progress to the community.

We want to give special thanks to all the people who allowed us to present such an outstanding program, and we would especially like to mention: the Program Committee members and additional reviewers; the community and publicity chairs; the session chairs; all the authors who submitted their papers to OSS 2017; the general chair (Roberto Di Cosmo), the Doctoral Consortium chairs (Imed Hammouda and Greg Madey), and the local organizers (Alejandra Garrido and Federico Balaguer). We are also grateful to a number of other people without whom this conference would not have happened, and with respect to preparing the proceedings we would like to specifically mention Stefano Zacchiroli for his support.

March 2017

Fabio Kon
Gregorio Robles

Organization

Organizing Committee

General Chair

Roberto Di Cosmo — Inria and Paris Diderot University, France

Program Chairs

Fabio Kon — University of São Paulo, Brazil
Gregorio Robles — Universidad Rey Juan Carlos, Spain

Local Organizing Chairs

Alejandra Garrido — LIFIA, Universidad Nacional de La Plata/CONICET, Argentina
Federico Balaguer — LIFIA, Universidad Nacional de La Plata, Argentina

Proceedings Chair

Stefano Zacchiroli — Paris Diderot University and Inria, France

Community Chair

Martin Michlmayr — HPE

Publicity Chairs

Latin America

Paulo Meirelles — UnB, Brazil

North America

Megan Squire — Elon University, USA

North Europe

Bjorn Lundell — HIS, Sweden

South Europe

Diomidis D. Spinellis — AUEB, Greece

Advisory Committee

Tony Wasserman   Carnegie Mellon University, USA
Imed Hammouda   Chalmers and University of Gothenburg, Sweden
Fulvio Frati   Università degli Studi di Milano, Italy

Program Committee

Chintan Amrit   University of Twente, The Netherlands
Alexandre Bergel   University of Chile, Chile
Cornelia Boldyreff   University of East London, UK
Jordi Cabot   ICREA – UOC (Internet Interdisciplinary Institute), Spain
Andrea Capiluppi   Brunel University, UK
Kevin Crowston   Syracuse University, USA
Jean Dalle   Pierre et Marie Curie University, France
Stéfane Fermigier   Nuxeo, France
Juan Galeotti   University of Buenos Aires, Argentina
Jesus Gonzalez-Barahona Universidad Rey Juan Carlos, Spain
Imed Hammouda   Chalmers and University of Gothenburg, Sweden
Ahmed Hassan   Queen's University, Canada
Akinori Ihara   Nara Institute of Science and Technology, Japan
Netta Iivari   University of Oulu, Finland
Terhi Kilamo   Tampere University of Technology, Finland
Stefan Koch   Bogazici University, Turkey
Fabio Kon   University of São Paulo, Brazil
Filippo Lanubile   University of Bari, Italy
Luigi Lavazza   Università degli Studi dell'Insubria, Italy
Walid Maalej   University of Hamburg, Germany
Tommi Mikkonen   Tampere University of Technology, Finland
Sandro Morasca   Università degli Studi dell'Insubria, Italy
John Noll   Lero – the Irish Software Engineering Research Centre, Ireland
Dirk Riehle   Friedrich Alexander University of Erlangen-Nürnberg, Germany
Gregorio Robles   Universidad Rey Juan Carlos, Spain
Barbara Russo   Free University of Bolzano/Bozen, Italy
Walt Scacchi   University of California, Irvine, USA
Diomidis Spinellis   Athens University of Economics and Business, Greece
Ioannis Stamelos   Aristotle University of Thessaloniki, Greece
Igor Steinmacher   Universidade Tecnológica Federal do Paraná, Brazil
Klaas Stol   Lero, Ireland
Davide Taibi   University of Bolzano-Bozen, Italy
Guilherme Travassos   COPPE/UFRJ, Brazil
Anthony Wasserman   Carnegie Mellon University Silicon Valley, USA
Jens Weber   University of Victoria, Canada

Sponsors

With the Support of

and

Contents

Projects, Communication, and Participation

Considering the Use of Walled Gardens for FLOSS Project Communication ... 3
   Megan Squire

Investigating Relationships Between FLOSS Foundations and FLOSS
Projects 14
   Juho Lindman and Imed Hammouda

Designing for Participation: Three Models for Developer Involvement
in Hybrid OSS Projects 23
   Hanna Mäenpää, Terhi Kilamo, Tommi Mikkonen, and Tomi Männistö

Principled Evaluation of Strengths and Weaknesses in FLOSS
Communities: A Systematic Mixed Methods Maturity Model Approach 34
   Sandro Andrade and Filipe Saraiva

Posters and Tools

Measuring Perceived Trust in Open Source Software Communities 49
   Mahbubul Syeed, Juho Lindman, and Imed Hammouda

The Open Source Officer Role – Experiences 55
   Carl-Eric Mols, Krzysztof Wnuk, and Johan Linåker

Digging into the Eclipse Marketplace 60
   Jacob Krüger, Niklas Corr, Ivonne Schröter, and Thomas Leich

Licensing, Strategies, and Practices

How are Developers Treating License Inconsistency Issues?
A Case Study on License Inconsistency Evolution in FOSS Projects 69
   Yuhao Wu, Yuki Manabe, Daniel M. German, and Katsuro Inoue

Addressing Lock-in, Interoperability, and Long-Term Maintenance
Challenges Through Open Source: How Can Companies Strategically
Use Open Source? 80
   Björn Lundell, Jonas Gamalielsson, Stefan Tengblad,
   Bahram Hooshyar Yousefi, Thomas Fischer, Gert Johansson,
   Bengt Rodung, Anders Mattsson, Johan Oppmark, Tomas Gustavsson,
   Jonas Feist, Stefan Landemoo, and Erik Lönroth

Understanding the Effects of Practices on KDE Ecosystem Health 89
  Simone da Silva Amorim, John D. McGregor,
  Eduardo Santana de Almeida, and Christina von Flach Garcia Chavez

Challenges in Validating FLOSS Configuration. 101
  Markus Raab and Gergö Barany

Case Studies

Progression and Forecast of a Curated Web-of-Trust:
A Study on the Debian Project's Cryptographic Keyring 117
  Gunnar Wolf and Víctor González Quiroga

Understanding When to Adopt a Library: A Case Study on ASF Projects . . . 128
  Akinori Ihara, Daiki Fujibayashi, Hirohiko Suwa,
  Raula Gaikovina Kula, and Kenichi Matsumoto

Adoption of Academic Tools in Open Source Communities:
The Debian Case Study 139
  Pietro Abate and Roberto Di Cosmo

Assessing Code Authorship: The Case of the Linux Kernel 151
  Guilherme Avelino, Leonardo Passos, Andre Hora,
  and Marco Tulio Valente

Project Management, Development and Evaluation

Release Early, Release Often and Release on Time.
An Empirical Case Study of Release Management 167
  Jose Teixeira

Technical Lag in Software Compilations: Measuring How Outdated
a Software Deployment Is 182
  Jesus M. Gonzalez-Barahona, Paul Sherwood, Gregorio Robles,
  and Daniel Izquierdo

OSSpal: Finding and Evaluating Open Source Software 193
  Anthony I. Wasserman, Xianzheng Guo, Blake McMillian, Kai Qian,
  Ming-Yu Wei, and Qian Xu

Longitudinal Analysis of the Run-up to a Decision to Break-up (Fork)
in a Community 204
  Amirhosein "Emerson" Azarbakht and Carlos Jensen

Author Index 219

Projects, Communication, and Participation

Considering the Use of Walled Gardens for FLOSS Project Communication

Megan Squire[✉]

Elon University, Elon, NC, USA
`msquire@elon.edu`

Abstract. At its core, free, libre, and open source software (FLOSS) is defined by its adherence to a set of licenses that give various freedoms to the users of the software, for example the ability to use the software, to read or modify its source code, and to distribute the software to others. In addition, many FLOSS projects and developers also champion other values related to "freedom" and "openness", such as transparency, for example in communication and decision-making, or community-orientedness, for example in broadening access, collaboration, and participation. This paper explores how one increasingly common software development practice - communicating inside non-archived, third-party "walled gardens" - puts these FLOSS values into conflict. If communities choose to use non-archived walled gardens for communication, they may be prioritizing one type of openness (broad participation) over another (transparency). We use 18 FLOSS projects as a sample to describe how walled gardens are currently being used for intra-project communication, as well as to determine whether or not these projects provide archives of these communications. Findings will be useful to the FLOSS community as a whole as it seeks to understand the evolution and impact of its communication choices.

Keywords: Open source · Free software · Communication · Email · Mailing list · IRC · Stack overflow · Slack · Apache · Wordpress · Teams · Chat

1 Introduction

A common denominator between all free, libre, and open source software (FLOSS) projects is that they provide users with a software license that allows the user some level of freedom to read, modify, or distribute the software source code. Echoing these freedoms, FLOSS software is also produced in such a way as to foster openness and collaboration. For example, transparency in decision-making and welcoming participation are key values that are common to many FLOSS projects. These values have been called "open from day one" [1], or a "bazaar" style of organization [2], and have been attributed to the "success of open source" [3]. More recently the so-called "open source way" [4] is described as "a way of thinking about how people collaborate within a community to achieve common goals and interests" when applied to non-software contexts.

One software development practice that has traditionally been cited in the literature to preserve this openness is using publicly archived mailing lists for decision-making and important project-related communication [5]. Mailing list archives preserve a **transparent** record of decision-making that can serve as an institutional memory and can help get new users up to speed quickly. Mailing lists also offer a **technological openness**, in other words a non-corporate-controlled, non-proprietary software system, ideally available under a FLOSS license. However, more recently, the FLOSS community has begun to ponder an additional perspective on openness: one that is defined by **inclusivity** and diversity of participation. [6–8] An industry publication recently bemoaned that older communication systems used in FLOSS (specifically IRC) are "complicated and unfriendly" and "the barrier to entry was a formidable challenge for the first time user" [9].

In this paper, we attempt to describe how one increasingly popular software development practice puts these openness values – openness through transparency and licensing, and openness through inclusivity – into conflict. Specifically, **communicating in "walled gardens"**, or non-open and corporate-controlled systems such as Slack or Stack Overflow, and **not keeping archives of this communication** puts the FLOSS goal of transparency into conflict with the goals of ease-of-use, inclusivity, and diversity of participation.

The remainder of this paper is organized as follows: first, we provide an overview of communication technologies used in FLOSS projects, and then we describe how a collection of 18 FLOSS projects currently relies on walled gardens for communication. For this, we use publicly available descriptions of existing FLOSS projects or repositories that are known to use walled gardens. By becoming aware of the size and scope of the practice of using walled gardens to communicate, the FLOSS community at large can choose how to react, including whether to embrace the practice, conduct additional research, take preventative measures, provide alternatives, or ignore the practice.

2 Communication Technology Used in FLOSS Projects

In keeping with the nature of FLOSS work as community-owned and community-driven, each individual software team makes the decisions about which communication technologies to use, and when to adopt or reject a new technology. Each team has its own requirements and makes its own determination of the positive and negative aspects of each communication choice. Here we describe two main types of technology, asynchronous and synchronous technologies, and how different FLOSS communities have used each one. For each category, we describe the alternatives in terms of the various "openness" values described previously: openness via transparency, openness via licensing and non-corporate control, and openness via inclusivity and ease-of-use.

2.1 Asynchronous Communication

Traditionally, many FLOSS communities have communicated using mailing lists. Some communities, such as the Apache project ecosystem, still require the use of mailing lists to conduct project business [10, 11]. There are several reasons for this preference. First, email is an **asynchronous** communication medium. Asynchronous communication allows for messages that can be sent and read at different times. (Other examples of asynchronous communication include paper mail, email, bulletin board systems, and Web sites.) Asynchronous communication works especially well for FLOSS teams that may be geographically distributed, since messages can be sent and read at the convenience of both parties.

Another feature of email mailing lists that is helpful to FLOSS development is the ease of creating browsable, searchable mailing list **archives**. Feller and Fitzgerald write, "Archived discussions, which represent 'self-documentation' of projects, are critical in OSS development."[5] Archives preserve a record of decisions and can help bring new contributors up to speed.

Finally, and significantly for many projects, generic email and mailing lists are **standards-based**, in that anyone can develop email software, and sending and receiving email requires no particular relationship or agreements with any single corporation. Email protocols and software are not owned or controlled by any one entity, corporate or otherwise. Generic email or mailing list systems can be contrasted with **proprietary**, but still asynchronous, systems such as the Google Groups web-based Usenet interface [12], or Stack Overflow, a web-based Question and Answer site increasingly used by many FLOSS projects to handle many kinds of technical support [13]. Colloquially, these closed, corporate-controlled systems are called **walled gardens**.

2.2 Synchronous Communication

Some FLOSS teams also elect to use **synchronous** communication technologies, such as chat or instant messaging, in which the users are communicating back and forth in real time. For example, FLOSS teams may conduct developer meetings using Internet Relay Chat (IRC) [14, 15]. Real-time chat systems, such as IRC (but also recently including new entrants into this space such as Rocketchat, Mattermost, Discord, or Slack), are also used to share ideas informally, to get immediate technical help, and to build camaraderie in the community [1]. Because of the ephemeral nature of chat, communities may not approach it with the same expectation of being a long-term archive as they would expect from an email mailing list. Still, some communities and IRC channels are archived, usually through the use of special archiving **bots**. One impressive example of chat archiving is the Ubuntu IRC log collection, which is available at http://irclogs.ubuntu.com. These archives cover discussions happening on nearly 300 different Ubuntu-related chat channels, starting in 2004.

As with email and asynchronous discussion systems, synchronous systems differ in whether they are a product of a single corporation, or whether they are a FLOSS-licensed or open protocol. For example, IRC is an application layer Internet protocol, and as such anyone can run a server or develop a client for it. In contrast, Slack (https://slack.com), is a synchronous chat system developed and operated by a corporation, and its rules about costs, archiving policies, data sharing, number of participants, and so on, are determined by the corporation alone. Slack has a single client, and a Terms of Service (ToS) that restrict its use. Slack is not FLOSS licensed. We therefore include corporate-controlled, non-FLOSS licensed synchronous messaging services such as Slack in our definition of **walled gardens**.

2.3 How FLOSS Values Conflict When Communicating in Walled Gardens

In 2015, FLOSS developer Drew Devault wrote a blog post entitled "Please don't use Slack for FOSS projects" which argued that Slack is a walled garden, and any trend toward adopting it should be curtailed in favor of continuing with IRC which he says is "designed to be open". [16] The comments section of this post illustrates the conflict between the value of open design on one hand, and the value of openness through ease-of-use and inclusivity on the other hand. In those 187 comments, the value of "openness" is invoked for both arguments. Similarly, the Wordpress project, in rationalizing their move to Slack for developer and user chat [17] gives six reasons for the move, and the first three of those have to do with the user interface: "Open for everyone, Friendly user interface, Easy asynchronous conversation". With their invocation of "open for everyone" they are certainly referring to usability and not licensing, since Slack is not open source [18]. Interestingly, they also laud the ability of Slack to function in an "asynchronous" way, specifically contrasting it with IRC and Skype (which they call "real-time"). For this paper, we will continue to refer to Slack as a synchronous technology.

A related values conflict is whether FLOSS projects using walled gardens are being "open" (in the sense of transparent) if they do not provide archives of their communications. Should FLOSS projects need to provide archives of their communications, and do certain communication technologies make archiving easier or harder? In general, the asynchronous communication technologies like web pages and mailing lists are stored as files, and as such, will be easier to archive. FLOSS email mailing lists are usually archived both by the projects themselves, and archives for many projects are also available for search/browsing/downloading via third-party web sites such as MarkMail (http://markmail.org) and Gmane (http://gmane.org). Even though IRC is a synchronous communication medium, since it was invented in 1988, it has had many years to develop logging and archiving features, including a diverse set of archive bots. Text-based IRC logs are publicly available for many large projects including Ubuntu, OpenStack, Puppet, Perl6, many Apache Software Foundation projects, and so on. Projects using third-party synchronous walled gardens like Slack have the technical capability to produce text logs, but as we will discuss in the next section, do not typically do so.

In the next section we begin to describe the increasing use of walled gardens by 18 popular FLOSS projects, including whether or not the communications are archived, and what the community's rationale is for using the walled garden.

3 Data on Walled Garden Usage in FLOSS Projects

The tables below show examples of FLOSS projects that have announced that they are using walled gardens as a primary communication channel. These tables focus on Slack as a walled garden since prior work already addressed the use of Stack Overflow for developer support [13], and because – as Sect. 4 will show – Stack Overflow's "garden walls" are substantially lower and more porous than the walls surrounding Slack.

In the tables, URLs containing references to the evidence are provided in the Appendix as [A1], [A2], and so on. Table 1 contains information for a general collection of FLOSS projects that rely on walled gardens for communication, and Table 2 contains information for only Apache Software Foundation (ASF) projects. We moved ASF projects into their own table so that they could be compared to each other, since they are all subject to the same rules about decision-making on mailing lists [10, 11].

Table 1. FLOSS projects using walled gardens for all or part of their communication

Community	Use of walled garden	Status of archives
Wordpress (all)	Moved from IRC to Slack. "Slack communication is used for contributing to the WordPress project, be it code, design, documentation, etc" [A1]	No consistent Slack archive. Occasional links to archives are posted (e.g. [A2]), but Slack login is required. The archives are not downloadable or searchable. IRC logs used to be available, but now only one channel is logged [A3]
Drupal (UX)	Uses Slack for "daily talk and weekly meetings" [A4]. Main site Drupal.org is still evaluating going to Slack in a two-year old thread still getting active comments [A5]	No Slack archive [A6]
Ghost	Users/devs "split between IRC and our forums" consolidated at Slack. Weekly meetings in Slack [A7]	Meeting summaries are available on [A8], but full logs require a Slack login
Socket.io	"Join our Slack server to discuss the project in realtime. Talk to the core devs and the Socket.IO community" [A9] [A10]	No Slack archive
Elementary OS	"we switched over to Slack from IRC/Google+ at … in the early summer. It's been a massive improvement." [A11] No links to join Slack on public web site [A12]. Uses Stack Exchange for "common questions" [A13] [A14] [A15]	No Slack archive. No local Stack Exchange archive
MidoNet	"We recently saw some other communities moving [IRC] over to Slack, and decided to make the jump ourselves" [A16]	Uses Slackarchive.io for archives. [A17]
Reactiflux/ React.js	Moved from Slack to Discord after getting too big and Slack refused new invites. [A18] Still has Freenode IRC channel. Stack Overflow recommended for questions [A19]	No Discord archive. No local Stack Exchange archive
Bitcoin-core	Most discussion happens on IRC. Mentions Slack in passing [A20]	Uses Slackarchive.io for archives. [A21]

Table 2. Apache Software Foundation projects using walled gardens for all or part of their communication

Community	Use of walled garden	Status of archives
Apache Cordova	Users can "Join the discussion on Slack" [A22], which "is a replacement for IRC, but not a replacement for decisions and voting, that still needs to be on the list" [A23]	No Slack archive
Apache Groovy	"The Slack channel is not endorsed by the Apache Software Foundation, It's run by Groovy enthusiasts in the community for casual conversations and Q&A. Official discussions must happen on the mailing lists only" [A24]	No Slack archive
Apache Hbase	Mailing lists still exist but "Our IRC channel seems to have been deprecated in favor of the above Slack channel" [A25] The Slack channel is only mentioned in Sect. 110.3 [A26] and 143.2 [A27] of the Reference Guide	No Slack archive
Apache Iota	"The user mailing lists … is the place where users of Apache iota ask questions and seek for help or advice.… Furthermore, there is the [apache-iota] tag on Stack Overflow if you'd like to help iota users there.… You are very welcome to subscribe to all the mailing lists. In addition to the user list, there is also an iota Slack channel that you can join to talk to other users and contributors" [A28]	No Slack archive
Apache Kudu	Slack is where "developers and users hang out to answer questions and chat" [A29]	No Slack archive
Apache Mesos and Aurora	Developers and users hang out in … Slack [A30] [A31] "Note that even if we move to Slack, we will make sure people can still connect using IRC clients and that the chat history is publicly available (per ASF guidelines)" [A32]	Mesos and Aurora both use Slackarchive.io for archives [A33]
Apache Spark	"For usage questions and help (e.g. how to use this Spark API), it is recommended you use the Stack Overflow tag apache-spark as it is an active forum for Spark users' questions and answers" [A34]	No local Stack Overflow archive
Apache Spot	"Getting started" link on Apache Spot project page [A35] links to Github [A36] which states "If you find a bug, have question or something to discuss please contact us: –Create an Issue.… –Go to our Slack channel"	No Slack archive
Apache Thrift	Slack not officially mentioned on product pages, but team created and channel mentioned in one email thread [A37]	Uses Slackarchive.io for archives [A38]

The last column in each table shows whether the community is providing archives of the communication that happens in the walled garden. To determine whether archives were available, we performed the following procedure. First we searched for archives via the public web site for the project, and if those were not available, we searched for archives via Google, using the following queries:

- [community name/project name] slack
- [community name/project name] chat
- [community name/project name] archive
- [community name/project name] logs
- [community name/project name] slackarchive.io

With a few exceptions, most of the projects that did have an archive put the link to it in an obvious place, so the archives were easy to find.

These tables show that the majority of projects which *are* using walled gardens are *not* creating archives of these communications. In the next section we discuss some options for communities that *do* want to create archives.

4 Archiving Walled Gardens

If a community does decide to move to walled garden for communication, there are some strategies it can take to combat the potential for a corresponding loss of transparency. Creating archives of the communications – as would have been available with a mailing list or IRC channels – is one obvious and familiar solution. We will first discuss the options for creating archives of Slack, and then we will briefly address Stack Exchange/ Stack Overflow archiving.

4.1 Archiving Slack

There are a few different options for archiving Slack conversations, each of which have different positive and negative aspects. First, as we noted in Tables 1 and 2, there are third-party services, such as Slackarchive.io (http://slackarchive.io), which can create and host Slack archives. Slackarchive.io lists many open source projects on its "who is using" list, including Bitcoin-core, Midonet, Apache Mesos, and Apache Thrift. The archives are searchable and browsable by date, but the archives are not easily downloadable. There are no Terms of Service posted on the Slackarchive.io site, nor is there a robots.txt file. The archives themselves are displayed in a JavaScript-driven responsive web interface, making downloads inconvenient and non-trivial to automate.

Another option for creating archives for Slack is to connect it to IRC via the Slack bridge [19] or via a third party tool (e.g. Sameroom, available at http://sameroom.io), and once the chat is on IRC, the archives can be created there using an IRC archive bot. Depending on the client, IRC may or may not be able to understand advanced features of Slack, including direct messages, code formatting features, and document attachments. Users who choose to use IRC will not see these aspects of the Slack experience, nor will an IRC bot be able to archive them.

Third, community managers can take the approach of Wordpress and simply point people to the in-Slack archive, for example [A2]. The downsides of that approach are:

- Viewers of the archive must be signed in members of the channel.
- The archives are only browsable on a day-to-day basis (a "pick a date" widget is also available).

- By default, the archives are not searchable or downloadable by a non-administrative user.
- Some communities with a lot of messages in the archive have reported seeing errors reading, "Your team has more than 10,000 messages in its archive, so although there are older messages than are shown below, you can't see them. Find out more about upgrading your team" [20].

4.2 Archiving Stack Exchange

The options for creating local archives of Stack Overflow and Stack Exchange sites are determined by a Creative Commons BY-SA 3.0 license [21] that allows reuse of Stack Exchange network data (for example questions, answers, and the like) as long as attribution rules are followed [22]. The site also periodically provides a CC-licensed Data Dump [23] with private identifying user data removed. Despite these generous terms, it does not appear that many FLOSS projects relying on Stack Overflow for developer or user support are creating their own archives of this data, nor are they providing context to Stack Overflow questions or answers from within their own ecosystems. Rather, the communities that are using Slack as a question-and-answer facility are simply pointing users to the relevant Stack Overflow tag or corresponding Stack Exchange subdomain.

5 Conclusion

This paper presents data on how 18 FLOSS projects (including 10 Apache Software Foundation (ASF) projects) use walled gardens to communicate with and between users and developers. We define walled gardens in terms of their ownership or control by a single corporation, as well as by their lack of FLOSS licensing to users. Examples of walled gardens include synchronous communication services like Slack, and asynchronous communication sites like Stack Overflow.

We posit that when walled gardens are chosen for communication, the community has decided to subjugate the FLOSS value of openness via transparent, non-corporate, FLOSS-licensed communication for a different - and equally compelling - definition of openness, namely an openness of easy participation and diverse contribution. One way that these competing values can both "win" is for the project to provide avenues for increased transparency after the walled garden is chosen, specifically by providing easy-to-find, publicly available, downloadable archives of the communication that happens inside the walled garden. This step would effectively open a "gate" into the walled garden and reassert the value of transparency once again.

Unfortunately, our data shows that only a handful of projects have made any attempt toward transparency by opening such a gate. This resistance to creating transparent archives of communication also persists in communities such as ASF that explicitly encourage archives and transparency in project communication.

By questioning the use of walled gardens for communication and evaluating their effects on multiple types of "openness", we hope to begin a dialogue within the FLOSS community about how to preserve and extend its unique values.

Appendix

Below are the URLs referenced in Tables 1 and 2 as [A1], [A2], and so on.

- A1. http://make.wordpress.com/chat
- A2. https://make.wordpress.org/polyglots/2015/04/16/chat-notes-https-wordpress-slack-com-archives-core/
- A3. https://irclogs.wordpress.org/
- A4. http://www.drupalux.org/tools-and-resources
- A5. https://www.drupal.org/node/2490332
- A6. https://www.drupal.org/node/2798167
- A7. https://blog.ghost.org/ghost-slack/
- A8. https://dev.ghost.org/public-dev-meeting-4th-october/
- A9. http://socket.io/slack/
- A10. http://rauchg.com/slackin/
- A11. https://news.ycombinator.com/item?id=8286291
- A12. https://www.reddit.com/r/elementaryos/comments/25t7cg/where_to_talk_to_the_developers/
- A13. https://elementary.io/support
- A14. https://elementary.io/get-involved
- A15. https://elementaryos.stackexchange.com/
- A16. https://blog.midonet.org/irc-chat-moved-slack/
- A17. http://midonet.slackarchive.io/
- A18. https://facebook.github.io/react/blog/2015/10/19/reactiflux-is-moving-to-discord.html
- A19. https://facebook.github.io/react/community/support.html
- A20. https://bitcoincore.org/en/contribute/
- A21. http://bitcoincore.slackarchive.io/
- A22. https://cordova.apache.org/contribute/
- A23. http://markmail.org/message/o6ltqszgeqykcuku
- A24. http://groovy-lang.org/community.html
- A25. https://issues.apache.org/jira/browse/HBASE-16413
- A26. https://hbase.apache.org/book.html#getting.involved
- A27. https://hbase.apache.org/book.html#trouble.resources
- A28. https://iota.incubator.apache.org/contribute.html
- A29. https://kudu.apache.org/community.html
- A30. http://mesos.apache.org/community/
- A31. http://aurora.apache.org/community
- A32. https://lists.apache.org/thread.html/a1c53250a94d96e3f4038a76f93db01c3cc4d649df861f762373ac0f@%3Cdev.mesos.apache.org%3E
- A33. http://mesos.slackarchive.io/
- A34. http://spark.apache.org/community.html
- A35. http://spot.incubator.apache.org/

A36. https://github.com/Open-Network-Insight/open-network-insight/tree/spot#contributing-to-apache-spot
A37. https://www.mail-archive.com/dev@thrift.apache.org/msg32757.html
A38. http://thrift.slackarchive.io/general/

References

1. Fogel, K.: Producing Open Source: How to Run a Successful Free Software Project. O'Reilly and Associates, Sebastopol (2005). http://producingoss.com
2. Raymond, E.: The Cathedral & the Bazaar: Musings on Linux and Open Source by an Accidental Revolutionary. O'Reilly & Associates, Sebastopol (2001)
3. Weber, S.: The Success of Open Source. Harvard University Press, Cambridge (2004)
4. Red Hat Community Architecture Team: The Open Source Way (2009). https://opensourceway.org/book
5. Feller, J., Fitzgerald, B.: Understanding Open Source Software Development. O'Reilly & Associates, Sebastopol (2002)
6. Daniel, S., Agarwal, R., Stewart, K.J.: The effects of diversity in global, distributed collectives: a study of open source project success. Inf. Syst. Res. **24**(2), 312–333 (2013)
7. Kuechler, V., Gilbertson, C., Jensen, C.: Gender differences in early free and open source software joining process. In: Hammouda, I., Lundell, B., Mikkonen, T., Scacchi, W. (eds.) OSS 2012. IAICT, vol. 378, pp. 78–93. Springer, Heidelberg (2012). doi: 10.1007/978-3-642-33442-9_6
8. Vasilescu, B., Posnett, D., Ray, B., van den Brand, M.G., Serebrenik, A., Devanbu, P., Filkov, V.: Gender and tenure diversity in GitHub teams. In: Proceedings of the 33rd Annual ACM Conference on Human Factors in Computing Systems, pp. 3789–3798 (2015)
9. Williams, O.: Slack is quietly, unintentionally killing IRC. The Next Web (2015). http://thenextweb.com/insider/2015/03/24/slack-is-quietly-unintentionally-killing-irc/
10. Apache Software Foundation (nd) Decision Making. https://community.apache.org/committers/decisionMaking.html
11. Apache Software Foundation (nd) Mailing Lists. http://apache.org/foundation/mailinglists.html
12. Braga, M.: Google, a Search Company, Has Made its Internet Archive Impossible to Search. Motherboard (2015). http://motherboard.vice.com/read/google-a-search-company-has-made-its-internet-archive-impossible-to-search. (Feb 13)
13. Squire, M.: Should we move to Stack Overflow? Measuring the utility of social media for developer support. In: Proceedings of the 37th International Conference on Software Engineering (ICSE 2015), vol. 2. pp. 219–228. IEEE Press (2015)
14. Shihab, E., Jiang, Z.M., Hassan, A.E.: On the use of Internet Relay Chat (IRC) meetings by developers of the GNOME GTK+ project. In: Proceedings of the 2009 Mining Software Repositories, pp 107–110 (2009)
15. Shihab, E., Jiang, Z.M., Hassan, A.E.: Studying the use of developer IRC meetings in open source projects. In: Proceedings of Software Maintenance (ICSM 2009), pp 147–156 (2009)
16. Devault, D.: Please don't use Slack for FOSS projects (2015). https://drewdevault.com/2015/11/01/Please-stop-using-slack.html. Accessed 1 Nov 2015
17. Make Wordpress, Chat (nd) https://make.wordpress.org/chat/
18. Baker, J.: 4 open source alternatives to Slack. Opensource.com (2016). https://opensource.com/alternatives/slack

19. Slack Help Center (nd) Connect to Slack over IRC and XMPP. https://get.slack.help/hc/en-us/articles/201727913-Connect-to-Slack-over-IRC-and-XMPP
20. FreeCodeCamp: So Yeah We Tried Slack... and We Deeply Regretted It (2015). https://medium.freecodecamp.com/so-yeah-we-tried-slack-and-we-deeply-regretted-it-391bcc714c81, Accessed 21 June 2015
21. Creative Commons. Attribution-ShareAlike 3.0 Unported (CC BY-SA 3.0) License. https://creativecommons.org/licenses/by-sa/3.0/
22. Stack Exchange Terms of Service. http://stackexchange.com/legal/terms-of-service
23. Stack Exchange, Inc.: Stack Exchange Data Dump (2016). https://archive.org/details/stackexchange. Accessed Dec 2016

Open Access This chapter is licensed under the terms of the Creative Commons Attribution 4.0 International License (http://creativecommons.org/licenses/by/4.0/), which permits use, sharing, adaptation, distribution and reproduction in any medium or format, as long as you give appropriate credit to the original author(s) and the source, provide a link to the Creative Commons license and indicate if changes were made.

The images or other third party material in this chapter are included in the chapter's Creative Commons license, unless indicated otherwise in a credit line to the material. If material is not included in the chapter's Creative Commons license and your intended use is not permitted by statutory regulation or exceeds the permitted use, you will need to obtain permission directly from the copyright holder.

Investigating Relationships Between FLOSS Foundations and FLOSS Projects

Juho Lindman[1] and Imed Hammouda[2(✉)]

[1] Applied IT, University of Gothenburg, Gothenburg, Sweden
juho.lindman@ait.gu.se
[2] Department of Computer Science and Engineering, Chalmers and University of Gothenburg, Gothenburg, Sweden
hammouda@chalmers.se

Abstract. Foundations function as vital institutional support infrastructures for many of the most successful open source projects, but the role of these support entities remains an understudied phenomenon in FLOSS research. Drawing on Open Hub (formerly known as Ohloh) data, this paper empirically investigates the different ways these entities support projects and interact with different projects and with each other.

Keywords: Open source · Open source foundations

1 Introduction

Continuing Free/Libre Open Source Software's (FLOSS) success is based on the evolution of FLOSS projects and contributors [1–5], but there is a research gap concerning the entities[1] that support FLOSS, such as foundations [6]. These entities support individual FLOSS projects in different ways, but the dynamics they are engaged in remains an understudied phenomenon. In addition, the cooperation of these entities and between developers poses several questions for further study.

We address these gaps in our empirical investigation of how these entities support and interact based on Open Hub data. In detail, our research question: *How FLOSS entities support FLOSS projects?* Our findings reveal traces of a complex interplay in this ecosystem when describing this dynamic.

The paper is organized as follows: Section 2 gives background on earlier related research. Section 3 presents the methodological details of data collection and analysis. Findings are then reported and discussed in Sect. 4, followed by Sect. 5, Discussion. Finally, future research directions and concluding remarks are presented in Sect. 6.

---

[1] In this work we call these "support entities" noting that in many cases "foundation" would also be applicable. However, we note that (1) not all of these entities are foundations and (2) even if they were, there are subtle differences regarding their legal and tax status in different jurisdictions. Thus, we limit these legal considerations outside the scope of this study and call these support entities.

2 Background

FLOSS foundations support their community projects in different ways. We explore FLOSS support entities ("Foundations," "Organizations") and their relationships to the projects they are affiliated with. Riehle [6] demonstrates how FLOSS support entities manage and ensure the long-term survival of their projects.

These entities are linked to projects and help by providing financial support and legal assurance. This makes the FLOSS projects a bit less dependent on the volunteer efforts. In addition, FLOSS support entities have other responsibilities related to the hosting and management of the FLOSS projects. Responsibilities include (i) organizing community projects (ii) marketing, (iii) managing intellectual property (IP) rights and (iv) setting strategic directions. Support entities may also provide means to protect community-generated content using IP legislation [6].

In this paper, we investigate empirically the FLOSS environment, the role of the supporting entities and the relationships between support entities.

3 Methodology

This study was conducted by using **Theoretical Saturation Grounded Theory** approach which is a form of a qualitative data collection and data analysis methodology. According to [7], theoretical saturation is associated with theoretical sampling for grounded theory. A grounded theory is a scientific research approach used by the researchers for the collection and analysis of qualitative data. The main purpose of choosing this research approach is to develop a theory (or) a model through a continuous comparative analysis of qualitative data collected by theoretical sampling process. This flexible research approach is required to collect huge volume of data because, data collection will be done simultaneously along with the data analysis process. A theory (or) a model can be formulated from the collected data. This research approach is also used to assess any sort of patterns (or) variations out of an investigated research area. The selection of cases during this research process will most likely produce the most relevant data that will evaluate emerging theories. However, each new case might offer a slightly different outcome. The researcher will be having a continued sampling of data and he/she will analyze the data until no new data emerges. The end point of theoretical saturation indicates that, the approach has reached a point where no new data were identified and it shows the researcher that the enough data were collected for data analysis purposes.

3.1 Data Collection

The **Open Hub data repository** (formerly known as Ohloh) is used as a primary data source for this study. This source holds key information about the support organizations concerning their sectors, development focuses, licensing policies, membership types and structure. The data repository also holds other information, such as projects and a committer's list, which can be used to determine the relationships between support entities and projects. Open Hub can be accessed using their **API keys** [8]. We use this repository to identify the relationship a support entity can have with another entity and a support entity's portfolio projects. We used Open Hub data from all FLOSS support entities that host at least one project.

Support entity websites are another main source of data. These websites hold key information about support and services, incubation processes, project governance, maintenance, project development practices, IP management, license agreement policies, hosting services and so on. This information is used to map out how the entities provide support for projects.

3.2 Data Analyses

We used a Java program to parse the API data from the XML data format to plain text and stored it in a database. We collected data from 88 FLOSS support entities ("Organizations"). We have set a criterion to analyze our sampling cases (i.e. data) that we collected from the support entities. Our criterion for data analysis is that, if we go through 20 sampling cases without no new data/findings, then it is our saturation point.

In the generated database, we identified whether entities with unique organization IDs have (1) connections with projects affiliated with other entities and (2) whether an organization's affiliated developers contribute to the projects of other entities. We also noted when developers contributed to some other projects (e.g., to their own projects). These different scenarios are described in Fig. 1 below.

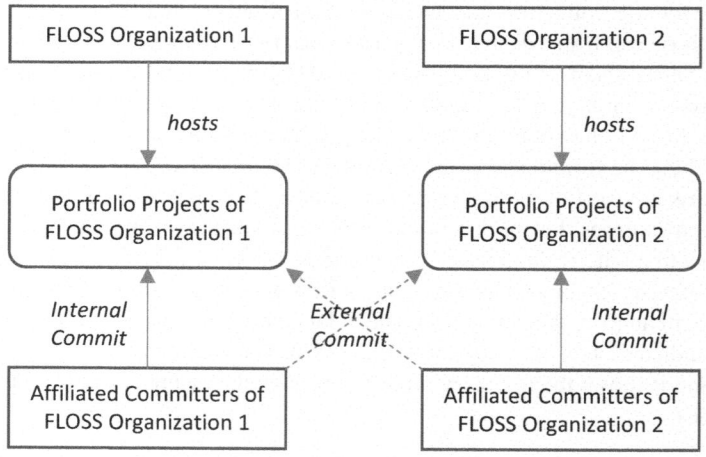

Fig. 1. The relationships between different FLOSS organizations.

We then used a manual approach to search for the appropriate information through relevant online sources—such as foundation websites and forums—to describe the identified the relationships between the FLOSS organizations. We investigated each relationship between any two support entities within the FLOSS relationship network.

Finally, we qualitatively analyzed the identified details of the relationships and grouped them.

4 Findings

We defined a FLOSS support entity taxonomy (Fig. 2) that describes some of support entities' characteristics. We then outlined the data of the different characteristics available.

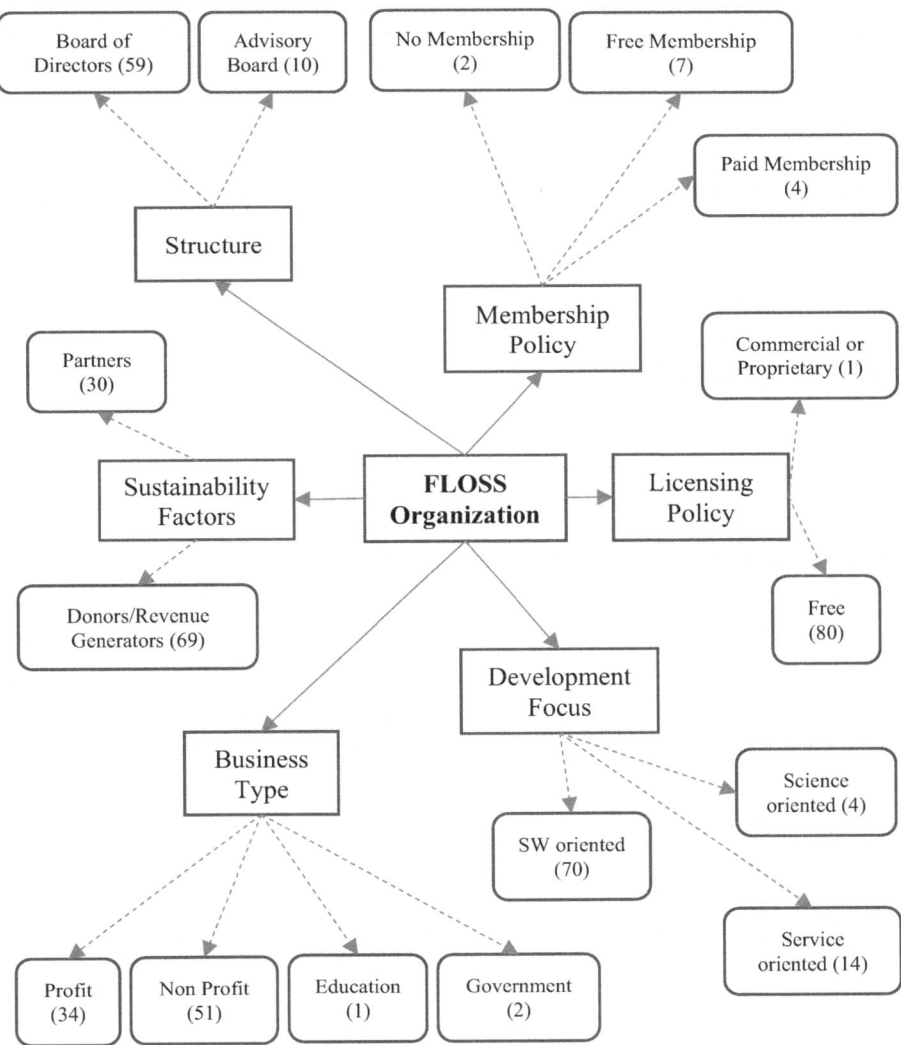

Fig. 2. FLOSS support entity taxonomy.

A **Profit (or) Commercial FLOSS** support entity generates revenue via sales of products, services and solutions. They collaborate with different corporations and technical partners. **Nonprofit** foundations are primarily sustained through volunteer donations. They collaborate with external companies, educational institutions and other stakeholders to get funds to support the projects. Most of these organizations are also primarily governed by the Board of Directors (BOD). **Government FLOSS** mostly consists of science-related projects. The funding for such projects comes mainly from public sources. **Education FLOSS** comprises primarily educational institutions. These support entities mainly focus on providing education to the general public and are sustained through donations from public sources and student fees.

Organizations list different development focuses. Options include **S/W orientated, service orientated** and **science orientated**. Most service-orientated support entities were of the profit type, while science-orientated support entities were often government based and educational.

FLOSS entities may support projects that use either **free software license** projects or **commercial or proprietary software license** projects. A free software license allows the user of a piece of software the extensive rights to modify and redistribute that software. A commercial or proprietary software license is produced for sale or to serve commercial purposes.

FLOSS support entities evolve through different kinds of **donors and revenue generators** and **partners**, such as volunteers, corporations, open-source organizations, software products, government agencies, educational institutes and investors.

FLOSS organizations are governed by two different governance modes: the (BOD) and the **Advisory Board** (AB). The BOD has the decision-making authority and responsibility for governing the support entity. BOD committee roles may include Founder, Investor and Director. In contrast, the AB does not have the decision-making authority, and they are only responsible for assisting or giving advice within the organization. AB committee members can have roles like Senior Manager, Executive, Volunteer and so on.

FLOSS organizations have different types of membership schemes. The **no membership** (NM) type does not have any members within the support entity. The **free membership** (FM) type allows any members to join without any membership fee. The **paid membership** (PM) type allows only the paid members to take part.

5 Discussion

To answer our research question (*How FLOSS entities support FLOSS projects?*), we explored how entities support FLOSS projects. We grouped our findings (described in detail in Table 1 below): services, incubation process, project governance, project maintenance, IP, project acceptance and hosting services. Table 1 summarizes the key support mechanisms.

Table 1. How foundations support FLOSS projects.

Support	Explanations
Services	FLOSS support entities can provide legal, financial and consulting services to their projects. Support entities can provide tools and offer advice on how to raise funds. Support entities can also provide essential support on how to protect the IP and financial contributions, and it can limit the legal exposure of an individual contributor in portfolio projects; for example, ASF and Gentoo
Incubation process	Support entities have different guidelines on how a portfolio project can be created. Many support entities require an incubation process. Created projects enter the incubation process. Some of the processes are mandatory quality control mechanisms. In some FLOSS organizations, incubation processes are used to create new versions of the existing projects and not for creating new projects. Some FLOSS projects start with pre-existing code before they go through the incubation process. These incubation processes are useful for new projects in learning community norms and processes. Projects in incubation will be monitored by the nominated mentors There are some variations: • The incubation process is only used to create the new versions of an existing project and not for creating entirely new projects; for example, the Wikimedia Foundation • Individuals are responsible for the creation of projects. However, under the Eclipse Foundation, a project can be started/created with some pre-existing code • A project can be started/created by anyone with the necessary skills
Project governance	Support entities may assign a project management committee (PMC) consisting of people to govern or manage projects and subprojects. Support entity mentors usually work with PMC to help in the evolution of the project; for example, ASF and Tryton
Project maintenance	Project data are maintained either by a PMC or by projects; for example, ASF
Intellectual Property (IP)	FLOSS support entities' IP management enables the participation of software developers from different organizations to develop software. Tried-and-true practices exist to support software IP management and to foster a growing community. FLOSS organizations protect the developer's contribution to portfolio projects when the developer signs a Contributor License Agreement (CLA). The CLA is specially designed to protect the developer's contribution. Organizations usually do not protect the hosted projects managed by third parties with the CLA; for example, Outercurve Foundation, Eclipse and Gentoo • A project might receive organization IP clearance for contributions and third-party libraries • IP management enables and encourages the participation of organization software developers to develop software collaboratively in a FLOSS community • When a CLA is signed by the developers, the entity protects the contributions on its portfolio projects; for example, Twitter and 52 NIFGOSS • However, third parties managing the hosted projects within the entity are not protected by the CLA
Project acceptance	Projects need to be championed by a sponsor (i.e., if the sponsor is the foundation board); for example, Outercurve Foundation
Hosting services	Organizations provide project hosting services and tools to promote FLOSS development; for example, OSGeo and Genivi Alliance • The support entity hosts projects and a wide variety of other mailing lists for projects, committees and special interest groups

Table 1 shows that FLOSS organizations like ASF, Gentoo and SpringSource provide various support and services to portfolio projects. Organization incubation processes are used in ASF, Wikimedia Foundation, Eclipse Foundation and the MirOS project. Foundations such as ASF and Tryton assigns a PMC to govern their projects. Some foundations, such as KDE, have limited hierarchical structures. Some support entities like the Outercurve Foundation, Eclipse and Gentoo and own IP rights to protect their portfolio projects while restricting their contributors.

Based on our qualitative analyses, we list the identified reasons that describe why the support entities interact. Two FLOSS support entities can have a relationship because of the following key reasons: plugins, sponsorship, tie-ups, packages, reliance, key persons and hosting (see Table 2 for more detailed descriptions).

Table 2. The relationship between two support entities.

Plugins/Add-ons	A FLOSS support entity may provide or produce plugins/add-ons to other FLOSS support entity projects and their produces; for example, the Xfce desktop provides add-on to Mozilla's Thunderbird application
Sponsorship	A FLOSS support entity may provide funding or sponsorship their contributors to other FLOSS support entities and portfolio projects; for example, Twitter provides financial funding and contributes to the Apache Software Foundation. Yahoo also provides financial funding to the OpenStack Foundation
Tie-up	FLOSS project software might have a tie-up with other FLOSS organizations' software. The Xfce and KDE desktops have tie-ups with Debian operating system
Packages	A FLOSS support entity may provide packages for other FLOSS products and services. For an example, Homebrew provides the packages for KDE desktop applications to install on OS X. Homebrew also provides packages to Mozilla's add-ons on OS X
Reliance	A FLOSS support entity might be using other FLOSS organization software, services, infrastructure, tools or products for its own business operations and services; for example, Sony Mobile and Yahoo are using the OpenStack platform infrastructure for their business purposes
Key person	A key person—such as the founder, lead developer, maintainer or manager—from one FLOSS support entity might be employed by other FLOSS foundations. Both FLOSS entities might have a single person as a common manager to manage FLOSS projects; that is, a single person acts as a manager for both organizations' projects. For example, Tarent solutions Gmbh and the MirOS project have a single person managing their projects and the same person is the founder of the MirOS project and is employed by Tarent Solutions Gmbh
Hosting	A FLOSS support organization might host and distribute other FLOSS organizations' products and services; for example, BlackBerry hosts and distributes Adobe apps on BlackBerry World to BlackBerry mobiles. A FLOSS organization may provide generic modules and functions to work with other FLOSS organizations' software implementations; for example, SaltStack is providing generic modules and functions to work with the Apache Software Foundation implementation

From the collected API data, we explored the relationship between two FLOSS organizations. We could not find any projects hosted under or claimed by multiple organizations as a portfolio project. We also explored whether there are relationships among different FLOSS support entities.

Based on the collected data, different FLOSS organizations have relationships when affiliated developers from one FLOSS organization contributes to other FLOSS entities' portfolio projects. As this study mainly focuses on the support entities, we did not consider the individual project information in-depth that could give more insight regarding specific projects and their committers.

6 Conclusions and Future Avenues for Research

This research study investigated FLOSS support entities, their role in FLOSS projects and the relationships among them within the FLOSS ecosystem. Based on our findings, we claim that our proposed methodology could identify the key attributes and values of a FLOSS support entity through a developed taxonomy and the FLOSS organizations key roles in FLOSS projects.

This research opens several new areas for further research. There are interesting research opportunities related to verifying and measuring the impacts of developer contribution and entities. Our methodology focuses on chosen parts of the interplay between the support entities, so we expect future studies to shed more light on their important and understudied role in supporting and governing FLOSS.

Acknowledgements. The authors would like to thank Bharat Kumar Mendu and Joshua Smith Soundararajan for their contribution to this research.

References

1. Godfrey, M., Tu, M.: Growth, evolution, and structural change in open source software. In: Proceedings of the 4th International Workshop on Principles of Software Evolution, pp. 103–106. ACM Press (2001)
2. Robles, G., Amor, J.J., Gonzalez Barahona, J.M., Herraiz, I.: Evolution and growth in large libre software projects. In: Proceedings of the Eighth International Workshop on Principles of Software Evolution (IWPSE 2005), pp. 165–174. IEEE Computer Society (2005)
3. Roy, C.K., Cordy, J.R.: Evaluating the evolution of small scale open source software systems. In: Proceedings of the 15th International Conference on Computing, Research in Computing Science (2006). Special issue on CIC
4. Succi, G., Paulson, J., Eberlein, A.: Preliminary results from an empirical study on the growth of open source and commercial software products. In: EDSER3 Workshop, pp. 14–15 (2001)
5. Aksulu, A., Wade, M.: A comprehensive review and synthesis of open source research. J. Assoc. Inf. Syst. **11**(1), 576–656 (2010)

6. Riehle, D.: The economic case for open source foundations. Computer **43**(1), 86–90 (2010)
7. Glaser, B., Strauss, A.L.: The Discovery of Grounded Theory: Strategies for Qualitative Research. Transaction Publishers (2009)
8. Gallardo Valencia, R.-E., Tantikul, P., Sim, S.-E.: Searching for Reputable Source Code on the Web. http://www.drsusansim.org/papers/group2010-gallardo.pdf

Open Access This chapter is licensed under the terms of the Creative Commons Attribution 4.0 International License (http://creativecommons.org/licenses/by/4.0/), which permits use, sharing, adaptation, distribution and reproduction in any medium or format, as long as you give appropriate credit to the original author(s) and the source, provide a link to the Creative Commons license and indicate if changes were made.

The images or other third party material in this chapter are included in the chapter's Creative Commons license, unless indicated otherwise in a credit line to the material. If material is not included in the chapter's Creative Commons license and your intended use is not permitted by statutory regulation or exceeds the permitted use, you will need to obtain permission directly from the copyright holder.

Designing for Participation: Three Models for Developer Involvement in Hybrid OSS Projects

Hanna Mäenpää[1](✉), Terhi Kilamo[2], Tommi Mikkonen[1], and Tomi Männistö[1]

[1] University of Helsinki, Helsinki, Finland
{hanna.maenpaa,tomi.mannisto}@cs.helsinki.fi, tommi.mikkonen@tut.fi
[2] Tampere University of Technology, Tampere, Finland
terhi.kilamo@tut.fi

Abstract. This paper reports governance practices of three profit oriented companies that develop OSS software with the help of their respective open development communities. We explore how the companies allow development contributions from external stakeholders, and what knowledge they let out of their internal software development activities. The results lay ground for further research on how to organize openness of the software development process in hybrid setups where the needs of different stakeholders are partly competing - yet complementary.

Keywords: Open source · Hybrid open source · Community management

1 Introduction

Open Source Software (OSS) projects are based on peer-production, self- organization of individuals, and consensus-based decision making [1]. They offer equal opportunities for both long-term members and newcomers in contributing to the development of the software product [2]. In the OSS environment, interactions and development decisions can take place in the absence of market-based or managerial models [1]. Still, active communities that are independent of commercial influence are rare. When companies engage with OSS communities, their corporate direction must be aligned to that of the community's peer production-based approach [3]. In this hybrid environment, the Bazaar truly meets the Cathedral [4], and the forces that drive the collaboration are partly defined by both.

Hybrid OSS collaborations can form around various kinds of software products [5], emerging organically when companies become interested in existing OSS projects or when the projects are initiated by companies themselves by releasing software source code out with an OSS-compliant license. This can be done with the aim of attracting external contributors, increasing the innovative capability of the company or by attracting a niche market that could later be expanded [3,6]. Engagement with OSS communities can be a means for strengthening brand awareness [3]. The strategy can be especially important for small and medium sized companies, helping to diversify their product offerings, taken that the companies have sufficient resources and technological competencies for building effective and reciprocal collaborations [7]. As Hybrid OSS communities consist of a mix of companies and independent developers with varying motivations [8], finding a mutually beneficial collaboration model poses various challenges.

Several calls exist for further research on management practises in the hybrid OSS arena (De Noni et al., 2013) [9]. Linåker et al. (2015) pinpointed the governance structures in open environments and the openness of the software product development process as interesting topics for future endeavors [10]. Hussan et al. (2016) invite research on practical implementations of the software development process to complement the current work in the academic landscape [11]. To address these calls, we investigate how three profit-oriented companies develop OSS-based products with their respective open source software development communities. We compare how they allow external contributors to access their development process and what knowledge they let out of the priorities and decisions that shape the future of the software. With this, we hope to provide new understanding on how the hybrid OSS development model can be formed and managed at the practical level and which factors can be used as design elements when organizing the community's collaboration model.

The rest of the paper is structured as follows. Section 2 describes typical characteristics of hybrid OSS communities, shedding light on the different styles of governance that companies can employ towards their communities. Section 3 presents our research approach for studying the collaboration practices of the case companies that are introduced in Sect. 4. Section 5 presents our findings, whereas Sects. 6 and 7 discuss and conclude the work.

2 Previous Work

Governance of OSS projects involves the means that are in place to steer the efforts of an autonomously working developer community [12]. The governance structure of a community should support collaboration in between the stakeholders, to enable efficient work coordination, and to create an environment where motivation of participants is fostered so that the community can operate in a sustainable manner [12]. It is not straightforward to create a productive and happy community - its boundaries and affordances must be consciously designed and managed [3]. This can take form in different governance configurations that can be mandated from a governing organization or emerge and evolve slowly as a result of a collective learning process [9].

While in community-driven projects decision-making power is distributed among the community's members, in hybrid set-ups a strong leader for the development project can emerge in the form of a non- or for-profit organization. This host can act as a sponsor, providing for the infrastructure needed for developing the software [8]. This role allows the host to control the community's activities to an extent [6]. Here, the host entity can define on what premises stakeholders can hold various positions, as well as what privileges and responsibilities these roles bring [6]. Implementing these decisions requires careful consideration of the versatile motivations of the contributors: if the community's members feel their values are being compromised or that their opinions are not being heard, their motivation can deteriorate [13,14]. Distributing knowledge and decision-making power aptly can help to achieve a symbiotic state where the community sees the company as an active co-developer of the software, rather than a "parasitic" business owner that outsources its selected tasks to the crowd [15].

2.1 Policies and Practices

The governance model of a community can vary from free-form and spontaneous to institutionalized, well defined and hierarchical [16]. While the history of an OSS project is reflected in the ways the community functions, fundamentals of how the community can form and evolve are largely defined by the license of the software source code [6]. A fully open licensing strategy increases the project's ability to attract new developers [6], increasing the attractiveness of the software product in the eyes of its potential users [17]. However, if the open development community is strong, this strategy may risk the host's influence on the software product [6,13], possibly creating an unclear legal relationship between the company and its contributors [18]. This risk can be managed by keeping selected software assets proprietary to the company, creating a "gate" for the external developers [13]. This allows the company to limit the open community's possibilities to modify and re-use the software and also to choose in which aspects of the development process it wants the open community to participate in [13].

In autonomous OSS projects, a set of freely accessible online tools are used to coordinate work, discuss its goals and deliver contributions [6,19]. These sociotechnical systems constitute 'boundary objects' of the community, helping its members to create personalized views on the status quo of the project. Principles according to which contributors should engage them can be implicitly known and embedded in the functionality the software platforms provide. Also, written guidelines and contributor agreements are used to establish how the community should work and what culture it should be built upon. When the development tools and related communications are openly accessible, the processes of requirements engineering, quality assurance and release management become transparent to the public. This, on its part, allows the external stakeholders to understand and practically influence the decisions that shape the software product. In this context, describing means for practical boundary-setting comprises the main contribution of this paper.

3 Research Approach

Case studies investigate phenomena in their natural context [20] and aim to generate case-grounded theory that can be extended, confirmed, or challenged through replication in future studies [20]. For this aim, we describe a mixed-method case study of practices that three for-profit companies use in building commercial OSS software in collaboration with their respective, hybrid developer communities. With this, we aim at answering the following research questions:

- RQ1: How can a software process be organized to allow a hybrid OSS collaboration model?
- RQ2: What factors can be used to affect openness of the collaboration model?

West and O'Mahony (2008), emphasize the role of accessibility of tasks and transparency of knowledge as important building blocks of the participation architecture in OSS communities [6]. Inspired by this, a research instrument of nine questions (See Table 1) was composed. First five questions (A–E) address accessibility, whereas the four additional questions (F–I) address what knowledge host companies let out of their internal development process.

Answers to these questions were sought by exploring of freely available online documentation, such as the project's wiki pages. Validity of the findings was evaluated by interviewing an employee of each case company, using the nine question research instrument as a basis for semi-structured interviews. Each answer was coded with a three-step scale from 0 to 2 where number zero represented that the matter is unconditionally closed from the open community. Number one was set to describe that the topic was open to the community to a limited degree. Number two was set to represent that the matter is fully open to the development community to know about or act upon independently. This triangulation of sources and viewpoints, is hoped to increase validity and fitness of the study design for replication in different environments [20].

4 Case Companies

This study focuses on the collaboration practices of three profit-oriented companies that base their businesses on products created in close collaboration with OSS communities. We describe how the companies have arranged their software development processes to allow receiving contributions from external stakeholders. The first case company, Qt Company Ltd., acts as a single vendor for the Qt software, a framework that can be used to develop applications for desktop computers, embedded systems and mobile devices. The Qt project was established in 1991 and was first incorporated by its original developers in 1993. After several commercial acquisitions, the current set-up emerged in 2014. Qt is distributed as free[1] commercial versions. While the source code of Qt is open for anybody to view, the commercial license grants full rights to develop and disseminate

---
[1] GPL, LGPLv3.

proprietary Qt applications. The company offers support and complementary software assets for its paying customers. Size of the community that develops the Qt framework is approximately 400 persons while the number of application developers ramps up to approximately a million.

The second case company, Vaadin Ltd. produces an application development framework that can be used to build interactive web applications that run on most operating systems and browsers. The software (Later: Vaadin) is offered with the Apache 2.0 license. It was initially developed as an add-on for an existing OSS product in 2002 from which an independent release was made in 2006. The development project has since been hosted by a company that offers online training, consultancy and sub-contracting of application projects. Development of Vaadin is dominated by the host company, and an application developer ecosystem of approximately 150 000 individuals exists. This is complemented by a developer community which has produced approximately 600 add-ons for the software.

Our third case is the Linux-based operating system Sailfish OS for mobile devices. Its history originates from a software that was released from Nokia as open source in 2011. The current host of Sailfish OS is Jolla Ltd., a startup that sells both proof of concept mobile devices and distributor licenses for the OS. The technical architecture of Sailfish OS is layered and parts of the software, including user interface libraries, are proprietary to the host company. The rest of the layers entail work from several OSS communities, such as Qt and the independent, community-driven project Mer. The Mer software alone comprises of packages that are using various FOSS licenses such as GPL, LGPL, BSD, and MIT. The company uses several crowdsourcing tactics for acquiring feedback about the quality of Sailfish OS. Even with only three projects, the cases reveal the versatility of possible governance configurations.

5 Findings

The Qt, SailfishOS and Vaadin open source communities were found to share significant similarities. For all, a central company acted as a host for the project, sponsored development platforms and participated in development tasks. All hosts advocated for dissemination of the software and arranged community-building activities. In all cases, the host company controlled contents, scope and timing of the software releases. All shared the practice of coupling an external, peer production driven development community with a company internal development process that was exposed to outsiders to a limited degree. Differences were found in which tasks external contributors can participate in and which parts of the development process was transparent for outsiders. Table 1 and Fig. 1 summarize these differences.

5.1 Access to Development Tasks

Host companies welcomed code contributions from the open community to varying degrees. In the Qt project, any person could access the workflow coordination

Table 1. Questions used for evaluating the collaboration models. 0 = The aspect is closed/hidden from the open community. 1 = Open to the community to a limited degree. 2 = The aspect is completely open to the community to know about or act upon.

		Qt	Vaadin	Sailfish
A	Who can contribute to software code?	2	2	1
B	Who can test code contributions?	2	2	1
C	Who can accept code contributions?	2	0	1
D	Who can verify defect reports?	2	1	1
E	Who can impact prioritization of work requests	2	2	1
F	Who knows about the integration process of code contributions?	2	2	1
G	Who knows what is on the product roadmap?	1	1	0
H	Who knows timing and content of releases?	1	1	0
I	Who knows priorities of work issues?	2	0	0

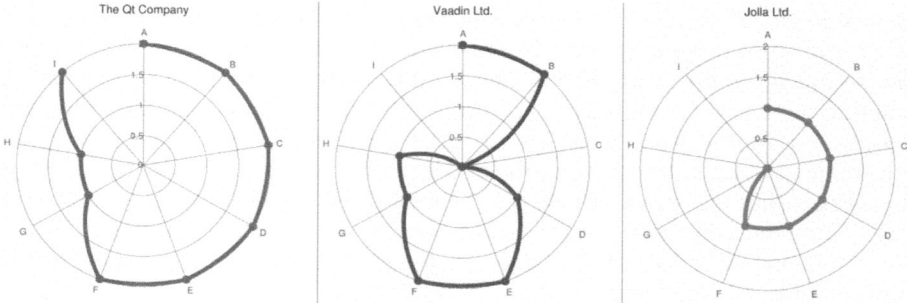

Fig. 1. Comparison of the three models.

tool[2] and assign oneself for a task. Also the tool that supported the code review process[3] was freely accessible. An approval from two humans was required for accepting a code contribution. Typically the code reviewers were, but were not required to be dedicated maintainers of the software. Partial automation of the testing process facilitated the work of code reviewers.

Vaadin Ltd. presented a more restrictive approach. The work flow coordination tool[4] was accessible for all, yet the company required code authors to write extensive test cases for their submissions. From there, the code was reviewed by dedicated employees of the host company. This arrangement limited community-drivenness of the development process considerably.

Jolla Ltd. did not offer access to work flow coordination tools of the complete Sailfish OS software. Instead it directed contributors to the Mer project's issue

---

[2] Jira.
[3] Gerrit.
[4] Git issues.

management tool[5]. From there, developers themselves needed to identify which part of the software's architecture their improvement considered, which required the developers to be moderately knowledgeable in terms of the software architecture before being able to contribute. A significant part of the development process was kept private by the host company, which did not let out knowledge about the status of the code integration process. To yield input from non-technical users, the company deployed a question and answer forum where users of the software could report and triage defects related to the user experience of the software, yet without any guarantees on the uptake or their work.

5.2 Influencing Development Priorities

As Qt and Vaadin received most of their requirements from users of their software, their internal development efforts were directed towards fulfilling the needs of their paying customers. In the Qt project, the openly accessible, detailed workflow management system[6] made development priorities clearly distinguishable. Development of Vaadin was largely carried out under the terms of the host company, however input for feature-level priorities were sought from the community by voting on a pre-selected set of features. In the Sailfish project, the development was driven by technical debts that become inherited from the software architecture's reliance on the external, independent OSS projects. The situation was largely focused on ensuring that the lower levels of architecture would support decisions made for the proprietary user interface layer.

5.3 Becoming an Actionable Developer

Practices on who can accept code contributions varied in between the projects. In the Qt project, both the core developer- and maintainer teams consisted of stakeholders of many organizational affiliations. These roles could be achieved through gaining individual merit and were open for anyone to pursue. In the case of Vaadin, the role was considered to be open for the community members, yet in practice the strict requirements for contributions made it very hard to enter the role. In the case of Jolla, the MerOS -community was genuinely community driven, welcoming many types of contributions from outsiders. However, the Mer consisted only a fraction of the Sailfish OS, and the host company's software developers occupied the many of the key positions in the community.

6 Discussion and Implications

The various hybrid OSS collaboration models assumed by the companies reflect the mission of the company and its business models. While origins of the project plays a role in how a hybrid community's governance model is built [21], licensing,

---

[5] Bugzilla.
[6] Jira.

technical architecture and development tools provide a framework in which the participation architecture of a community can be built [6]. Based on our study, we can provide some implications for the factors that can be used to affect the ways in which a host company can manage its boundaries in terms of accepting contributions from open communities.

The participation of external stakeholders can be restricted by licensing [6] or by regulating access to the source code by keeping selected software assets proprietary to the company [13]. Employing a distributed repository strategy proved effective in limiting the possibility of less knowledgeable hobbyists to take up development tasks. Opportunities for becoming a developer can be limited to a specific group of people by requiring a certain level of personal merit and initial or complementary contributions. At an extreme, contributors may be subject to a personal selection by members of the community or even by the host company before becoming an actionable developer.

An important design factor is what tasks a certain role withholds and who are allowed to perform them. Prioritization of tasks can at be the sole responsibility of the host company, or of a selected group of people such as maintainers who have gained their position through personal merit. At an extreme, prioritization can be open to anybody who can access the socio-technical systems or it can be acquired from unrelated, non-technical users by establishing e.g. online customer communities. In all cases, the host company can always define which input from the community it will use in its internal processes.

Community-drivenness requires a critical mass of external contributors [22]. This requirement can be eased by partial automation of the development process such as requirements prioritization or quality assurance. Even though testing and integration processes are supported with automation, it can be required that the final decisions are made in consensus by humans. Limiting this set of people provides a means for adjusting community drivenness of these processes. In this context, strength of the initiation rite for acquiring a certain role could be an interesting topic for future research.

Considering the level of openness: While the Qt company clearly pushed openness to the extreme, its community was found to be the most mature of the three we studied. While Qt started as a community-created project – although arguably with business reasons to do so – the company-created Vaadin project migrated to the open development model only after the it had gained a competitive edge. Sailfish, the newest entrant to the OSS market, was found to be very restricted when dealing with contributions that come from outside of the company. Vaadin represented the middle ground, although they put even more weight on the developers' views regarding direction of development and maturity of the product. In align with Schaarsmidt et al. [21], we find that these company-created projects seemed to maintain more control when compared to their community-driven counterparts.

Limitations. This study dealt with three OSS development communities that were selected to be as different as possible in terms of both age and purpose of their software products. Therefore, the generalizability of the results is limited and further research on projects that are both more similar in nature and of a larger scale is required. The question of representativeness limits the possibilities to generalize the study results. However, this limitation neither invalidates the findings nor prevents future studies from replicating the approach to evaluate whether they apply fully or partially in other types of hybrid OSS communities.

7 Conclusions

In this paper, we have investigated how hybrid OSS communities can be built to acquire contributors from company-external individuals. These communities, relying on open source software but mixing commercial and volunteer-based activities in their operations, have become an important way to create software systems for various contexts.

Based on the findings, it is clear that companies that use the hybrid OSS development model can act in different ways, leveraging either closed or open practices to support their business interests. A trend in the cases we have studied, it seems as the community matures, the level of openness increases, fostering community-driven peer production. However, the number of companies in the study is far too low to propose conclusive results.

The role of the open development community and the principles according to which individuals can meaningfully participate in the development are essential design factors of the hybrid OSS development model. How these should be defined and managed requires careful consideration on how much knowledge and influence should be released to the open development community, how different roles and privileges can be gained and how autonomously the community should be allowed to steer the development of the software product.

References

1. Benkler, Y.: Coase's penguin, or linux, the nature of the firm. http://arxiv.org/abs/cs/0109077
2. Riehle, D., Ellenberger, J., Menahem, T., Mikhailovski, B., Natchetoi, Y., Naveh, B., Odenwald, T.: Open collaboration within corporations using software forges. IEEE Softw. **26**(2), 52–58 (2009)
3. Dahlander, L., Magnusson, M.: How do firms make use of open source communities? Long Range Plan. **41**(6), 629–649 (2008)
4. Raymond, E.: The cathedral and the bazaar. Knowl. Technol. Policy **12**(3), 23–49 (1999)
5. Bosch, J.: From software product lines to software ecosystems. In: Proceedings of the 13th International Software Product Line Conference, pp. 111–119. Carnegie Mellon University (2009)
6. West, J., O'Mahony, S.: The role of participation architecture in growing sponsored open source communities. Ind. Innov. **15**(2), 145–168 (2008)

7. Colombo, M.G., Piva, E., Rossi-Lamastra, C.: Open innovation and within-industry diversification in small and medium enterprises: The case of open source software firms. Res. Policy **43**(5), 891–902 (2014). open Innovation: New Insights and Evidence, http://www.sciencedirect.com/science/article/pii/S0048733313001601
8. Gonzalez-Barahona, J.M., Robles, G.: Trends in free, libre, open source software communities: from volunteers to companies. Inform. Technol. **55**(5), 173–180 (2013)
9. De Noni, I., Ganzaroli, A., Orsi, L.: The evolution of oss governance: a dimensional comparative analysis. Scand. J. Manag. **29**(3), 247–263 (2013)
10. Linåker, J., Regnell, B., Munir, H.: Requirements engineering in open innovation: a research agenda. In: Proceedings of the 2015 International Conference on Software and System Process, pp. 208–212. ACM (2015)
11. Munir, H., Wnuk, K., Runeson, P.: Open innovation in software engineering: a systematic mapping study. Empirical Softw. Eng. **21**(2), 684–723 (2016)
12. Markus, M.L.: The governance of free/open source software projects: monolithic, multidimensional, or configurational? J. Manage. Gov. **11**(2), 151–163 (2007). http://dx.doi.org/10.1007/s10997-007-9021-x
13. Shah, S.K.: Motivation, governance, and the viability of hybrid forms in open source software development. Manage. Sci. **52**(7), 1000–1014 (2006)
14. O'Mahony, S.: The governance of open source initiatives: what does it mean to be community managed? J. Manage. Gov. **11**(2), 139–150 (2007)
15. Dahlander, L., Wallin, M.W.: A man on the inside: Unlocking communities as complementary assets. Res. Policy **35**(8), pp. 1243–1259 (2006). special issue commemorating the 20th Anniversary of David Teece's article, "Profiting from Innovation", in Research Policy. http://www.sciencedirect.com/science/article/pii/S0048733306001387
16. de Laat, P.B.: Governance of open source software: state of the art. J. Manag. Gov. **11**(2), 165–177 (2007). http://dx.doi.org/10.1007/s10997-007-9022-9
17. Toral, S.L., Martínez-Torres, M.R., Barrero, F.J.: Virtual communities as a resource for the development of oss projects: the case of linux ports to embedded processors. Behav. Inform. Technol. **28**(5), 405–419 (2009)
18. Wolfson, S.M., Lease, M.: Look before you leap: Legal pitfalls of crowdsourcing. Proc. Am. Soc. Inform. Sci. Technol. **48**(1), 1–10 (2011)
19. Mockus, A., Fielding, R.T., Herbsleb, J.D.: Two case studies of open source software development: apache and mozilla. ACM Trans. Softw. Eng. Methodol. (TOSEM) **113**, 309–346 (2002)
20. Yin, R.K.: Case Study Research: Design and Methods. Sage publications, Thousand Oaks (2014)
21. Schaarschmidt, M., Walsh, G., von Kortzfleisch, H.F.O.: How do firms influence open source software communities? a framework and empirical analysis of different governance modes. Inf. Organ. **25**(2), 99–114 (2015)
22. Dahlander, L.: Penguin in a new suit: a tale of how de novo entrants emerged to harness free and open source software communities. Ind. Corp. Change **16**(5), 913–943 (2007)

Open Access This chapter is licensed under the terms of the Creative Commons Attribution 4.0 International License (http://creativecommons.org/licenses/by/4.0/), which permits use, sharing, adaptation, distribution and reproduction in any medium or format, as long as you give appropriate credit to the original author(s) and the source, provide a link to the Creative Commons license and indicate if changes were made.

The images or other third party material in this chapter are included in the chapter's Creative Commons license, unless indicated otherwise in a credit line to the material. If material is not included in the chapter's Creative Commons license and your intended use is not permitted by statutory regulation or exceeds the permitted use, you will need to obtain permission directly from the copyright holder.

Principled Evaluation of Strengths and Weaknesses in FLOSS Communities: A Systematic Mixed Methods Maturity Model Approach

Sandro Andrade[1](✉) and Filipe Saraiva[2]

[1] GSORT Distributed Systems Group, Federal Institute of Education, Science, and Technology of Bahia (IFBA), Salvador, Bahia, Brazil
sandroandrade@ifba.edu.br
[2] Institute of Exact and Natural Sciences,
Federal University of Pará (UFPA), Belém, Pará, Brazil
saraiva@ufpa.br

Abstract. *Context:* Free and Open Source Software usually results from intricate socio-technical dynamics operating in a diverse and geographically dispersed community. Understanding the fundamental underpinnings of healthy and thriving communities is of paramount importance to evaluate existing efforts and identify improvement opportunities. *Objective:* This paper presents a novel reference model for evaluating the maturity of FLOSS communities by mixing quantitative and qualitative methods. *Method:* We build upon established guidelines for Design Science research in order to devise a well-informed and expressive maturity model, describing how those methods and procedures were used in the design and development of such a model. *Results:* We present the model structure and functions, as well as instructions on how to instantiate it as evaluations of FLOSS communities. The use of the proposed maturity model is demonstrated in four FLOSS communities. *Conclusion:* Whilst instantiating the model may be burdensome if aiming at sketchy evaluations, results indicate our model effectively captures the maturity regardless aspects such as community size and lifetime.

Keywords: FLOSS communities evaluation · Discourse communities · Maturity models · Design science research · Mixed methods research

1 Introduction

Free/Libre Open Source Software (FLOSS) has been recognized, over the past years, as a promising socio-technical approach to deliver high quality technology in spite of being usually developed by a diverse, often decentralized, and geographically distributed community [7,37]. Understanding the social dynamics, work practices, methods, and tools adopted by such communities has been of interest not only to the canonical software industry but also to researchers from distinct fields [12], such as Management Science [20], Information Systems [10], Economics [6], and Social Sciences [17], just to mention a few.

Healthy and thriving FLOSS communities rely on effective communication [22], powerful socio-technical infrastructure [30], and refined hacker culture [23] to manage decentralization issues, attenuate contribution barriers, and delivery quality software in a timely way to a usually vast userbase. Capturing such refined socio-technical practices in systematic models for evaluating FLOSS communities enables a more rigorous and well-informed basis to compare distinct FLOSS efforts, reveal improvement opportunities for a given FLOSS community, and support researchers in figuring out the characteristics of the FLOSS community they are investigating. Nowadays, such evaluations are hampered by the lack of expressive and systematic maturity models particularly designed to take into account the subtleties of FLOSS development culture.

The scarcity of such maturity models hinders the thorough realization of many activities. First, when undertaking empirical observations of FLOSS communities, researchers may want to insulate confounding factors by ensuring that observed communities have similar maturity. Second, although some incipient FLOSS projects with low maturity may be seen as promising opportunities, FLOSS investors usually prefer to sponsor seasoned communities, where risks are lower and ROI is more likely. Third, it usually takes some time to young community managers start understanding what makes a thriving FLOSS community. Knowing beforehand the many facets that FLOSS community maturity encompasses, how to measure them, and possible improvement opportunities is quite useful to shorten the time required to reach enhanced maturity.

Existing software development maturity models, while effective in capturing general process areas and key practices, are usually inapt or limited in coping with and assessing idiosyncrasies commonly found in FLOSS projects [32,36]. Most of the available methods for evaluating FLOSS communities entail the use of quantitative approaches usually expressed as metrics for aspects such as community activeness, size, diversity, and performance [9,11,21,27,28,31]. Whilst useful to investigate how community performance has been evolving over time, metrics by themselves provide no guidance regarding improvement opportunities and may be tricky to be applied across different FLOSS communities.

The work presented in this paper has been driven by two major long-term research questions: (RQ1) to which extent refined socio-technical practices of thriving FLOSS communities can be captured as a maturity model? and (RQ2) is such a maturity model of any help when investigating the achievements of different FLOSS communities or identifying opportunities for enhanced maturity? We believe existing approaches are still ineffectual in addressing the particularities of FLOSS development, rigorously supporting the replication of evaluations, and providing a well-informed artifact for revealing improvement opportunities.

This paper presents a novel maturity model for the systematic evaluation of FLOSS communities, particularly designed to capture those – sometimes ingenious – socio-technical activities that induce healthiness, long-term sustainability, and quality of delivered technologies. The model is slightly influenced by CMMI [34] and its structure encompasses nine maturity domains (named *improvement areas*). Each improvement area, in its turn, brings together a set of socio-technical activities (named *disciplines*) expected to be found in thriving communities. The realization degree of a discipline is evaluated by its corresponding (quantitative or qualitative) *metric*. Finally, our model specifies six distinct *maturity levels* and which disciplines are required by each level. A FLOSS community is said to be on a given maturity level when it exhibits all level's disciplines, each one with a metric value that satisfies a particular condition (named *acceptance criteria*) for such a discipline in that particular maturity level.

The process of instantiating the maturity model as a new FLOSS community evaluation is described and, afterwards, demonstrated for four communities (KDE Plasma, Apache HTTP, Poppler, and Inkscape) with different sizes and lifetimes. Results show that the model is able to identify maturity in spite of such differences and that the adopted mixed methods (quantitative/qualitative) approach helps mitigating issues presented by existing evaluation techniques.

The remainder of this paper is organized as follows. Section 2 details the Design Science and mixed methods approaches that guided this research. Section 3 explains the notion of maturity of FLOSS communities, the problem of evaluating such communities, and the requirements for the proposed maturity model. Section 4 discusses related work, while Sect. 5 explains the design (structure and functions) of our model. In Sect. 6, we demonstrate how our maturity model was used to evaluate four distinct FLOSS communities. In Sect. 7, we discuss the strengths and weaknesses of our proposal and present venues for future research. Finally, Sect. 8 draws the concluding remarks.

2 Method

This work was carried out in accordance with the research framework presented by Johannesson and Perjons in [16] and supported by the guidelines for mixed methods research introduced by Creswell in [8].

Johannesson&Perjons' (JP) framework aims at creating an artifact and producing knowledge about how such an artifact helps sorting out a problem that recurrently appears in a given intended practice. Their framework defines five main activities (with associated input and output) and provides guidelines for carrying out such activities, selecting suitable research strategies, and relating the research to an existing knowledge base. The five activities are: *explicate problem* (described, for this work, in Sect. 3), *define requirements* (also in Sect. 3), *design and develop artifact* (Sect. 5), *demonstrate artifact* (Sect. 6), and *evaluate artifact* (not addressed in this paper and subject of future work).

The structure of the maturity model we propose herein entails a set of quantitative and qualitative metrics which evaluate different aspects of a given community. Therefore, using our model to create a new evaluation of a particular community can be seen as conducting a mixed methods research, where both quantitative and qualitative data collection and analysis techniques are simultaneously applied. We build on the guidelines provided by Creswell in [8] in order to define how the proposed model should be used to evaluate a community.

3 Problem and Requirements

In consonance with the JP framework, we carried out the *explicate problem* activity by undertaking two sub-activities: *define precisely* and *position and justify*.

Define precisely. Before defining the problem of assessing FLOSS communities maturity, it is crucial to explain what we mean by *maturity* in this work and its impact on community's healthiness. By maturity we mean the degree of accomplishment a FLOSS community exhibits in reaching the goals of delivering high quality technology and becoming an ecosystem which supports socio-technical advances for all of its constituent actors. We elaborate this concept of maturity around three major underpinnings: *(i)* userbase management; *(ii)* long-term sustainability; and *(iii)* inner/outer communication.

Userbase management encloses all practices which ease the delivery of high quality technology to an ever increasing userbase. This includes, for instance, quality assurance, software localization, and the availability of user-friendly installers or binary packages. *Long-term sustainability* refers to those practices which try to keep the community's health in spite of disturbances in the underlying socio-technical infrastructure, such as contributors leaving the project, disruptive strategical changes, or internal conflicts. Finally, *inner/outer communication* includes all practices which enable the effective communication inside the community and between the community and other ecosystem actors. Such maturity underpinnings represent overarching views of maturity and are further detailed as a set of disciplines that make up the model we propose herein.

With that view of maturity in mind, the problem addressed in this work can be defined: how should one proceed to assess the maturity degree of a given FLOSS community? How to make such evaluations more systematic and replicable across different researchers? How to identify improvement opportunities in a given FLOSS community to enhance its maturity degree?

Position and justify. We believe that assessing FLOSS communities maturity is a significant and challenging problem of general interest. It may appear in quite diverse practices. For example, knowing about a community maturity is an important decision-making information for a FLOSS investor selecting a community to support. Community managers may benefit from such a maturity model by carrying out self-assessments and identifying improvement opportunities. Social sciences researchers doing ethnographic studies may want to deliberately choose a mature community or an incipient one depending on their research goals. FLOSS educators may select communities with established mentoring programs (and, therefore, with increased maturity) to push their students into initial contributions. End users or companies may want to assess maturity to decide about the adoption of competing FLOSS solutions. Software Engineering researchers may undertake maturity assessment as an early exploratory/descriptive study and then, afterwards, decide about future research.

The *define requirements* activity was carried out by undertaking the two sub-activities proposed in JP framework: *outline artifact* and *elicit requirements*.

Outline artifact. The artifact proposed herein is a model which captures prescriptive knowledge about how to create new community evaluations.

Elicit requirements. On the basis of the aforementioned drawbacks of existing approaches, we defined the following requirements for the proposed maturity model: (R1) *model generality*: the model must be effective in evaluating the maturity of FLOSS communities regardless their size and lifetime; (R2) *model expressiveness*: the model must encompass socio-technical activities particularly relevant to FLOSS; (R3) *model predictability*: the model must support, as much as possible, systematic and replicable evaluations.

4 Related Work

In [25], authors studied 40 successful and 40 unsuccessful FLOSS projects from SourceForge and analyzed their respective maturities by verifying the (lack of) adoption of some important processes/tools like mailing lists, version control systems, documentation, and more. The successful projects exhibited the adoption and continuous use of such processes, as opposed to those unsuccessful projects.

The work presented in [21] performs a study on maturity models for FLOSS communities in order to decide whether a software can be used for commercial solutions. In such a work, they assume there is a correlation between the maturity level of a FLOSS community and the products (software systems) delivered by this community: if the community has a high maturity level then the software created by them will exhibit a high maturity as well. Their approach is heavily based on CMMI [34], using the same levels and descriptions.

Sony Mobile has been developing studies on FLOSS maturity models for a similar context. Their model, described in [3], defines five levels of maturity for adoption of open source technologies: from "accidental" and "repetitive" – when FLOSS use is driven by individual initiatives, through "directed" – when FLOSS adoption has gained support from executive management, to "collaborate" and "prevail" – when a full-fledged FLOSS culture is already in place. This model initially supported the decision of Sony Mobile about the use of Android OS in their smart-phone products. Later, they have extended such model into a general tool for evaluation of FLOSS projects.

In [28], the authors propose an assessment model for FLOSS development processes named *Open Source Maturity Model*. Such a model resembles CMMI in many aspects and it is aimed to be used by both companies and FLOSS communities. In their work, a given FLOSS can be classified in one of three levels and the classification process is carried out by analyzing whether some elements of the management and development process are used by the community. For instance, they verify whether the community yields product documentation, the popularity of the software, contributions from companies, and more.

The QualOSS model, described in [32], evaluates qualitative aspects of software products and their communities in order to verify software quality and maintainability. In [15], a qualitative model based on metrics extracted from source code repositories, mailing lists, and issues tracking tools is proposed. QSOS (Qualification and Selection of Open Source Software) [2] is a maturity assessment methodology that aims to compare and select FLOSS projects to be used by companies. QSOS evaluations are carried out in four steps. In the "define" step, users must define different elements to be evaluated (e.g. features, license, and community). The "evaluate" step assigns scores to each one of such elements. In the "qualify" step, users apply filters/weights to scores in order to verify whether a project is good enough to be adopted. Finally, the "select" step verifies whether the software fulfill the needs defined by the user.

In spite of such a variety of models already available, we believe that some capabilities, not tackled by previous work, are important enough to justify the need for a new model. First, most of existing models provide no systematic instruments for measuring activities performance and, therefore, are highly dependent of a skilled evaluator to succeed. Second, social aspects are usually not addressed (except in People-CMM). Third, such models usually evaluate very specific subjects, such as product's quality or benefits of FLOSS adoption, being helpful only for those particular goals. Finally, mixing qualitative and quantitative metrics to improve model's accuracy is rarely adopted in existing work.

5 The Maturity Model

The sub-activities defined in JP framework for the *design and develop artifact* activity are: *imagine and brainstorm, assess and select, sketch and build*, and *justify and reflect*.

Table 1. Maturity model's improvement areas and corresponding categories

Acronym	Improvement Area (IA)	Category
CA	Community activeness	Inner/outer communication
FM	Financial management	Long-term sustainability
OG	Open governance	Inner/outer communication
QA	Process and product quality assurance	Userbase management
PR	Public relations	Inner/outer communication
SI	Social infrastructure	Long-Term Sustainability
SM	Strategic management	Long-term sustainability
UR	User reachability	Userbase management

Imagine and brainstorm. In this work, the maturity model requirements and the activities it encompasses were elicited by using the participant observation

[33] method. The authors of this paper have been contributing to communities such as Qt [35], KDE [18], and Mageia [24] for nearly ten years, working on activities that span coding, promotion, artwork, finances, community management, and strategic management. In order to elicit the socio-technical activities captured in our model, we carried out a brainstorm which resulted in an extensive enumeration of practices we think highly impacts community maturity.

Assess and select. After having a list of prospective socio-technical activities, we ranked each activity regarding its impact on community maturity and its likelihood of being generically carried out in any FLOSS community (global practice). We systematically discarded those ones with minor impact on maturity or those whose adoption makes sense only in particular scenarios. Whilst brainstorming is obviously amenable to research bias, we consider that the rank-discard operation alleviates some threats and makes it acceptable for this paper's purposes. The adoption of more rigorous techniques for selecting those socio-technical activities are subject of future work.

Sketch and build. We carried out this sub-activity in many iterations, where the model constructs, structure, and functions were incrementally refined as we gained knowledge about the proposed artifact. The model is slightly influenced by CMMI (in particular, by CMMI-Dev [34] and People-CMM [4] models), since it also defines levels of maturity and expected disciplines for each level. The following paragraphs explain the final model's structure and behavior, as well as the decisions we took in order to fulfill the requirements mentioned in Sect. 3.

The proposed maturity model is defined as a tuple $MM = \langle C, IA, D, L \rangle$; where $C = \{userbase\ management,\ long\text{-}term\ sustainability,\ inner/outer\ communication\}$ is a set of *categories* representing the three maturity underpinning presented in Sect. 3, IA is a set of *improvement areas*, D is a set of *disciplines*, and L is a set of *levels* of increasingly maturity. An improvement area $ia_i \in IA$ is defined as a tuple $ia_i = \langle a, n, c \rangle$; where a is the improvement area's *acronym*, n is the improvement area's *name*, and $c \in C$ is the improvement area's associated *category*. Table 1 presents the categories and improvement areas of our model.

A discipline $d_i \in D$ is defined as a tuple $d_i = \langle a, n, t, \mu, pv, ia \rangle$; where a is the discipline's *acronym*, n is the discipline's *name*, $t \in \{T\text{-}technical,\ S\text{-}social,\ S/T\text{-}socio\text{-}technical\}$ is the discipline's *type*, μ is the discipline's *metric*, pv is the discipline's *preferable value*, and ia is the discipline's associated *improvement area*. Each metric $d_i.\mu$ is defined in a quantitative (QT) or qualitative (QL) way. A preferable value $d_i.pv$ specify whether maturity increases with greater ($\uparrow$) or smaller ($\downarrow$) values, for quantitative metrics, or with which specific values (e.g. Yes/No), for qualitative metrics. Table 2 presents the model's disciplines.

Finally, a level $l_i \in L$ is defined as a tuple $l_i = \langle n, CP \rangle$; where n is the level's name and CP is the level's set of *compliance points*. A compliance point $cp_{ij} \in l_i.CP$, in its turn, is defined as a tuple $\langle rd, ac(rd.\mu) \rangle$; where $rd \in D$ is the compliance point's *requested discipline* and $ac(rd.\mu)$ is a corresponding predicate named *acceptance criteria* that, when evaluated as true, denotes that

Table 2. Some maturity model's disciplines for each improvement area (IA)

IA	Acronym	Discipline	Type	Metric ($\mu_{Acronym}$)	Type
QA	QA1	Static code analysis	T	% codebase analyzed	QT ($\uparrow$)
	QA2	Code review	T	% codebase reviewed	QT ($\uparrow$)
	QA3	Continuous integration	T	% codebase under CI	QT ($\uparrow$)
	QA4	Documentation policy	T	Qualitative evidence	QL (Yes)
	QA5	Release schedule	T	Qualitative evidence	QL (Yes)
CA	CA1	Mailing list activity	S/T	Norm. threads/month	QT ($\uparrow$)
	CA2	Mailing list resp. Rate	S/T	% threads answered	QT ($\uparrow$)
	CA3	Bug fixing	T	% bugs fixed/month	QT ($\uparrow$)
	CA4	Activity diversity	S/T	Norm. pony factor	QT ($\uparrow$)
OG	OG1	Public repository	T	Qualitative evidence	QL (Yes)
	OG2	Public roadmap	T	Qualitative evidence	QL (Yes)
	OG3	Open release process	T	Qualitative evidence	QL (Yes)
	OG4	Open QA process	T	Qualitative evidence	QL (Yes)
UR	UR1	Localized content	T	Qualitative evidence	QL (Yes)
	UR2	Binary packages	T	Qualitative evidence	QL (Yes)
	UR3	Cross-Platf. support	T	Qualitative evidence	QL (Yes)
PR	PR1	Website	S	Completeness degree	QT ($\uparrow$)
	PR2	Release announces	S	Qualitative evidence	QL (Yes)
SI	SI1	Regular sprints	S/T	#sprints/year	QT ($\uparrow$)
	SI2	Newcomers program	S/T	Qualitative evidence	QL (Yes)
FM	FM1	NGO/Foundation	S	Qualitative evidence	QL (Yes)
	FM2	Sponsorship strategy	S/T	Qualitative evidence	QL (Yes)
SM	SM1	Board of directors	S/T	Qualitative evidence	QL (Yes)
	SM2	Advisory board	S/T	Qualitative evidence	QL (Yes)

the discipline rd is carried out with a maturity degree that is good enough for the level l_i. The model's levels and disciplines are presented in Table 3.

The maturity of a given FLOSS community FC is defined as the name of the maximum level l_m that has all its compliance points satisfied in FC:

$$M(FC) = l_m.n; \text{ where } m = \max_{i: l_i \in L \wedge \forall cp \in l_i.CP: cp.ac(cp.rd.\mu)} i$$

Justify and reflect. In order to cope with the subtleties of our definition of maturity and leverage the fulfillment of requirement R2 (model expressiveness), we adopted a mixed methods approach where all quantitative and qualitative data collection/analysis steps are carried out simultaneously. A last analysis step converges the partial results and come up with an ultimate outcome. In our model, this is implemented by a set of acceptance criteria defined for each level. We address requirement R1 (model generality) by ensuring all metrics use

Table 3. Maturity model's Levels with required disciplines and acceptance criteria

Level	Disciplines	Acceptance criteria
1 (operational)	CA[1–3]	$\mu_{CA1} \geq 0.1 \land \mu_{CA2} \geq 0.5 \land \mu_{CA3} \geq 0.1$
2 (proactive)	QA2, OG1	$\mu_{QA2} \geq 0.1 \land \mu_{OG1} = Yes$
	PR[1–2]	$\mu_{PR1} \geq 2 \land \mu_{PR2} = Yes$
3 (established)	QA[2, 4, 5]	$\mu_{QA2} \geq 0.5 \land \mu_{QA4} = Yes \land \mu_{QA5} = Yes$
	CA[1–4]	$\mu_{CA1} \geq 0.5 \land \mu_{CA2} \geq 0.8 \land \mu_{CA3} \geq 0.6 \land \mu_{CA4} \geq 0.05$
	UR[1–2], PR[1–2]	$\mu_{UR1} = \mu_{UR2} = \mu_{PR2} = Yes \land \mu_{PR1} \geq 3$
4 (managed)	QA[1–3], SI2	$\mu_{QA1} \geq 0.8 \land \mu_{QA2} \geq 0.75 \land \mu_{QA3} \geq 0.5 \land \mu_{SI2} = Yes$
	OG[2], UR[3]	$\mu_{OG2} = \mu_{UR3} = Yes$
5 (sustainable)	OG[3–4], SM[1–2]	$\mu_{OG3} = \mu_{OG4} = \mu_{SM1} = \mu_{SM2} = Yes$
	FM[1–2]	$\mu_{FM1} = \mu_{FM2} = Yes$

normalized values, insulating the effect of community size/lifetime. For example, the normalized Pony Factor is defined as the canonical Pony Factor [26] divided by the total number of core developers. Most of metrics presented in Table 2 are straightforward and may be evaluated by mining data sources such as version control systems, mail archives, code review platforms, and bug tracking systems. The metric *completeness degree* assigns an integer value in [0, 5] to the community's website, depending on how many information is made available.

6 Artifact Demonstration

As mentioned in Sect. 2, in this work we evaluated the proposed maturity model by demonstration. JP framework defines two sub-activities for the *demonstrate artifact* activity: *choose or design cases* and *apply artifact*.

Choose or design cases. We chose four representative FLOSS communities to demonstrate to use of the proposed maturity model: KDE Plasma [19], Apache HTTP [1], Poppler [29], and Inkscape [14]. Such communities were selected because they exhibit different characteristics regarding size and lifetime, which makes it possible a more thorough investigation on how successful our model is in addressing requirement R1 (model generality).

Apply artifact. All quantitative metrics defined for our maturity model's disciplines have been evaluated, in the aforementioned FLOSS communities, manually, by using tools such as `git_stats` [13] or by scripts developed as part of this work. We collected evidence for the qualitative metrics by observing documents such as project's website, wiki pages, and mailing list archives. Table 4 presents the evaluations of some maturity model's metrics.

Table 4. Some metric values for the four FLOSS communities evaluated

Metric	KDE plasma	Apache HTTP	Poppler	Inkscape
μ_{QA1}	0.82	0.00	0.00	0.87
μ_{QA2}	0.93	0.96	0.12	0.77
μ_{QA3}	1.00	1.00	1.00	0.52
μ_{CA4}	0.19	0.16	0.83	0.21
μ_{OG3}	Yes	Yes	Yes	No
μ_{OG4}	Yes	No	Yes	No
μ_{PR1}	3	5	2	5
μ_{SI1}	2	1	0	1
μ_{FM1}	Yes (KDE e.V.)	Yes (ASF)	No	Yes (Inkscape)
μ_{FM3}	No	Yes	No	Yes

7 Discussion and Future Work

The maturity evaluation data presented in Table 4 allows one to classify the investigated FLOSS communities in the following maturity levels: KDE Plasma (4: managed), Apache HTTP (3: established), Poppler (2: proactive), and Inkscape (4: managed). In spite of having nice politics for code review ($\mu_{QA2} = 0.96$) and continuous integration ($\mu_{QA3} = 1.00$), Apache HTTP fails in reaching higher maturity mostly because of the lack of static code analysis ($\mu_{QA1} = 0.00$) – important to reduce bugs density. Poppler got a low maturity level because of the lack of quality assurance practices such as code review, documentation policy, and release schedule – probably a consequence of its small size (biggest normalized Pony Factor: $\mu_{CA4} = 0.83$). Finally, KDE Plasma and Inkscape fail in having increased maturity because of the lack of sponsorship strategy ($\mu_{FM3} = No$) and open release and QA processes ($\mu_{OG3} = \mu_{OG4} = No$), respectively.

At this point, some important considerations can be drawn about the maturity model's limitations when evaluating FLOSS communities and threats to the validity of the demonstration presented herein. First, the model's acceptance criteria have been defined to assign different fulfillment degrees of disciplines into increasingly levels of maturity. Obviously, different acceptance criteria may lead to different results and are subject of further investigation. Second, the lack of more systematic information about how to carry out the qualitative evaluations may also imply in different results when replicating evaluations. Third, exceptional scenarios such as lack of community activeness because of heavy codebase stabilization (and, therefore, high maturity) are not currently addressed.

As for future work, a number of improvement venues may be identified. Creating new evaluations may be burdensome, specially for seasoned communities with a lot of data to be analyzed. We plan to provide better support by creating a new tool or extending initiatives like Biritergia's Grimoire Lab [5]. Advanced empirical studies are also planned, aimed at providing fundamental knowledge for enhancing the capture of socio-technical activities, refining the acceptance criteria, and evaluating maturity model quality attributes.

8 Conclusion

This paper presented a systematic mixed methods approach for evaluating the maturity of FLOSS communities. The novelty of our approach is the definition of a maturity model which captures socio-technical practices endemic to FLOSS ecosystems and mixes quantitative and qualitative metrics to systematically support the assessment of maturity and identification of improvement opportunities. We described the model structure and behavior, and demonstrated how to use the proposed artifact to evaluate four FLOSS communities with distinct characteristics. We believe this work advances the field of open source research by providing a generic artifact which enables the systematic capture of refined FLOSS-related socio-technical activities and supports researchers in carrying out replicable FLOSS communities evaluation experiments.

References

1. Apache Foundation: The Apache HTTP Server Project (2017). http://httpd.apache.org
2. Atos: Qualification and Selection of Open Source software (QSOS) (2013). http://backend.qsos.org/download/qsos-2.0_en.pdf
3. Bergman, O.: Report from the SCALARE project - sony mobile's involvement in open source. Technical report 1, Sony Mobile (2014). http://scalare.org/sony-mobiles-involvement-in-open-source/
4. Curtis, B., Hefley, W.E., Miller, S.: People Capability Maturity Model (P-CMM), version 2.0, second edition. Technical report CMU/SEI-2009-TR-003, Software Engineering Institute, Carnegie Mellon University, Pittsburgh, PA (2010). http://cmmiinstitute.com/resources/people-capability-maturity-model-p-cmm
5. Bitergia: Grimoire Lab - OpenSource Development Analytics toolkit (2017). http://grimoirelab.github.io/
6. Bitzer, J., Schröder, P.: The economics of open source software development. Elsevier (2006). https://books.google.com.br/books?id=obex6Fkrc18C
7. Capiluppi, A., Lago, P., Morisio, M.: Characteristics of open source projects. In: 7th European Conference on Software Maintenance and Reengineering (CSMR 2003), 26–28, 2003, Benevento, Italy, Proceedings, p. 317. IEEE Computer Society (2003). http://dx.doi.org/10.1109/CSMR.2003.1192440
8. Creswell, J.W.: Research Design: Qualitative, Quantitative, and Mixed Methods Approaches, 4th edn. SAGE Publications Inc., Thousand Oaks (2013)
9. Crowston, K., Howison, J.: Assessing the health of open source communities. IEEE Comput. **39**(5), 89–91 (2006). http://dx.doi.org/10.1109/MC.2006.152
10. Fitzgerald, B.: The transformation of open source software. MIS Q. **30**(3), 587–598 (2006). http://misq.org/the-transformation-of-open-source-software.html
11. Franco-Bedoya, O.: Open source software ecosystems: towards a modelling framework. In: Damiani, E., Frati, F., Riehle, D., Wasserman, A.I. (eds.) OSS 2015. IAICT, vol. 451, pp. 171–179. Springer, Cham (2015). doi:10.1007/978-3-319-17837-0_16

12. Gacek, C., Arief, B.: The many meanings of open source. IEEE Softw. **21**(1), 34–40 (2004). http://dx.doi.org/10.1109/MS.2004.1259206
13. Gieniusz, T.: GitStats is a git repository statistics generator (2017). https://github.com/tomgi/git_stats
14. Inkscape Community: Inkscape - Draw Freely (2017). http://inkscape.org
15. Izquierdo-Cortazar, D., González-Barahona, J.M., Dueñas, S., Robles, G.: Towards automated quality models for software development communities: the QualOSS and FLOSSMetrics case. In: e Abreu, F.B., Faria, J.P., Machado, R.J. (eds.) Quality of Information and Communications Technology, 7th International Conference on the Quality of Information and Communications Technology (QUATIC 2010), Porto, Portugal, 29 September - 2 October, 2010, Proceedings, pp. 364–369. IEEE Computer Society (2010). http://dx.doi.org/10.1109/QUATIC.2010.66
16. Johannesson, P., Perjons, E.: An Introduction to Design Science. Springer, Heidelberg (2014). http://dx.doi.org/10.1007/978-3-319-10632-8
17. Karanović, J.: Free software and the politics of sharing. In: Digital Anthropology, p. 185 (2013)
18. KDE Community: KDE - Experience Freedom! (2017). http://www.kde.org
19. KDE Community: Plasma Desktop (2017). http://plasma-desktop.org
20. von Krogh, G., von Hippel, E.: The promise of research on open source software. Manage. Sci. **52**(7), 975–983 (2006). http://dx.doi.org/10.1287/mnsc.1060.0560
21. Kuwata, Y., Takeda, K., Miura, H.: A study on maturity model of open source software community to estimate the quality of products. In: Jedrzejowicz, P., Jain, L.C., Howlett, R.J., Czarnowski, I. (eds.) 18th International Conference in Knowledge Based and Intelligent Information and Engineering Systems (KES 2014), Gdynia, Poland, 15–17, Procedia Computer Science, vol. 35, pp. 1711–1717. Elsevier (2014). http://dx.doi.org/10.1016/j.procs.2014.08.264
22. Lanubile, F., Ebert, C., Prikladnicki, R., Vizcaíno, A.: Collaboration tools for global software engineering. IEEE Softw. **27**(2), 52–55 (2010). http://dx.doi.org/10.1109/MS.2010.39
23. Lin, Y.: Hacker culture and the FLOSS innovation. IJOSSP **4**(3), 26–37 (2012). http://dx.doi.org/10.4018/ijossp.2012070103
24. Mageia Community: Home of the Mageia project (2017). http://www.mageia.org
25. Michlmayr, M.: Software process maturity and the success of free software projects. In: Software Engineering: Evolution and Emerging Technologies, pp. 3–14. IOS Press (2005). http://www.booksonline.iospress.nl/Content/View.aspx?piid=1139
26. Nalley, D.: The tragedy of open source (2017). http://opensource.cioreview.com/cxoinsight/the-tragedy-of-open-source-nid-23375-cid-92.html
27. Ortega, F., González-Barahona, J.M.: Quantitative analysis of the wikipedia community of users. In: Désilets, A., Biddle, R. (eds.) Proceedings of the 2007 International Symposium on Wikis, Montreal, Quebec, Canada, 21–25 October 2007, pp. 75–86. ACM (2007). http://doi.acm.org/10.1145/1296951.1296960
28. Petrinja, E., Nambakam, R., Sillitti, A.: Introducing the opensource maturity model. In: Proceedings of the 2009 ICSE Workshop on Emerging Trends in Free/Libre/Open Source Software Research and Development (FLOSS 2009), pp. 37–41 (2009). http://dx.doi.org/10.1109/FLOSS.2009.5071358
29. Poppler Community: Poppler (2017). https://poppler.freedesktop.org
30. Scacchi, W.: Socio-technical interaction networks in free/open source software development processes. In: Acuña, S.T., Juristo, N. (eds.) Software Process Modeling, pp. 1–27. Springer, Heidelberg (2005)

31. Sigfridsson, A., Sheehan, A.: On qualitative methodologies and dispersed communities: reflections on the process of investigating an open source community. Inf. Softw. Technol. **53**(9), 981–993 (2011). http://dx.doi.org/10.1016/j.infsof.2011.01.012
32. Soto, M., Ciolkowski, M.: The QualOSS open source assessment model measuring the performance of open source communities. In: Proceedings of the Third International Symposium on Empirical Software Engineering and Measurement (ESEM), 15–16, 2009, Lake Buena Vista, Florida, USA, pp. 498–501. ACM/IEEE Computer Society (2009). http://doi.acm.org/10.1145/1671248.1671316
33. Spradley, J.P.: Participant Observation. Waveland Press, Long Grove (2016)
34. CMMI Product Team: CMMI for development, v1.3. Technical report CMU/SEI-2010-TR-033, Software Engineering Institute, Carnegie Mellon University, Pittsburgh, PA (2010). http://resources.sei.cmu.edu/library/asset-view.cfm?AssetID=9661
35. The Qt Company: Qt—cross-platform software development for embedded & desktop (2017). http://www.qt.io
36. von Wangenheim, C.G., Hauck, J.C.R., von Wangenheim, A.: Enhancing open source software in alignment with CMMI-DEV. IEEE Softw. **26**(2), 59–67 (2009). http://dx.doi.org/10.1109/MS.2009.34
37. Wilson, T.D.: Understanding Open Source Software Development. Addison-wesley, London, xi, p. 211 (2002). ISBN 0-201-73496-6. http://informationr.net/ir/reviews/revs046.html. Review of: Jodeph feller & Brian Fitzgerald

Open Access This chapter is licensed under the terms of the Creative Commons Attribution 4.0 International License (http://creativecommons.org/licenses/by/4.0/), which permits use, sharing, adaptation, distribution and reproduction in any medium or format, as long as you give appropriate credit to the original author(s) and the source, provide a link to the Creative Commons license and indicate if changes were made.

The images or other third party material in this chapter are included in the chapter's Creative Commons license, unless indicated otherwise in a credit line to the material. If material is not included in the chapter's Creative Commons license and your intended use is not permitted by statutory regulation or exceeds the permitted use, you will need to obtain permission directly from the copyright holder.

Posters and Tools

Measuring Perceived Trust in Open Source Software Communities

Mahbubul Syeed[1], Juho Lindman[2], and Imed Hammouda[3(✉)]

[1] American International University-Bangladesh, Dhaka, Bangladesh
mahbubul.syeed@aiub.edu
[2] Chalmers and University of Gothenburg, Gothenburg, Sweden
juho.lindman@ait.gu.se
[3] University of Gothenburg, Gothenburg, Sweden
imed.hammouda@cse.gu.se

Abstract. We investigate the different aspects of measuring trust in Open Source Software (OSS) communities. In the theoretical part we review seminal works related to trust in OSS development. This investigation provides background to our empirical part where we measure trust in a community (in terms of *kudo*). Our efforts provide further avenues to develop trust-based measurement tools. These are helpful for academics and practitioners interesting in quantifiable traits of OSS trust.

1 Introduction

Trust can be perceived as the relationship between people where one person is taking a risk to accept other persons' action [1]. Such trust is one of the fundamental traits of a successful collaborative development environment, e.g., OSS projects [3–6].

Trust is directly linked to securing a functioning development community, community governance and on-going group work [3,4]. A community with such attributes can attract new developers to join and contribute in the project [4]. Therefore, the sustainability of an OSS project much depends on trust-related questions [2].

Alongside, third party organizations often try to ensure the quality and re-usability of an OSS component before adoption. Such verification is strongly coupled with the trust rating of the developers who developed those modules [9–11]. Therefore, assessing trust among the developers is a seminal question in OSS research. Recent study in [5] infer trust among developers based on their contributions. Others measured developers' contributions in Man-Month to investigate trust among them [7].

This study address the following two issues related to trust: first, we investigate the relationship between developers' contribution in OSS projects and their trust rating in the community, which is formulated as follows, *RQ1: How likely a trust rating of a developer changes when contributing to OSS projects?* Second, we investigate how community status affects members endorsing each others' contribution. Status difference may arise due to: (a) different trust levels in the community, and (b) homophilic elements [8], e.g., same project, country, location, programming language and same community status. Therefore we investigate the following, *RQ2: How likely developers with different community status will endorse each others' contribution?*

2 Methodology

2.1 Data Collection and Presentation

Our data is from OpenHub [12] which records the evaluation information (popularly known as *kudo*) sent or received by the developers over time. Developers are ranked according to their kudo scores, known as *kudo ranks*. Data is collected using the offered open APIs, which returns results in XML. Relevant information is then extracted and stored in database for further analysis.

Developer Account information. This study extracts 563,427 registered developer account information [13] that includes the following: developers account id, name, post count, and kudo rank. *Kudo rank* (a number between 1 and 10) defines ranking of the member based on certain criteria, e.g., kudo received from other members and history of contributions in OSS projects [9].

Project information. This study extracted 662,439 OSS project data which holds the following information: project id, name, and total user.

Contributor information. A contributor dataset holds project specific contributions made by each developer. A total of 844,012 contribution records were collected, each of which holds, project specific contributor's id and name, personal account id and name, project id in which contribution is made, time of first and last commit, total number of commits and the man month (i.e., the number of months for which a contributor made at least one commit). In the context of OpenHub *Man Month* represents the accumulated contributions made by a developer in OSS projects.

Kudo sent and received history. Following information related to kudo sent and received by a member for a given period of time is collected: sender or receiver account id and name, receiver or sender account id and name, project id and name, contributors id, name and date when the kudo was sent or received. A total of 46,926 kudo received records and 57,458 kudo sent records are collected.

Kudo sent and received history data is then combined to generate a uniform dataset that has the following data items: Sender account id and account name, receiver account id and name, project id and name to which the kudo was sent, contributor id and name, and the date when kudo was sent.

2.2 Data Analysis

RQ1: To determine the extent to which a developer is trusted against his contributions in OSS projects, following approach is adopted. First, contributors (or

Table 1. Developers count on first commit date

First commit date	No of developers committed
2012-03-26	40
2012-07-05	39
2012-05-10	36

developers) are grouped based on the first commit date. Then the three dates in which maximum number of developers count found are taken for further analysis, as shown in Table 1.

Then, the contributions (Sect. 2.1) and the kudo rank (Sect. 2.1) of every developer under each of the three dates are measured. This measurement is done from the first commit date till the last. In this study, the *man month* (Sect. 2.1) is used to measure developer contributions. Alongside, *Kudo rank* is used to represent the trust value of a developer. Additionally, following logical assumptions are made: (a) each of the developers starts with a kudo rank 1 at their first commit date, and (b) change in this kudo rank or trust rating is associated with the amount of contributions made by that developer over a given period of time.

RQ2: Next we examine how often developers of different community status endorse each others contributions. For this, developers are clustered according to their kudo ranks. Example clusters are, kudo rank (9 and 10), (7 and 8), (5 and 6), (3 and 4) and (1 and 2). Then, the log of kudo sent and received (Sect. 2.1) among developers in different clusters is recorded. This will offer a holistic view on the exchange of kudo among developers of different trust values.

Second, exchange of kudo is examined from two perspectives, namely, sending/receiving kudo (a) directly to developers' personal account and (b) in the contributors' project specific account in which the developer has contributed. This will portray a deeper understanding on how developers of different trust value recognize each others' contributions.

Third, kudo exchange log was generated based on developers who worked in the same project, distinct project, and both. This will provide insight whether working on the same projects stimulate higher kudo exchange.

3 Result and Synthesis

RQ1: How likely that a trust rating of a developer changes when contributing to the OSS projects?
The underlying assumption of this research question is that a developer should start with a kudo rank 1 (or trust rating 1) at the first committing date. And this kudo rank keeps changing along with his contributions in projects over time.

As per the reported results it is observed that 78% to 100% developers who have kudo rank 9 contributed to projects for more than 24 man-months.

Whereas, 54% to 79% developers at kudo rank 8 contributed more than 24 man-months. Likewise, the man-months contribution goes down along with low kudo ranks. For instance, none of the developers at kudo rank 5 has contribution record of more than 24 man-months. To summarize our findings, developers trust rating in the community is associated with the contributions they made in the projects over time and the amount of contributions has an impact on the trust value they attain at a given point of time.

RQ2: How likely that developers with different community status will endorse each others' contribution?
We aim to identify the dynamics between the community status of the developers and endorsing each others' contributions. In order to do so, this study analyzed the collected data from three different perspectives as presented in Sect. 2.2. First perspective is to study the kudo exchange pattern among the developers who belong to different kudo rank clusters. Reported results show that almost all the kudos are sent to the developers who belong to the kudo rank between 7 and 10. For instance, developers having kudo ranks between 9 and 10 sent almost all of their kudos to the developer having kudo rank between 7 and 10. This pattern holds for all other kudo rank clusters as well.

This outcome leads to several observations: First, developers living at higher kudo ranks are often the ones who commit the most significant contributions to the projects, hence, the majority of kudos are attributed to them as a token of appreciation. Second, these group of developers are the ones who are trusted by all the community members irrespective of their ranking in the community. Third, developers residing at lower kudo ranks (e.g., ranking between 1 and 6) rarely receive kudos for their contributions.

Investigation on the second perspective reveals that developers with higher kudo ranking or trust rating most often receive their kudos directly to their personal account. In a very few occasions, kudos are attributed to their project specific accounts. For instance, about 83% to 93% of the kudos received by developers having rank between 7 and 10 are attributed to their personal accounts. This highlights how high ranked developers are often appreciated irrespective of the projects they have contributed to. However, Low kudo ranked (e.g., rank between 1 and 5) developers are not investigated due to lack of sample data.

Finally, the study on one of the homophilic factors, e.g. the effect of working on same or different projects, on exchanging kudo rank reveals inconclusive results. For instance, developers who work on the same and distinct projects at the same time, share kudo more frequently than developers working in either distinct or same projects. Therefore, this study does not conclusively support the earlier research on homophilic factors [8] which claims that such factors have positive impact on endorsing each others contributions.

Acknowledgments. The authors would like to thank Ally Tahir Bitebo for his contribution to this research.

References

1. Golbeck, J.: Analyzing the social web, Chap. 6, p. 76. ISBN-13: 978–0124055315
2. Sirkkala, P., Hammouda, I., Aaltonen, T.: From proprietary to open source: Building a network of trust. In: Proceedings of Second International Workshop on Building Sustainable Open Source Communities (OSCOMM 2010), pp. 26–30 (2010)
3. Stewart, K.J., Gosain, S.: The impact of ideology on effectiveness in open source software development teams. MIS Q. **30**(2), 291–314 (2006)
4. Lane, M.S., Vyver, G., Basnet, P., Howard, S.: Inter-preventative insights into interpersonal trust and effectiveness of virtual communities of open source software (OSS) developers (2004)
5. de Laat, P.B.: How can contributors to open-source communities be trusted? On the assumption, inference, and substitution of trust. Ethics Inf. Technol. **12**(4), 327–341 (2010)
6. Dabbish, L., Stuart, C., Tsay, J., Herbsleb, J.: Social coding in GitHub: transparency and collaboration in an open software repository, pp. 1277–1286 (2012)
7. Arafat, O., Riehle, D.: The commit size distribution of open source software, pp. 1–8 (2009)
8. Hu, D., Zhao, J.L., Cheng, J.: Reputation management in an open source developer social network: an empirical study on determinants of positive evaluations. Decis. Support Syst. **53**(3), 526–533 (2012)
9. Gallardo-Valencia, R.E., Tantikul, P., Elliott Sim, S.: Searching for reputable source code on the web. In: Proceedings of the 16th ACM international conference on Supporting group work, pp. 183–186 (2010)
10. Orsila, H., Geldenhuys, J., Ruokonen, A., Hammouda, I.: Trust issues in open source software development. In: Proceedings of the Warm Up Workshop for ACM/IEEE ICSE, pp. 9–12 (2010)
11. Gysin, F.S., Kuhn, A.: A trustability metric for code search based on developer karma. In: Proceedings of 2010 ICSE Workshop on Search-Driven Development: Users, Infrastructure, Tools and Evaluation, pp. 41–44 (2010)
12. OpenHub data repository. http://www.openhub.net/
13. OpenHub API documentation. https://github.com/blackducksw/ohloh_api

Open Access This chapter is licensed under the terms of the Creative Commons Attribution 4.0 International License (http://creativecommons.org/licenses/by/4.0/), which permits use, sharing, adaptation, distribution and reproduction in any medium or format, as long as you give appropriate credit to the original author(s) and the source, provide a link to the Creative Commons license and indicate if changes were made.

The images or other third party material in this chapter are included in the chapter's Creative Commons license, unless indicated otherwise in a credit line to the material. If material is not included in the chapter's Creative Commons license and your intended use is not permitted by statutory regulation or exceeds the permitted use, you will need to obtain permission directly from the copyright holder.

The Open Source Officer Role – Experiences

Carl-Eric Mols[1], Krzysztof Wnuk[2(✉)], and Johan Linåker[3]

[1] Sony Mobile, Lund, Sweden
Carl-eric.mols@sonymobile.com
[2] Blekinge Institute of Technology, Karlskrona, Sweden
krzysztof.wnuk@bth.se
[3] Lund University, Lund, Sweden
johan.linaker@cs.lth.se

Abstract. This papers describe the Open Source Officer role and the experiences from introducing this role in several companies. We outline the role description, main responsibilities, and interfaces to other roles and organizations. We investigated the role in several organization and bring interesting discrepancies and overlaps of how companies operate with OSS.

Keywords: Open source governance · Inner-source · Maturity models

1 Introduction

Several companies have discovered and utilized the extensive benefits that Open Source Software (OSS) brings to their product development activities and processes. As any OSS adoption is an organizational change and often a cultural shift, there is a need for supporting role that ensures these transformations are smooth and directed towards achieving higher maturity models in operating with OSS [1].

In this paper, we present the Open Source Officer Role and discuss the experiences from establishing this role in three organizations. We outline the most important challenges that the role installation brings and outline the research agenda for further research activities.

2 The Open Source Officer Role Description

The Open Source Officer (OSO) role at Sony Mobile is a response for the need to support governance, organizational development and education activities that increase Sony Mobile's ability in OSS-based development and business. The role connects the management, legal/IPR and software organizations around the open source operations, see Fig. 1. It provides an important communication point for these three organizations, ensures that the processes and activities are synchronized and the potential questions are timely resolved. The OSO interfaces with executive management and participates in the daily work of the Open Source Board which scope and responsibilities can be set for a single business organization or the entire corporate. The OSO officer reports directly to the Head of Open Source Software and interfaces with software developers, architects, managers and lawyers working directly in the same organization and also roles responsible for the IPR questions. At the same time, it can happen that OSO works directly with corporate legal organizations on matters that are impacting several business units, e.g. license committee or inner-source governance organizations.

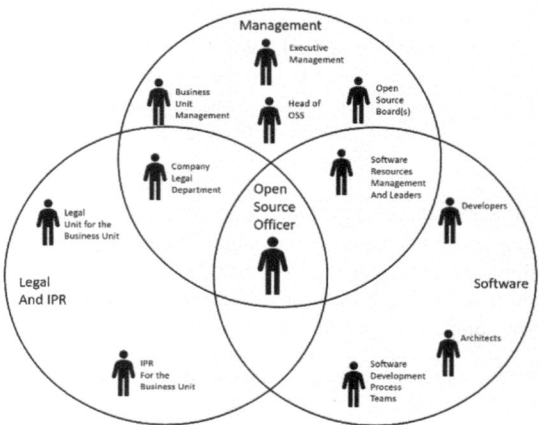

Fig. 1. The Open Source Officer role and the other roles that it interfaces in the organization.

The sourcing organization plays an important role here as it is responsible for negotiating contracts with component suppliers for the non-OSS components and for hardware components that come with software that can be proprietary and/or OSS. The sourcing organization has the task to secure that suppliers are fulfilling the obligation of the OSS licenses (are OSS compliant) in the delivered software. It also can support the search and selection of the best sourcing strategy (with the OSS as the priority) given the set of functional and quality requirements that a given component should deliver.

Scope of operations and main working areas include:

Governance and support systems - The Open Source Officer is a part of Open Source Operations and in charge for governance and support, including processes etc.
Education - the officer identifies the education needs in an organization as well as ensures that needed education is provided to the organization.
Developer Engagement - The OSO leads and mentors the software organizations in the engagement in OSS projects (maturing and taking on their responsibilities). The organizations take the formal responsibility for the OSS engagement activities.
Business Models - although having no direct responsibility, the OSO should engage in business strategy development discussions to influence, support, and advice business entities to enable a full advantage of using OSS in generating and sustain business.
Leadership and Culture - The OSO can support and advice in the creation of organization and leadership culture that is suitable for ensuring extensive benefits from OSS. The actual task of creating an organization is the top management responsibility.

Key Competences include:

Strong leadership skills are required as a central part of the role is to develop and manage governance and support systems as well as the education program required to advance in the open source maturity.

Communication skills - strong written and verbal English skills are required as the role involves communication with local and global organizations – including company external organizations, e.g. purchasing a training course from an external company.

Functional and technical skills - good change management skills are required as the role supports the changes in the mindset of individuals, support required transformation of organizational structures as well as influence the culture of the organization. Good understanding of OSO that is reaching beyond the basic copyright issues or OSS compliance, business and market logic implications as well. Good understanding on the fundamentals of software engineering.

Technology knowledge - the OSO need to be a very good generalist and understand the technological aspects of software as well as other aspects. This is particularly important for OSOs not originating from software organizations.

Key Responsibilities include:

Engage actively in the Open Source Board operations - the Open Source Board is the governing function for Open Source within the company or a business unit. The two main tasks for the board involve: (1) Maintaining the corporate policies set by the executive management regarding OSS operations and ensuring that the documentation is up to date, and (2) Vetting and approving contribution proposals and ensuring that both business needs and IPR are taken into consideration.

Ensure that Open Source related processes and trainings are provided - that includes ensuring that the processes are defined, documented and implemented in relevant organizations and that the training is provided.

Act as an interpreter between engineers and lawyers - ensure that OSS related questions gets timely answered and that engineers and developers are proactive and positive about using OSS components without unnecessary license related fears.

Act as the company's external interface in Open Source related questions - especially for the questions related acquisitions and compliance of the released products.

Act as an internal management consultant - that reacts to any request for help or support about the OSS operations or knowledge.

Authorities - the OSO has a deciding voice as one of the members of the Open Source Board and can propose changes to OSS related directives and processes.

3 Experiences from Three Software-Intensive Organizations

Company A is the develops software-intensive products for global market in a matured market where several strong vendors established their position. The company joined the OSS ecosystem in 2007 and within three years dropped all other platforms and based all the product on this OSS platform. The company is currently on level 4 in of OSS maturity [1]. The scope and responsibility of the OSO role is described in Fig. 1 and in

Sect. 2. One important remark is that the OSO in this case does not take the responsibility for compliance or running OSS-related software projects.

Company B is a direct competitor to company A and apart from software-intensive embedded systems the company is also active in several other business units that produce home electronics, automotive, chemical and heavy industry. Our analysis is based on an interview with the OSO from the same business unit as company A. The main difference at company B is that OSO is also responsible for a group of about 80 developers that maintain the critical components based on OSS code that are reused in several business units. The OSO is a project manager for these activities. Another difference is that the OSO acts as an authority regarding legal and IPR questions and have no dedicated OSS-knowledgeable lawyer to closely collaborate with.

Company C manufactures trucks, buses and engines for heavy transport applications for a global market and experienced an increased dependence on software and is currently transforming into a software-intensive product development organization. The OSO role differs in two aspects: (1) the OSO is also a project manager that is responsible for running OSS-based software projects (not the core part like at company B) and (2) the OSO needs to have the required technical knowledge about software and its architecture to support the transformation to a software-intensive company.

Related Work. Kemp [3] suggests the introduction of an OSS Compliance Officer (OSSCO) with the responsibility of developing and implementing the OSS governance mechanisms, agree on an internal OSS strategy (e.g., expressing where and why to use OSS) and oversee that it is followed, mainly from the possible IP leakage and compliance issues. Much of the responsibilities of an inner-source champion [2] align with the role of an OSSCO as proposed by Kemp [3] and with the OSO role.

4 Conclusion and Future Work

In this experience report we have described the role of an Open Source Officer (OSO). The OSO role offers a central authority and champion that can help an organization to both introduce and mature in their use of OSS. The presented role description is based on knowledge and experience gained from Sony Mobile and confronted with interviews at two other large organizations that use OSS in their products. Future work will further investigate how the role description may fluctuate in organizations with differing characteristics, but also how the surrounding organizational structure of the OSO can be defined, e.g., in regards to OSS governance board.

Acknowledgements. This work was funded by the ITEA2 project 12018 SCALARE, and by the IKNOWDM project [grant number 20150033] from the Knowledge Foundation in Sweden.

References

1. Mols, C.E.: The open source maturity model. http://scalare.org/rag/open-source-maturity-model
2. Stol, K.J., Avgeriou, P., Barbar, M.A., Lucas, Y., Fitzgerald, B.: Key factors for adopting inner source. Trans. Softw. Eng. Methodol. **23**(2), 18 (2014)
3. Kemp, R.: Open source software (OSS) governance in the organisation. Comput. Law Secur. Rev. **26**(3), 309–316 (2010)

Open Access This chapter is licensed under the terms of the Creative Commons Attribution 4.0 International License (http://creativecommons.org/licenses/by/4.0/), which permits use, sharing, adaptation, distribution and reproduction in any medium or format, as long as you give appropriate credit to the original author(s) and the source, provide a link to the Creative Commons license and indicate if changes were made.

The images or other third party material in this chapter are included in the chapter's Creative Commons license, unless indicated otherwise in a credit line to the material. If material is not included in the chapter's Creative Commons license and your intended use is not permitted by statutory regulation or exceeds the permitted use, you will need to obtain permission directly from the copyright holder.

Digging into the Eclipse Marketplace

Jacob Krüger[1,2(✉)], Niklas Corr[1], Ivonne Schröter[2,3], and Thomas Leich[1,3]

[1] Harz University of Applied Sciences, Wernigerode, Germany
{jkrueger,tleich}@hs-harz.de
[2] Otto-von-Guericke University, Magdeburg, Germany
ivonne.schroeter@ovgu.de
[3] METOP Gmbh, Magdeburg, Germany

Abstract. Eclipse is an integrated development environment that can be extended with plug-ins. Thanks to Eclipse's success, a diverse community has been established with members coming from industry, open-source projects, and others, and a marketplace with more than 1.700 different plug-ins developed. Hence, the question arises how this marketplace is composed: *Who contributes plug-ins? Which plug-ins are successful? Are there common characteristics or trends?* To answer these questions, extensive investigations are necessary. In this paper, we present *(i)* an initial approach for corresponding analyses and *(ii)* preliminary results. Overall, we aim to pave the way for further research addressing, for example, motivations to participate in, or the evolution of, open marketplaces.

Keywords: Eclipse IDE · Eclipse Marketplace · Open source · Empirical study

1 Introduction

Open-source systems gained momentum in software engineering mainly because of free use, accessibility, and fast innovation speed [16,17,20,21]. As a result, many companies use such systems as basis for their own products [6], wherefore commercial and open-source software are more and more used concurrently [1,2,10,17]. A good example for this co-existence is the de facto standard *Eclipse*[1] [6,7,19].

Eclipse became the dominant integrated development environment (IDE) for Java used by developers from industry, universities, and open-source communities [5–7,9,19,23]. To support Eclipse and plug-in developers, the Eclipse Foundation implemented platforms to manage projects [5,16]. These platforms are support measures and drive the evolution of the community. As a result, the amount of plug-ins is steadily increasing from 1.385 in 2007 [23] to 1.762 at the beginning of 2017. In the context of this paper, the marketplace, in which these plug-ins are provided, will be the area of analysis.

---

[1] http://www.eclipse.org/, 02.01.2017.

While the Eclipse marketplace brings together diverse communities it has rarely been analyzed. However, such an analysis can help researchers to understand what motivates developers with different backgrounds (e.g., open-source and industry) to participate and collaborate. Furthermore, the findings can support to scope plug-ins and initiate cooperation. In this paper, we describe a preliminary analysis of the Eclipse marketplace and corresponding results. Overall, we aim to provide a glance on open marketplaces and initiate more detailed research.

2 Research Method

Different approaches can be used to analyze the Eclipse marketplace, for instance, empirical studies based on interviews or questionnaires. However, to scope further research, we propose to mine and assess data available in the marketplace, providing a starting point based on the users' perspective. To this point, we address two research questions within this article:

RQ-1 Which topics are addressed by successful plug-ins? Plug-ins and topics that accumulate more attention (i.e., more downloads) indicate practical acceptance. This analysis can help to select suitable plug-ins or to scope further development, for instance to improve existing approaches.

RQ-2 Who contributes to these plug-ins? Based on the previous question, we investigate who develops these plug-ins. This can help to identify leading developers and communities for specific topics, potentially indicating collaborations and new research directions.

We automatically crawled the marketplace and manually analyzed the data. For this, we limited our analysis to the 100 most downloaded plug-ins until October 2016, covering approximately 80.3% of all downloads until then. We remark, that our methodology in this article is preliminary and shall only provide a starting point for further research.

3 Preliminary Results

In Fig. 1, we illustrate the topics we identified within our sample and their categorized owners. Furthermore, we show the distribution of downloads for each topic, and especially for open-source communities.

RQ-1: Which topics are addressed by successful plug-ins? Developers often use several and synonymous terms to describe their plug-ins, hampering an automated categorization. Thus, we manually assessed the purpose of the 100 most downloaded plug-ins and derived 10 initial categories: `Revision control`, `IDE extension` (integrating programming languages or frameworks), `code analysis`, `build tool`, `user interface`, `database`, `editor`, `optimization` (of Eclipse), `documentation`, and `server`. As we show in Fig. 1, revision control and

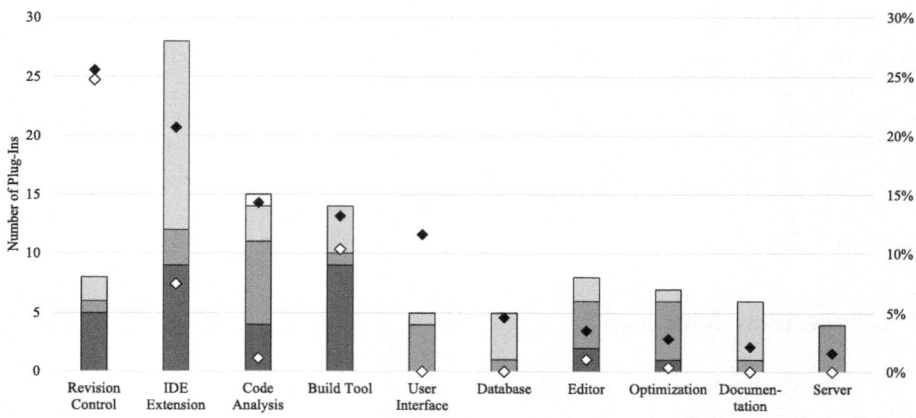

Fig. 1. Categorized projects of the 100 most downloaded plug-ins in the Eclipse marketplace.

IDE extensions accumulate most downloads. However, we also see that there is a difference in the number of available plug-ins for these two categories.

Only 8 plug-ins address revision control but are responsible for over a quarter of all downloads. This might be explained with a small set of established approaches, similar to the situation for user interfaces. Still, this result can be distorted, for instance because communities may require identical tooling, forcing participants to use a specific system even if they prefer another one.

In contrast, IDE extensions, similar to several remaining categories (e.g., code analysis, or build tools), provide far more plug-ins (28) while accumulating fewer downloads. A potential explanation is that these plug-ins often require adaptations to specific programming languages and development processes. Hence, their overall applicability is limited to specific communities and they compete with other IDEs.

RQ-2: Who contributes to these plug-ins? To gain an impression of Eclipse's community, we categorized the owners of plug-ins into four groups: `open-source`, `private`, `industrial`, and `university`. As we see in Fig. 1, open-source communities are leading in revision control and build tools, accumulating most plug-ins and downloads. Especially in revision control, which is used for distributed work and collaboration, they seem to benefit from their diversity [5]. However, open-source communities do not, or rarely, contribute to some other topics in our sample.

In contrast, private and industrial owners provide plug-ins for almost all topics. Private developers seem to dominate the development of user interfaces, optimization, and server integration, which facilitate using Eclipse. However, such plug-ins provide less utility besides comfort than, for example, customized build tools or revision control. For this reason, industrial and open-source communities might be less interested in developing these. We support this argument due to the fact that industrial owners provide most plug-ins in IDE extensions, databases, and documentation. These are essential aspects of software development in companies. Finally, we remark that universities own only a single plug-in in our sample, potential reasons being that they provide innovative but immature projects.

4 Research Agenda

The results presented in this work are preliminary and further analysis on how such marketplaces are composed are necessary. More detailed investigations may help to understand, why communities do or do not provide plug-ins and what motivates them. We emphasize that this requires extensive analyses and additional empirical studies. In future work, we aim to assess the following aspects:

How to assess the success of a plug-in? In this paper, we solely focused on the number of overall downloads. This is a significant limitation and other metrics are necessary to provide a more detailed view. For instance, to consider the marketplace's evolution, a plug-in's downloads in recent periods, integration into Eclipse packages, or the number of its developers are interesting.

Are there common characteristics of successful plug-ins? Different communities successfully participate in the Eclipse marketplace. Hence, success may depend on the topic and also certain characteristics, for example, used licenses [13,17,18], necessity to pay, or maturity. For community managers and developers such information are important to design and provide their software.

How do users select plug-ins? The previous two questions may indicate, and can be validated by investigating how, users select plug-ins. Besides these points, the users' selection also depends on their experiences and background. The results can help to understand how new techniques emerge and establish.

Why and how are plug-ins developed? An important question in the context of open-source software is the motivation of developers. In particular, it is interesting who initiates plug-ins for which reason, who contributes to these, or which connections exist. The corresponding results may provide insights into motivations to collaborate and participate in communities and open marketplaces.

5 Related Work

Several authors investigate the evolution of Eclipse or its plug-ins, focusing, for instance, on their architecture or API usage [3,4,14,22]. Further works investigate the laws of software evolution [12] in open-source systems [8,11]. In contrast to the systems themselves, our scope is how a potential marketplace for these evolves and is composed. Still, both approaches are complementary and can be combined, for instance to assess how a plug-ins evolution affects its popularity and status. Finally, Murphy et al. [15] empirically evaluate how developers use the Eclipse IDE. It seems interesting to utilize this approach to also assess how plug-ins are used.

6 Conclusions

Eclipse is one of the most prominent and widely used Java IDEs. Due to its success, a large and diverse community of plug-in developers established. They provide their plug-ins at the Eclipse marketplace, allowing other users to use them.

In this paper, we proposed to analyze the Eclipse marketplace. The preliminary results show that some topics, such as revision control or IDE extensions, are often demanded by users and that different owners participate. Finally, we described further research directions to deepen the understanding of open marketplaces and their communities.

Acknowledgments. This research is supported by DFG grant LE 3382/2-1 and Volkswagen Financial Services AG. We thank Heike Fischbach for commenting on drafts of this paper.

References

1. Bonaccorsi, A., Rossi, C.: Why open source software can succeed. Res. Policy **32**(7), 1243–1258 (2003). doi:10.1016/S0048-7333(03)00051-9
2. Bonaccorsi, A., Rossi, C.: Comparing motivations of individual programmers and firms to take part in the open source movement: from community to business. Know. Technol. Policy **18**(4), 40–64 (2006). doi:10.1007/s12130-006-1003-9
3. Businge, J.: Co-evolution of the Eclipse SDK framework and its third-party plug-ins. In: European Conference on Software Maintenance and Reengineering, CSMR, pp. 427–430. IEEE (2013). doi:10.1109/CSMR.2013.64
4. Businge, J., Serebrenik, A., van den Brand, M.: An empirical study of the evolution of Eclipse third-party plug-ins. In: Joint Workshop on Software Evolution and International Workshop on Principles of Software Evolution, IWPSE-EVOL, pp. 63–72. ACM (2010).doi:10.1145/1862372.1862389
5. des Rivières, J., Wiegand, J.: Eclipse: a platform for integrating development tools. IBM Syst. J. **43**(2), 371–383 (2004). doi:10.1147/sj.432.0371
6. Ebert, C.: Open source software in industry. IEEE Softw. **25**(3), 52–53 (2008). doi:10.1109/MS.2008.67
7. Geer, D.: Eclipse becomes the dominant java IDE. Computer **38**(7), 16–18 (2005). doi:10.1109/MC.2005.228
8. Godfrey, M.W., Tu, Q.: Evolution in open source software: a case study. In: International Conference on Software Maintenance, ICSM, pp. 131–142. IEEE (2000). doi:10.1109/ICSM.2000.883030
9. Goth, G.: Beware the March of this IDE: Eclipse is overshadowing other tool technologies. IEEE Softw. **22**(4), 108–111 (2005). doi:10.1109/MS.2005.96
10. Hars, A., Ou, S.: Working for free? Motivations for participating in open-source projects. In: Hawaii International Conference on System Sciences, HICCS, pp. 1–9. IEEE (2001). doi:10.1109/hicss.2001.927045
11. Koch, S.: Software evolution in open source projects - a large-scale investigation. J. Softw. Maint. Evol. **19**(6), 361–382 (2007). doi:10.1002/smr.348
12. Lehman, M.M., Ramil, J.F.: Rules and tools for software evolution planning and management. Ann. Softw. Eng. **11**(1), 15–44 (2001). doi:10.1023/A:1012535017876

13. Manabe, Y., German, D.M., Inoue, K.: Analyzing the relationship between the license of packages and their files in free and open source software. In: Corral, L., Sillitti, A., Succi, G., Vlasenko, J., Wasserman, A.I. (eds.) OSS 2014. IAICT, vol. 427, pp. 51–60. Springer, Heidelberg (2014). doi:10.1007/978-3-642-55128-4_6
14. Mens, T., Fernández-Ramil, J., Degrandsart, S.: The evolution of Eclipse. In: International Conference on Software Maintenance, ICSM, pp. 386–395. IEEE (2008). doi:10.1109/ICSM.2008.4658087
15. Murphy, G.C., Kersten, M., Findlater, L.: How are java software developers using the elipse IDE? IEEE Softw. **23**(4), 76–83 (2006). doi:10.1109/MS.2006.105
16. Parreiras, F.S., Gröner, G., Schwabe, D., de Freitas Silva, F.: Towards a marketplace of open source software data. In: Hawaii International Conference on System Sciences, HICSS, pp. 3651–3660. IEEE (2015). doi:10.1109/HICSS.2015.439
17. Ramanathan, L., Iyer, S.K.: A qualitative study on the adoption of open source software in information technology outsourcing organizations. In: Damiani, E., Frati, F., Riehle, D., Wasserman, A.I. (eds.) OSS 2015. IAICT, vol. 451, pp. 103–113. Springer, Cham (2015). doi:10.1007/978-3-319-17837-0_10
18. Ruffin, M., Ebert, C.: Using open source software in product development: a primer. IEEE Softw. **21**(1), 82–86 (2004). doi:10.1109/MS.2004.1259227
19. Vaughan-Nichols, S.J.: The battle over the universal java IDE. Computer **36**(4), 21–23 (2003). doi:10.1109/MC.2003.1193223
20. von Hippel, E.: Innovation by user communities: learning from open-source software. Sloan Manage. Rev. **42**(4), 82–86 (2001)
21. Watson, R.T., Boudreau, M.-C., York, P.T., Greiner, M.E., Wynn Jr., D.: The business of open source. Commun. ACM **51**(4), 41–46 (2008). doi:10.1145/1330311.1330321
22. Wermelinger, M., Yu, Y.: Analyzing the evolution of Eclipse plugins. In: International Working Conference on Mining Software Repositories, MSR, pp. 133–136. ACM (2008). doi:10.1145/1370750.1370783
23. Yang, Z., Jiang, M.: Using Eclipse as a tool-integration platform for software development. IEEE Softw. **24**(2), 87–89 (2007). doi:10.1109/MS.2007.58

Open Access This chapter is licensed under the terms of the Creative Commons Attribution 4.0 International License (http://creativecommons.org/licenses/by/4.0/), which permits use, sharing, adaptation, distribution and reproduction in any medium or format, as long as you give appropriate credit to the original author(s) and the source, provide a link to the Creative Commons license and indicate if changes were made.

The images or other third party material in this chapter are included in the chapter's Creative Commons license, unless indicated otherwise in a credit line to the material. If material is not included in the chapter's Creative Commons license and your intended use is not permitted by statutory regulation or exceeds the permitted use, you will need to obtain permission directly from the copyright holder.

Licensing, Strategies, and Practices

How are Developers Treating License Inconsistency Issues? A Case Study on License Inconsistency Evolution in FOSS Projects

Yuhao Wu[1(✉)], Yuki Manabe[2], Daniel M. German[3], and Katsuro Inoue[1]

[1] Graduate School of Information Science and Technology,
Osaka University, Osaka, Japan
{wuyuhao,inoue}@ist.osaka-u.ac.jp
[2] Faculty of Advanced Science and Technology,
Kumamoto University, Kumamoto, Japan
y-manabe@cs.kumamoto-u.ac.jp
[3] Department of Computer Science, University of Victoria, Victoria, Canada
dmg@uvic.ca

Abstract. A license inconsistency is the presence of two or more source files that evolved from the same original file containing different licenses. In our previous study, we have shown that license inconsistencies do exist in open source projects and may lead to potential license violation problems. In this study, we try to find out whether the issues of license inconsistencies are properly solved by analyzing two versions of a FOSS distribution—Debian—and investigate the evolution patterns of license inconsistencies. Findings are: license inconsistencies occur mostly because the original copyright owner updated the license while the reusers were still using the old version of the source files with the old license; most license inconsistencies would disappear when the reusers synchronize their project from the upstream, while some would exist permanently if reusers decide not to synchronize anymore. Legally suspicious cases have not been found yet in those Debian distributions.

Keywords: Software license · Code clone · License inconsistency

1 Introduction

Free and open source software (FOSS) is software that can be freely used, changed, and shared (in modified or unmodified form) by anyone. FOSS should always be distributed under certain open source software licenses, otherwise they cannot be reused by others. The license of a source file usually resides in its header comment.

Many studies in software engineering have been done on software license. Some approaches for software license identification have been proposed [3,6,8]. Vendome et al. investigated the reasons on when and why developers adopt and change licenses by conducting a survey with the relevant developers [10].

We have developed a method to detect *license inconsistencies* in large-scale FOSS projects [11]. A license inconsistency is defined as two or more source files that evolved from the same original file containing different licenses. For example, file A and file B have the same program code, but the header of A includes GPL-2.0 and B includes Apache-2.0[1]. We have applied our detection method to Debian 7.5[2], one of the Linux distributions, and discovered different reasons that caused license inconsistencies and determined whether they are potentially illegal or not.

Although this work has provided us clues that some license inconsistencies indicate potential legal issues, this one-time analysis is not enough to understand how developers are dealing with the issues: whether developers are putting their efforts on eliminating license inconsistencies or they simply ignore the issues. The investigation of the evolution of license inconsistencies can help us understand whether the legal issues of license inconsistency discovered in the previous work are handled by developers. Therefore, we conducted this research and try to answer the following questions:

- **RQ1.** *What are the evolution patterns of license inconsistencies and the underlying reasons?* Analyzing the evolution patterns of license inconsistencies might gives us insight on the reasons that caused them to appear and disappear. The findings are: license inconsistencies appear, persist and disappear due to different reasons. They appear mostly because the original author updates the license while the reusers still use the old version of the files; they persist mostly because the downstream project is not synchronized with the upstream project yet; and they disappear when the downstream project is synchronized with the upstream project.
- **RQ2.** *Is the issue of license inconsistencies properly handled by developers?* The findings are: license inconsistencies are mainly caused by distribution latency, and they will disappear when the developers synchronize their projects from the upstream projects. They persist because the reusers are still using an old version of the files and do not perform the synchronization. We do not consider this as a legal issue.

In order to address these questions, we apply our license inconsistency detection method to Debian 8.2 (which was the newest version when we started this study) in addition to Debian 7.5, and investigate the evolution of license inconsistencies between theses two versions.

The rest of this paper is organized as follows: Sect. 2 introduces the methodology we employ to address our research questions. Section 3 describes the result we got from our analysis. A discussion of this result is given in Sect. 4. Section 5 introduces the related work. Finally, we conclude our paper in Sect. 6.

---

[1] Note that pairs of no license and any license, and different license versions are reported as license inconsistency.
[2] https://www.debian.org/.

2 Methodology

In this section we describe how we design our study.

2.1 Obtain License Inconsistency Groups for Debian 7.5 and Debian 8.2

A *license inconsistency group* is a group of multiple files that have same code contents but with different licenses. As introduced in our previous paper [11], we use the following steps to reveal license inconsistency groups:

1. **Create groups of file clones:** For all the source files in the target projects, we apply `CCFinder` [7] to extract the normalized token sequences of each file. The normalized token sequences is a token sequence of the source code, removing comments and whitespaces and changing all user-defined identifiers to a special token. Note that, although `CCFinder` itself is a clone detection tool, we do not utilize the full functionality of `CCFinder` and we only use it to generate the normalized token sequences of source files. By computing and categorizing the hash value of these token sequences, we then create a group for files that have the same normalized token sequences. We call them *license inconsistency groups*, or *group* for short in the rest of this paper. Each group contains at least two different files; i.e., a unique file is not contained in any group.
2. **Identify licenses for files in each group:** For each group of file clones, `Ninka` [3] is used to identify the license(s) of each file. `Ninka` identifies the license sentences in the comment parts of each file, and compares those with its license database. It can identify more than 110 different OSS licenses and their different versions with 93% accuracy. Meanwhile, it will report "NONE" if the file has no license and "UNKNOWN" if the license sentence of the file does not match the database. The result is a list of licenses for each file group.
3. **Report groups that contain a license inconsistency and calculate the inconsistency metrics:** We compare the license list of each file group. File groups are reported to have license inconsistencies unless all the licenses on the list are exactly the same. The result is a list of file groups that contain one or more types of license inconsistencies.

We apply these steps to Debian 7.5 and 8.2 respectively and obtain the file groups that contain license inconsistencies.

2.2 Compare the Difference of Groups

All the files in one group have the same token sequences, from which we calculate the hash value as the id for that group. We then compare the id of the groups in each version and get the set of groups that exist: (*a*) only in Debian 7.5; (*b*) only in Debian 8.2; (*c*) in both versions.

The result of this step would be three sets of file groups.

Table 1. Number of packages and files in Debian 7.5 and 8.2.

Number of packages	Debian 7.5	Debian 8.2
Source packages	17,160	20,577
Total files	6,136,637	13,124,700
.c files	472,861	767,006
.cpp files	224,267	335,269
.java files	365,213	477,154

Table 2. License inconsistency groups between two versions on Debian.

Number of groups	Debian 7.5	Debian 8.2
Intersection[a]	4062	4062
Relative complement[b]	2701	2947
Total	6763	7009

[a]Groups that exist in both versions
[b]Groups that exist in either version only

2.3 Investigate the Groups Manually

The groups that only exist in Debian 7.5 imply that they are eliminated from the new version; those that only exist in Debian 8.2 imply that new license inconsistency cases appears in this new version; those that exist in both versions indicate that they remain during these two versions. We manually examine the different groups and present the results in the next section.

3 Results

The number of packages and files in Debian 7.5 and 8.2 are shown in Table 1. We only consider `.c`, `.cpp` and `.java` files which are the supported types of our detection method. The detection result of license inconsistency groups in Debian 7.5 and 8.2 is shown in Table 2. In this table, intersection means that both two versions of Debian contain that group of license inconsistency; relative complement means only that version of Debian contain that group of license inconsistency. Thus there are 4062 groups of license inconsistencies detected in both versions; 2701 groups only in Debian 7.5; and 2947 groups only in Debian 8.2. By examining the groups that are only in Debian 7.5 we can find out how and why license inconsistencies disappeared in Debian 8.2; while examining the groups that are only in Debian 8.2 we can understand how and why license inconsistencies appeared. The intersection part indicates that these groups of license inconsistencies persisted in Debian 8.2.

How are Developers Treating License Inconsistency Issues? 73

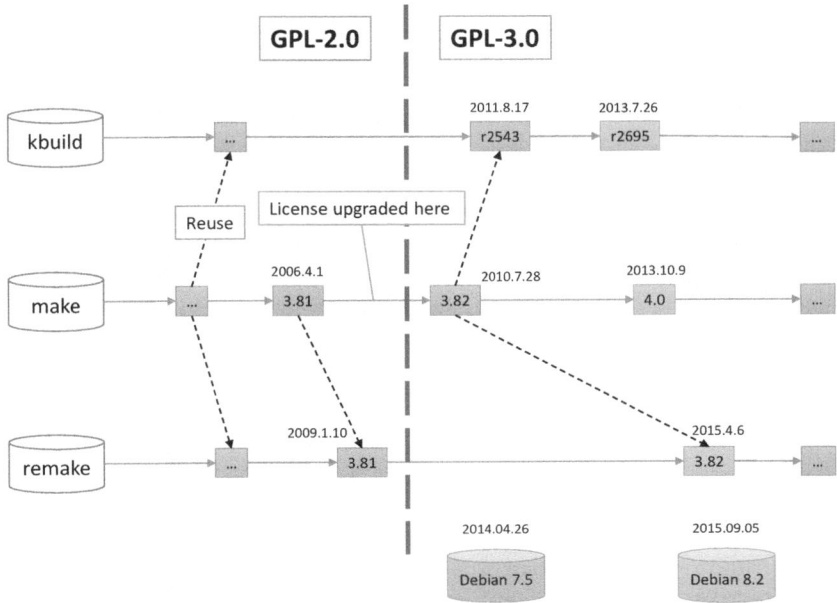

Fig. 1. A case of license inconsistency evolution which involves project `make`, `remake` and `kbuild`.

3.1 Why Do License Inconsistencies Appear?

There are several reasons that license inconsistencies appear. The key point is that there are multiple copies of the same source file with different licenses in the same distribution. We describe the general reasons that license inconsistency appears, thus the examples given in this section are not limited to those that appear in Debian 8.2. We categorize them into three types according to the reason that caused the copy of files.

- **Internal copy-and-paste of source files but their licenses are different.** If copies of the same file exist in one project (we call these internal copies), they should also exist in the final distribution (e.g. Debian 7.5). Thus a case of license inconsistency will be reported by our method if they contain different licenses.

  For example, in a project named `FreeMedForms`, some source files in a `plugins` directory are under BSD3 license. These files are copied to other directories with their licenses changed to GPL-3.0+.

  This type of license inconsistency could exist for just a short time, if the difference of license was due to mistakes and was later on fixed by developers. On the other hand, if developers decided to distribute these source files under different licenses, it would exist permanently.

- **Different versions of the same project are included in the same distribution.** Similar to the previous reason, if different versions of the same project which causes license inconsistencies are included in the final distribution, those license inconsistencies will be reported by our method.

For example, there is a project named `groovy` which contains files that had no license in version 1.7.2, and were then added a Apache-2.0 license in version 1.8.6. Both of these two versions of this project are included in Debian 7.5, thus this license inconsistency is reported.

- **Upstream and downstream projects both exist in the same distribution.** In this research, if project B reuses source files from project A by copy-and-paste, we call project B the downstream project and project A the upstream project. While the previous two reasons are about the same project, this reason involves multiple projects. Files from the upstream project are reused in the downstream project, and the license of these files were changed either by the original author or the reuser. If both of these projects are included in the same distribution, the license inconsistency will be reported by our method.

An example is shown in Fig. 1. As we can see from this graph, several source files in `remake` and `kbuild` project were originally from the `make` project, where license upgrade occurred in year 2010. Debian 7.5 includes older versions of `make` and `remake`, where the license was still GPL-2.0, while the newer version of `kbuild` contains the GPL-3.0 license. Thus license inconsistency is reported for this case.

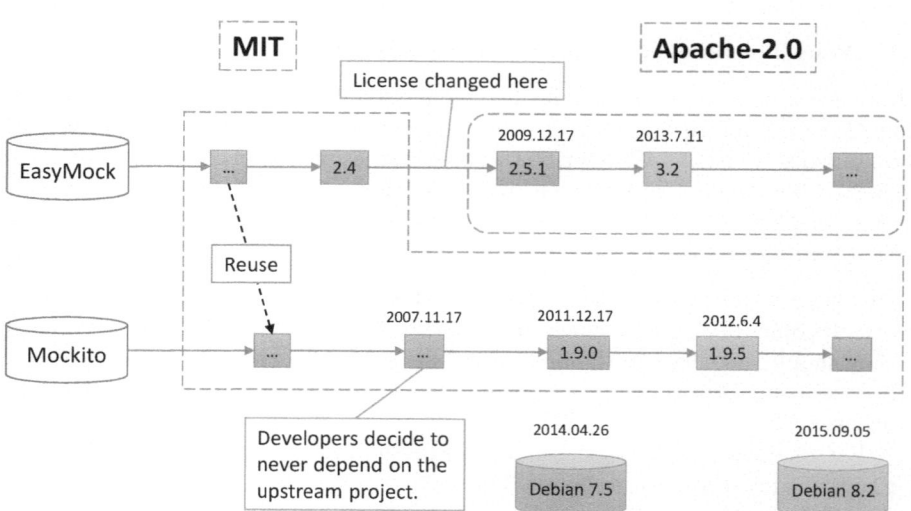

Fig. 2. A case of license inconsistency evolution which involves project `EasyMock` and `Mockito`.

3.2 Why Do License Inconsistencies Persist?

License inconsistencies usually exist in several continuous versions of a distribution. Some of them disappear soon, some exist for a long time, while some even persist forever. From the result in this research, we can summarize them into two reasons.

- **Source files are not yet synchronized, but license inconsistencies will eventually disappear when they are.** This type of license inconsistencies occurred because the downstream project has not yet been synchronized with the upstream project where the license of source files were changed. However, since the developers of the downstream projects are still synchronizing the project from the upstream regularly, this type of license inconsistencies will be eliminated eventually.

  For example, in the case of the project JSON-lib and jenkins-json described earlier, although license inconsistencies appeared in Debian 7.5 (where jenkins-json still uses source files under Apache-2.0/MIT dual license), they disappeared in Debian 8.2, where developers of jenkins-json project synchronized from the upstream project and the license all become Apache-2.0 only. Though this case of license inconsistency disappeared in Debian 8.2, we consider it as a typical example to explain why license inconsistencies would exist for only a period of time and disappear when the source files are synchronized.

- **Downstream project no longer synchronizes from upstream, and license inconsistencies will likely exist permanently.** In this case, developers of downstream project chose to no longer synchronize from the upstream project, thus the license inconsistencies are likely to exist forever, unless the synchronization resumes.

  As shown in Fig. 2, among the results we found a project named Mockito which copy-and-owned several source files from a project named EasyMock. The license of these files in the upstream project were changed from MIT to Apache-2.0 in year 2009, however the Mockito project still uses the original MIT license. Besides, Mockito project made some changes to the source code of these files by their own, and never again synchronized from EasyMock. After checking the history of these files in Mockito project, we found that one of the commit in year 2007 contains the following commit message: *"umbilical cord between mockito package and easymock package is cut!"*, which implies that they will never synchronize from the upstream project. Thus this case of license inconsistency is likely to exist permanently, unless Mockito project decides to synchronize from EasyMock again.

3.3 Why Do License Inconsistencies Disappear?

We observed several cases where license inconsistencies disappeared from Debian 8.2. The reasons are summarize as follows.

– **Downstream project synchronized from upstream project.** When the downstream project synchronized from the upstream project, the license of the source files becomes the same, thus the license inconsistencies disappear.

Again, from Fig. 1 we can see that Debian 8.2 updated all these three projects to a newer version where all of their licenses are upgraded to GPL-3.0, thus this license inconsistency disappears.

The case of project JSON-lib and jenkins-json discussed earlier also applies here.

– **The source code that contained the license inconsistency was removed or changed—thus no longer identical.** In this research since we only inspect identical files, only files that contain the same token sequences are considered that they are from the same origin. If the source code of a file changed dramatically which made their token sequences different from the corresponding files, or if the relevant source file was removed in the new version, then the license inconsistencies will no longer be reported by our method.

For example, there is a file in project icu which is under IBM copyrights in both versions of Debian. This file was reused in project openjdk-7 but with a GPL-2.0 license in Debian 7.5. Thus this case of license inconsistency was reported in Debian 7.5. However, the source code of the file in openjdk-7 was changed in Debian 8.2 while the license remained the same. Our method no longer not consider them as file clones since they have different token sequences, thus the license inconsistency disappears in the newer version of Debian.

4 Discussion

4.1 Revisiting the Research Questions

The answer to our research questions are as follows:

RQ1: *What are the evolution patterns of license inconsistencies and the underlying reasons?*

– **Appear.** (*i*) Internal copy-and-paste of source files in a project but their licenses are different; (*ii*) Different versions of the same project are included in the same distribution; (*iii*) Upstream and downstream projects both exist in the same distribution.
– **Persist.** (*i*) Source files are not yet synchronized, but license inconsistencies will eventually disappear when they are; (*ii*) Downstream project no longer synchronize from upstream, and license inconsistencies are likely to persist permanently.
– **Disappear.** (*i*) Downstream project synchronized from upstream project; (*ii*) Source code which contained license inconsistency was removed or changed and we consider them as different files.

RQ2: *Is the issue of license inconsistency properly handled by developers?* The evolution of license inconsistencies in Debian shows that, they are mainly caused by distribution latency and will be eliminated when the downstream projects get synchronized. We found license inconsistencies appear mostly because the original author modified the license while the reusers were still using the old version of the file; they disappear because the files are synchronized with the upstream projects; and they persist if the downstream projects were not synchronized.

4.2 Effectiveness of This Approach

This approach is effective to analyze how developers are addressing the issues of license inconsistency in a certain software ecosystem. As shown in the results, we could use this method to reveal how license inconsistency groups evolved over time. By analyzing different groups we could have a basic idea on how developers are treating license inconsistency issues. For example, by analyzing the license inconsistency groups that only exists in the old version, we could learn why license inconsistencies disappeared in the newer version and what efforts did the developers put to eliminate them.

We could apply this same approach to other software systems to study how different communities are dealing with license inconsistency issues.

4.3 Threats to Validity

Internal Validity. We use the same methodology as our previous study to detect license inconsistency cases, which relies on the token sequence generation from CCFinder and the license identification from Ninka. For file clone detection, we use normalized token sequences as the metric to decide clones. If source files are modified a lot (e.g. add/remove several statements), they might not be recognized as clones. We could use approaches that detect similar source files to mitigate this problem. Regarding license identification, Ninka is state-of-the-art license identification tool which has an accuracy of 93% [3]. As shown in Sect. 3, our manual analysis also proves its high accuracy and precision.

External Validity. This study focuses on the license inconsistency issues in Debian. The results and analysis may not be generated to other software systems. And we plan to study other software systems in the future.

5 Related Work

Many studies in software engineering have been done on software license. Some approaches for software license identification have been proposed [3,6,8]. Using these approaches, some researches analyzed software licenses in open source projects and revealed some license issues. Di Penta et al. provided an automatic method to track changes occurring in the licensing terms of a system and did an exploratory study on license evolution in six open source systems and explained the impact of such evolution on the projects [2]. German et al. proposed a method to understand licensing compatibility issues in software packages [4].

They mainly focused on the compatibility between license declared in packages and those in source files. In another research, they analyzed license inconsistencies of code siblings (a code clone that evolves in a different system than the code from which it originates) between Linux, FreeBSD and OpenBSD, but they did not explain the reasons underlying these inconsistencies [5]. Alspaugh et al. proposed an approach for calculating conflicts between licenses in terms of their conditions [1]. Vendome et al. performed a large empirical study of Java applications and found that changing license is a common event and a lack of traceability between when and why the license of a system changes [9]. In their following research [10], they investigated the reasons on when and why developers adopt and change licenses during evolution of FOSS Java projects on GitHub by conducting a survey with the relevant developers. They concluded that developers consider licensing as an important task in software development.

In our previous research [11], we proposed a method to detect license inconsistencies in large-scale FOSS projects. We then applied this method to Debian 7.5 and examined the results manually and discovered various reasons that caused these license inconsistencies, among which some were legally suspicious and deserved further investigation. As far as we know, no research has been done to investigate the evolution of license inconsistencies.

6 Conclusions

In this research we have applied our license inconsistency detection method to both Debian 7.5 and Debian 8.2. By comparing the results of these two versions of Debian, we identified three evolution patterns of license inconsistencies. With a manual analysis of the license inconsistency cases we discovered various reasons that caused the evolution. Although license inconsistencies are detected in both versions of Debian, from our manual analysis we concluded that these reported license inconsistencies are caused because the upstream project updated the license while the downstream project has not been synchronized yet. These findings suggest that in our target ecosystem, Debian, license inconsistencies are caused by distribution latency and they will disappear when the downstream projects get synchronized.

For future work, we would apply this approach to other software ecosystems and see whether there are different patterns of license inconsistency evolution and whether the license inconsistency issues are properly handled.

Acknowledgments. This work is supported by Japan Society for the Promotion of Science, Grant-in-Aid for Scientific Research (S) "Collecting, Analyzing, and Evaluating Software Assets for Effective Reuse"(No.25220003) and Osaka University Program for Promoting International Joint Research, "Software License Evolution Analysis".

References

1. Alspaugh, T., Asuncion, H., Scacchi, W.: Intellectual property rights requirements for heterogeneously-licensed systems. In: Proceedings of the 17th International Requirements Engineering Conference (RE2009), pp. 24–33 (2009)

2. Di Penta, M., German, D.M., Guéhéneuc, Y.G., Antoniol, G.: An exploratory study of the evolution of software licensing. In: Proceedings of the 32nd International Conference on Software Engineering (ICSE2010), pp. 145–154 (2010)
3. German, D.M., Manabe, Y., Inoue, K.: A sentence-matching method for automatic license identification of source code files. In: Proceedings of the 25th International Conference on Automated Software Engineering (ASE2010), pp. 437–446 (2010)
4. German, D., Di Penta, M., Davies, J.: Understanding and auditing the licensing of open source software distributions. In: Proceedings of the 18th International Conference on Program Comprehension (ICPC2010), pp. 84–93 (2010)
5. German, D., Di Penta, M., Gueheneuc, Y.G., Antoniol, G.: Code siblings: technical and legal implications of copying code between applications. In: Proceedings of the 6th Working Conference on Mining Software Repositories (MSR2009), pp. 81–90 (2009)
6. Gobeille, R.: The FOSSology project. In: Proceedings of the 5th Working Conference on Mining Software Repositories (MSR2008), pp. 47–50 (2008)
7. Kamiya, T., Kusumoto, S., Inoue, K.: CCFinder: a multilinguistic token-based code clone detection system for large scale source code. IEEE Trans. Softw. Eng. **28**(7), 654–670 (2002)
8. Tuunanen, T., Koskinen, J., Kärkäkinen, T.: Automated software license analysis. Autom. Softw. Eng. **16**(3–4), 455–490 (2009)
9. Vendome, C., Linares-Vásquez, M., Bavota, G., Di Penta, M., Germán, D.M., Poshyvanyk, D.: License usage and changes: a large-scale study of java projects on github. In: The 23rd IEEE International Conference on Program Comprehension, ICPC 2015 (2015)
10. Vendome, C., Linares-Vásquez, M., Bavota, G., Di Penta, M., German, D.M., Poshyvanyk, D.: When and why developers adopt and change software licenses. In: 2015 IEEE International Conference on Software Maintenance and Evolution (ICSME), pp. 31–40. IEEE (2015)
11. Wu, Y., Manabe, Y., Kanda, T., German, D.M., Inoue, K.: Analysis of license inconsistency in large collections of open source projects. Empirical Softw. Eng. (accepted)

Open Access This chapter is licensed under the terms of the Creative Commons Attribution 4.0 International License (http://creativecommons.org/licenses/by/4.0/), which permits use, sharing, adaptation, distribution and reproduction in any medium or format, as long as you give appropriate credit to the original author(s) and the source, provide a link to the Creative Commons license and indicate if changes were made.

The images or other third party material in this chapter are included in the chapter's Creative Commons license, unless indicated otherwise in a credit line to the material. If material is not included in the chapter's Creative Commons license and your intended use is not permitted by statutory regulation or exceeds the permitted use, you will need to obtain permission directly from the copyright holder.

Addressing Lock-in, Interoperability, and Long-Term Maintenance Challenges Through Open Source: How Can Companies Strategically Use Open Source?

Björn Lundell[1(✉)], Jonas Gamalielsson[1], Stefan Tengblad[1], Bahram Hooshyar Yousefi[1], Thomas Fischer[1], Gert Johansson[2], Bengt Rodung[3], Anders Mattsson[4], Johan Oppmark[5], Tomas Gustavsson[6], Jonas Feist[7], Stefan Landemoo[8], and Erik Lönroth[9]

[1] University of Skövde, Skövde, Sweden
{bjorn.lundell,jonas.gamalielsson,stefan.tengblad,
bahram.hooshyar.yousefi,thomas.fischer}@his.se
[2] Combitech AB, Linköping, Sweden
gert.johansson@combitech.se
[3] Findwise AB, Gothenburg, Sweden
bengt.rodung@findwise.com
[4] Husqvarna AB, Huskvarna, Sweden
anders.mattsson@husqvarnagroup.com
[5] JAK, Skövde, Sweden
johan.oppmark@jak.se
[6] PrimeKey Solutions AB, Solna, Sweden
tomas@primekey.se
[7] RedBridge AB, Stockholm, Sweden
jfeist@redbridge.se
[8] Saab AB, Linköping, Sweden
stefan.landemoo@saabgroup.com
[9] Scania IT AB, Södertälje, Sweden
erik.lonroth@scania.se

Abstract. This industry paper reports on how strategic use of open source in company contexts can provide effective support for addressing the fundamental challenges of lock-in, interoperability, and longevity of software and associated digital assets. The fundamental challenges and an overview of an ongoing collaborative research project are presented. Through a conceptual model for open source usage in company contexts we characterise how companies engage with open source and elaborate on how the fundamental challenges can be effectively addressed through open source usage in company contexts.

1 Introduction

Over the years, researchers have identified a number of different motivations for companies and individuals to engage with open source [4, 21, 29]. Open Source Software (OSS) is software made available under a software license which has been approved by the Open Source Initiative [25] and with OSS the nature of development and competition in the software sector has significantly impacted on this sector [7]. This, in turn, has led to increased opportunities for organisations basing their business on open source and in 2007 it was found that in the context of the Norwegian software industry "more than 30% of the companies get over 40% of their income from OSS related services or software" [11]. Further, open source goes beyond software and important aspects of open source have influenced licensing in the hardware domain [12] and as a development model for standardisation [19].

Open source constitutes an early exemplar of open innovation [20] and its strategic use by companies is increasing [23]. Software maintained in open source projects is external to specific company contexts. Therefore, to maintain control of R&D resources it is critical for any company to participate and utilise effective work practices for involvement in open source communities, something which calls for technical and strategic considerations. Hence, companies must be prepared to counter and adapt their way of working in order to stay competitive in an increasingly competitive market.

Building and organising communities around OSS projects involves a number of challenges (e.g. [1, 3, 8]) and previous research shows "that effective governance and work practices that are appreciated by community members is fundamental for long-term sustainability" for open source projects [8]. A number of OSS projects are governed by a foundation (e.g. the Eclipse Foundation, the Linux Foundation, and the Document Foundation), which "are associations that serve to protect, not define, their respective communities' core technologies as well as the advancement of the commons through technical, social, and educational services" [9]. Previous studies have analysed Eclipse-projects and investigated how "software firms can apply different types of governance approaches to open source software development projects" [27]. Further, several widely adopted OSS projects are also governed in other ways and many companies seek guidance concerning how to establish effective strategies for governance and company involvement in open source projects.

This industry paper makes three principle contributions. First, we elaborate on the three fundamental challenges: lock-in, interoperability, and long-term maintenance of software and associated digital assets. Second, we present an overview of an industrial collaborative research project which aims to establish effective strategies for how companies can (and should) strategically engage with open source projects in order to successfully address the three fundamental challenges. Third, through an evolved conceptual model and associated strategies for company involvement with open source we illustrate how companies seek to strategically use and engage with open source projects in different ways.

2 On Fundamental Challenges: Lock-in, Interoperability, and Long-Term Maintenance

Over the years we have witnessed more widespread deployments of complex IT-systems and associated increased demands for longevity of software [8, 19]. This causes organisations to vary concerning different types of lock-in and inability to provide long-term maintenance of critical systems and digital assets [16, 19]. Further, OSS is often deployed in a legacy situation where there is a lot of proprietary software and closed file formats. This leads to the need for migrations between different file formats and establishment of interoperable systems. Interoperability supports systems heterogeneity, thereby increasing options for organisations [2, 10, 13].

Use of an open standard, especially when implemented in OSS, contributes to interoperability in that it "ensures that data and systems can be interpreted independently of the tool which generated it" [17]. This is relevant for scenarios in both commercial [18] and public sector [19] organisations. The Swedish National Procurement Services has published a list of open standards, which all can be referenced as mandatory requirements in public procurement [24]. An open standard is a standard which conforms to the definition presented in the European Interoperability Framework (EIF) version 1.0 [24] and such standards can be implemented and distributed under different licenses for proprietary software and under all OSI-approved licenses for OSS.

To allow for competition and stimulate innovation the Framework agreements established by the Swedish National Procurement Services [24] require that only open standards can be referenced as mandatory requirements in public procurement. A recent study commissioned by the Swedish Competition Authority found that many IT-projects in the Swedish public sector refer to closed standards which cannot be implemented in open source software, and the Director General for the Swedish Competition Authority states in the foreword to the report from the study that "From a competition perspective it is often problematic when public sector organisations conduct IT procurement and express requirements for closed standards" [19]. Further, the study shows that there is a widespread practice to refer to standards, trademarks, and proprietary software and IT-solutions which only specific manufacturers and suppliers can provide [19].

Many companies and organisations need to preserve their systems and associated digital assets for more than 30 years [22], and in some industrial sectors (e.g. avionics) even more than 70 years [3, 26]. In such usage scenarios "there will be problems if the commercial vendor of adopted proprietary software leaves the market" with increased risks for long-term availability of both software and digital assets [22].

Open source projects with healthy ecosystems can be an appropriate way to address risks related to lock-in and long-term maintenance of commodity software [15]. Further, use of open standards reduces the risk to an organisation of being technologically locked-in since they increase control by supporting migration, thereby reducing an organisation's reliance on a single product or supplier [6, 10, 13, 16, 28]. Further, previous research claims that support for interoperability should not require compatibility with existing software systems (since it tends to favour specific providers of those systems), but rather promote "interoperability with software from multiple vendors", something which can be achieved through use of OSS and open standards [10]. Despite such recommendations, recent results from a study commissioned by the Swedish Competition Authority show that many Swedish governmental organisations undertake projects for development and procurement of IT-systems which inhibit competition and use of open source solutions since there are mandatory requirements for compatibility with specific proprietary technology and closed standards that (perhaps) unintentionally inhibit interoperability and create a number of very problematic lock-in effects.

There is limited prior research concerning effective strategies for how companies can successfully address the three challenges through use and involvement in open source software projects. The ongoing collaborative research project LIM-IT is one notable exception which aims to advance the existing body of knowledge concerning effective strategies for company involvement with open source in order to successfully address these challenges.

3 Addressing Fundamental Challenges Through Open Source: An Overview of the LIM-IT Project

The overarching goal of the LIM-IT project is to develop, use, and scrutinise effective work practices and strategies for development, procurement, and organisational implementation of software systems in a number of complex application domains, where such software systems with associated digital assets (provided in a number of different open and closed standards and file formats) typically involve several open source projects as well as proprietary software, often depending on many different legacy systems. To address this goal, practitioners and researchers are committed to investigate the following core question: *"How can companies develop and utilise effective work practices for achieving long-term strategic benefits from participation in open collaborative projects?"*

To successfully address the core question there is a need to thoroughly understand motivations and expectations from all relevant (private and public sector) stakeholder groups, which inherently encompass a complex web of interdependencies (with a variety of different, sometimes conflicting, motivations and goals) between different stakeholders involved in, and affected by, a coopetative marketplace, i.e. a marketplace with competition on top of (open) collaboration.

Researchers from different research specialisations (including open source, software engineering, organisational science, and intellectual property rights) address the fundamental challenges from multi-disciplinary perspectives in collaboration with practitioners in a number of innovative organisations. Partner organisations include (small and large) companies from the primary software sector that all have extensive experience from development and use of (proprietary and open source) software, as well as software intensive organisations from the secondary software sector, representing businesses in different domains such automotive, avionics, finance, and outdoor power products. The primary software sector companies are all service providers with many years of experience from providing services and delivering open source solutions to the private- and public sector. Several of these are international and have also been contracted in framework agreements by the Swedish National Procurement Services at Kammarkollegiet (a governmental authority) for delivering open source solutions to the Swedish public sector organisations in public procurement. Amongst the companies in the software intensive secondary sector, several are recognised as globally leading enterprises in their respective fields.

The research project seeks to investigate how the fundamental challenges lock-in, interoperability, and long-term maintenance of software and associated digital assets can be successfully addressed in different usage context. Investigation involves systematic scrutiny, through use of an action-case study approach [5], of a number of usage contexts which are of relevance for partner organisations.

4 Strategic Use of Open Source in Different Company Contexts

When companies succeed in establishing long-term symbiotic relationships with external open source communities and projects, such relationships can significantly strengthen the company's own missions in addition to strengthen involved open source communities which govern development in open source projects that may be of strategic importance for the own company.

In Fig. 1 we present a conceptual model for how companies can exploit, and engage with, open source based on previous and ongoing research. The model, which initially was presented in the context of product lines [14], has evolved through collaborative research with representatives for partner organisations involved in the LIM-IT project. Arrows (labelled 1, 2, 3, 4a, 4b, and 5 in Fig. 1) represent principle strategies (strategies 1, 2, 3, 4a, 4b, and 5 in Table 1) for how companies can exploit, and engage with, open source in order to seek long-term benefit for their own organisation in different usage contexts. It should be noted that our research has in particular evolved strategy 4a compared to the initial model [14].

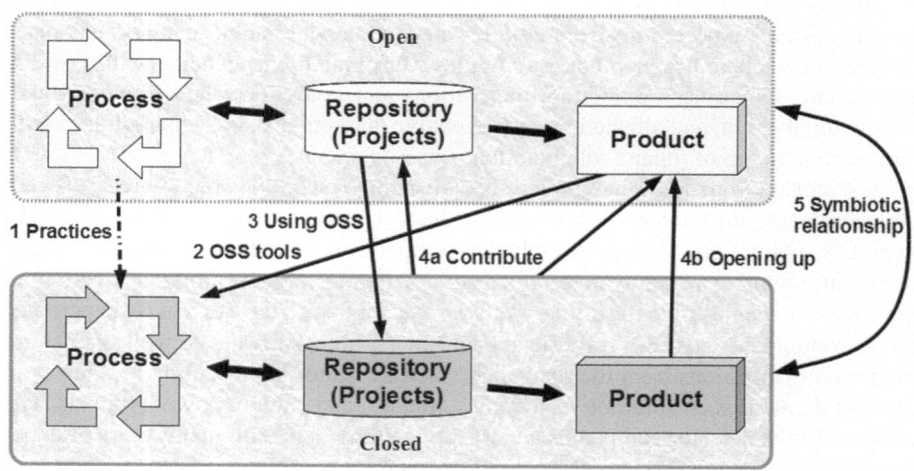

Fig. 1. Leveraging Open Source opportunities

Through conduct of research in the LIM-IT project, we have for all these strategies identified a number of specific instances for how companies exploit and are engaged with open source in different usage contexts in the primary and secondary software sector. By drawing from the identified instances in which partner companies exploit and engage with open source, we present some illustrative examples of the identified instances in order to characterise all principle strategies which have been evolved in collaboration with partner companies. The presented strategies and illustrative examples show how companies utilise (and can utilise) open source software for long-term strategic benefits.

Table 1. Principle strategies for how a company can engage with open source projects

Strategy 1	Adopt open development practices within closed company contexts. This has been referred to as inner source development [15]
Strategy 2	Use open source software tools in a company's own development process
Strategy 3	Use open source software components in the IT- and software products[a] which are deployed to customers and other usage contexts outside the own company context
Strategy 4	Contribute to existing open source projects and open up proprietary software products and release those as new open source projects: (4a) Contribute to existing open source projects and to existing open source products (that have been released from those open source projects) (4b) Open up software products that were initially developed as proprietary software in the own closed company context and release those products as new open source projects
Strategy 5	Establish symbiotic relationships between development projects in the closed company context and strategically important open source projects maintained and governed outside the company's own context. Such mutually beneficial relationships are strategically important for strengthening a company's business and technical development. Further, such relationships are also beneficial for open source projects

[a]Stable releases from open source projects that are deployed for use in different contexts are often referred to as software products

All five principle ways for use and engagement with open source projects can be identified amongst the partner organisations in the LIM-IT research project. All companies have, to some extent, adopted open source work-practices into their own development process (strategy 1), and all use a variety of different open source software in their own company context (strategy 2). For example, several companies use the Eclipse-based modelling tool Papyrus in development projects undertaken in their own company context, and companies in the primary software sector also provide services and training related to specific open source tools. Further, companies also internally use the open source licensed ROS (Robotic Operating System) for simulations in their own development processes and there are also experiences from use of many other open source licensed solutions, such as Apache Solr, Elastic, PostgreSQL, and MongoDB.

Companies use various open source implementations in their own software and hardware offerings (strategy 3). For example, open source implementations of the LWM2 M protocol is adopted for wireless communication with machines for use in different product offerings and several companies include several open source software components in solutions provided to customers. Several companies use a combination of proprietary and open source software, and organisations have experience from distribution of solutions under different terms (including open source software, SaaS, and a combination of proprietary and open source software).

Amongst partner organisations there are experience from releasing proprietary software as open source software (strategy 4b) and also from providing contributions to established open source projects (strategy 4a), such as Apache Solr, SignServer, and EJBCA.

Organisations seek to establish a long-term symbiotic relationship between different interests in open and closed contexts which is beneficial for both companies and open source projects (strategy 5). Such relationships can be effective means for influencing the formation of long-term goals and thereby support strategic collaborations. For example, organisations in the LIM-IT project has experience from involvement in open source industrial working groups, such as Eclipse and the Papyrus Industry Consortium. Further, amongst partners there are also experiences from initiation of and engagement with independent open source projects (e.g. SignServer and EJBCA) which include all relevant roles.

It should be noted that a combination of the above strategies may be utilised for utilising opportunities with open source in a specific company context. Besides strategic and technical benefits from utilising the five strategies for engaging with open source there are also other potential benefits. For example, from a perspective of personnel policy, a company engaged with open source may be perceived as a much more attractive employer, which may significantly ease recruitment of new staff.

5 Conclusion

This paper has elaborated on how companies can strategically use open source for addressing lock-in, interoperability, and long-term maintenance of software and associated digital assets. Through a conceptual model for how companies can use and leverage from open source we have presented an overview of a collaborative research project which aims to establish effective strategies for how companies can use and strategically engage with open source projects in different ways. In so doing, we have illustrated how organisations, through adoption of different strategies, currently use and are involved with open source projects in order to achieve long-term strategic benefits for their own organisation.

Through systematic research investigations of how companies can successfully address the fundamental challenges lock-in, interoperability, and long-term maintenance of software and associated digital assets in different usage contexts we seek to advance practically useful recommendations for use and engagement with open source projects, whilst also contributing to advancing the existing body of knowledge in the field.

Acknowledgements. This research has been financially supported by the Swedish Knowledge Foundation (KK-stiftelsen) and participating partner organisations in the LIM-IT project. The authors are grateful for the stimulating collaboration and support from colleagues and partner organisations.

References

1. Ågerfalk, P.J., Fitzgerald, B.: Outsourcing to an unknown workforce: exploring opensourcing as a global sourcing strategy. MIS Q. **32**(2), 385–409 (2008)
2. Bird, G.B.: The business benefit of standards. StandardsView **6**(2), 76–80 (1998)
3. Blondelle, G., Arberet, P., Rossignol, A., Lundell, B., Labezin, C., Berrendonner, R., Gaufillet, P., Faudou, R., Langlois, B., Maisonobe, L., Moro, P., Rodriguez, J., Puerta Pena, J.-M., Bonnafous, E., Mueller, R.: Polarsys: towards long-term availability of engineering tools for embedded systems. In: ERTS 2012, 8 p. (2012)
4. Bonaccorsi, A., Rossi, C.: Comparing motivations of individual programmers and firms to take part in the open source movement: from community to business. Knowl. Technol. Policy **18**(4), 40–64 (2006)
5. Braa, K., Vidgen, R.: Interpretation, intervention, and reduction in the organizational laboratory: a framework for in-context information system research. Account. Manag. Inf. Technol. **9**, 25–47 (1999)
6. EU: Communication from the commission to the european parliament, the council, the european economic and social committee and the committee of the regions, Against lock-in: building open ICT systems by making better use of standards in public procurement, COM(2013) 455 final, European Commission, Brussels, 25 June 2013
7. Fitzgerald, B.: The transformation of Open Source software. MIS Q. **30**(4), 587–598 (2006)
8. Gamalielsson, J., Lundell, B.: Sustainability of Open Source software communities beyond a fork: how and why has the LibreOffice project evolved? J. Syst. Softw. **89**, 128–145 (2014)
9. Germonprez, M., Allen, J.P., Warner, B., Hill, J., McClements, G.: Open Source communities of competitors. Interactions **20**(6), 54–59 (2013)
10. Ghosh, R.A.: Open standards and interoperability report: an economic basis for open standards, FLOSSPOLS, Deliverable D4, 12 December, Maastricht (2005). www.flosspols.org
11. Hauge, Ø., Sørensen, C.-F., Conradi, R.: Adoption of Open Source in the software industry. In: Russo, B., Damiani, E., Hissam, S., Lundell, B., Succi, G. (eds.) OSS 2008. IFIPAICT, vol. 275, pp. 211–221. Springer, Heidelberg (2008)
12. Katz, A.: Towards a functional licence for open hardware. Int. Free Open Source Softw. Law Rev. **4**(1), 41–62 (2012)
13. Krechmer, K.: The meaning of open standards. In: Proceedings of the 38th Hawaii International Conference on System Sciences, 10 p. IEEE Computer Society, Los Alamitos (2005)
14. van der Linden, F.: Applying Open Source software principles in product lines. Upgrade **10**(2), 32–40 (2009). http://www.cepis.org/upgrade/files/issue%20III-2009-vanderlinden.pdf
15. van der Linden, F., Lundell, B., Marttiin, P.: Commodification of industrial software: a case for Open Source. IEEE Softw. **26**(4), 77–83 (2009)
16. Lundell, B.: e-Governance in public sector ICT-procurement: what is shaping practice in Sweden? Eur. J. ePract. **12**(6) (2011). https://joinup.ec.europa.eu/sites/default/files/76/a7/05/ePractice%20Journal-%20Vol.%2012-March_April%202011.pdf
17. Lundell, B.: Why do we need open standards? In: Orviska, M., Jakobs, K. (eds.) Proceedings of the 17th EURAS Annual Standardisation Conference 'Standards and Innovation'. The EURAS Board Series, Aachen, pp. 227–240 (2012). ISBN: 978-3-86130-337-4
18. Lundell, B., Gamalielsson, J., Mattsson, A.: Exploring tool support for long-term maintenance of digital assets: a case study. In: Fomin, V., Jakobs, K. (eds.) Proceedings of the 16th EURAS Annual Standardization Conference, European Academy of Standardisation, The EURAS Board, pp. 207–217 (2011)

19. Lundell, B., Gamalielsson, J., Tengblad, S.: IT-standarder, inlåsning och konkurrens: En analys av policy och praktik inom svensk förvaltning, Uppdragsforskningsrapport 2016:2, Konkurrensverket (2016). http://www.konkurrensverket.se/nyheter/problem-med-slutna-standarder-vid-it-upphandlingar/ (in Swedish, with an English Executive Summary). ISSN: 1652-8089
20. Lundell, B., van der Linden, F.: Open Source software as open innovation: experiences from the medical domain. In: Eriksson Lundström, J.S.Z., et al. (eds.) Managing Open Innovation Technologies, pp. 3–16. Springer, Berlin (2013)
21. Lundell, B., Lings, B., Lindqvist, E.: Open Source in Swedish companies: where are we? Inf. Syst. J. **20**(6), 519–535 (2010)
22. Lundell, B., Lings, B., Syberfeldt, A.: Practitioner perceptions of Open Source software in the embedded systems area. J. Syst. Softw. **84**(9), 1540–1549 (2011)
23. Northbridge: 2016 the future of open source, North Bridge (2016). http://www.slideshare.net/blackducksoftware/2016-future-of-open-source-survey-results
24. NPS: Open IT-standards, National Procurement Services (Kammarkollegiet), 7 March, Dnr 96-38-2014 (2016). http://www.avropa.se/globalassets/open-it-standards.pdf
25. OSI: Open Source Initiative (2017). https://opensource.org/
26. Robert, S.: On-board software development - The open-source way, IST/ARTEMIS workshop, Helsinki, 22 November 2006
27. Schaarschmidt, M., Walsh, G., von Kortzfleisch, H.F.O.: How do firms influence Open Source software communities? A framework and empirical analysis of different governance modes. Inf. Organ. **25**(2), 99–114 (2015)
28. UK: Open standards principles: for software interoperability, data and document formats in government IT specifications. Cabinet Office, UK, 1 November 2012
29. Wichmann, T.: FLOSS Final Report – Part 2, Free/Libre Open Source Software: Survey and Study Firms' Open Source Activities: Motivations and Policy Implications, Burleson Research GmbH, July, Berlin (2002)

Open Access This chapter is licensed under the terms of the Creative Commons Attribution 4.0 International License (http://creativecommons.org/licenses/by/4.0/), which permits use, sharing, adaptation, distribution and reproduction in any medium or format, as long as you give appropriate credit to the original author(s) and the source, provide a link to the Creative Commons license and indicate if changes were made.

The images or other third party material in this chapter are included in the chapter's Creative Commons license, unless indicated otherwise in a credit line to the material. If material is not included in the chapter's Creative Commons license and your intended use is not permitted by statutory regulation or exceeds the permitted use, you will need to obtain permission directly from the copyright holder.

Understanding the Effects of Practices on KDE Ecosystem Health

Simone da Silva Amorim[1(✉)], John D. McGregor[2],
Eduardo Santana de Almeida[3], and Christina von Flach Garcia Chavez[3]

[1] Federal Institute of Education, Science and Technology of Bahia,
Salvador, Bahia, Brazil
simone.amorim@ifba.edu.br
[2] Clemson University, Clemson, SC, USA
johnmc@cs.clemson.edu
[3] Federal University of Bahia, Salvador, Bahia, Brazil
esa@dcc.ufba.br, flach@ufba.br

Abstract. Open source software ecosystems have adjusted and evolved a set of practices over the years to support the delivery of sustainable software. However, few studies have investigated the impacts of such practices on the health of these ecosystems. In this paper, we present the results of an ethnographic-based study conducted during the Latin-American KDE users and contributors meeting (LaKademy 2015) with the goal of collecting practices used within the KDE ecosystem and understanding how they affect ecosystem health. The analysis was based on softgoal interdependency graphs adapted to represent practices and relate them to non-functional requirements and goals. Our results provide a preliminary insight to understand how KDE ecosystem community interacts, which working practices have been adopted and how they affect ecosystem health.

Keywords: Open source software ecosystems · Ethnographic studies · Software practices · Software ecosystem health

1 Introduction

The software ecosystem (SECO) strategy has been used with great success for several years [1,2]. This strategy has facilitated the emergence of communities surrounding hardware and software computing platforms, such as the Apple iOS community, and certain configurable products, such as the Eclipse Rich Client Platform. Each organization joining a SECO is looking to fill a role in the community that will foster its business objectives. The community members leverage the work of other members to grow bigger products faster than they could have on their own.

Within a SECO, one or more platform providers work to attract product developers to use the provider's platform as the foundation for products. The platform organization shares some degree of control over their platform, provides tools that make product development easier on their platform, and provides access to information about the current structure and future changes to the platform. The dominant organization in the ecosystem, usually the platform owner, heavily influences the culture of the ecosystem.

The *health* of a SECO stands for *the growing and continuity of the software ecosystem remaining variable and productive over time* [11]. The assessment of SECO health can be performed with respect to different aspects, including robustness, productivity, and niche creation [11]. Some studies present quantitative assessment on SECO health [13].

Practices can be useful to understand a SECO and assess its health. For instance, the practice *"review all code before accepting into the release"* may impact several quality indicators and contribute to increasing productivity while avoiding rework. However, to our knowledge, there is no qualitative study that focuses on software practices and their relation to SECO health.

In this paper, we present the results of an ethnographic-based study conducted with the purpose of investigating the practices used by a SECO from three perspectives [5] – business, social, and technical – and their impact on SECO health. The selected research method, ethnography, has been used to study software practices in different contexts [16,17]. The object of our study was KDE[1], an open source SECO that gathers a set of platforms and products for Linux distributions. During the Latin-American KDE users and contributors meeting (LaKademy 2015), we collected day-to-day practices and analyzed them to understand their impact on SECO health. Softgoal interdependency graphs (SIG) [7] extended with practices, support the analysis of KDE practices and their influence on health aspects of SECO such as productivity and robustness.

The remainder of the paper is organized as follows: Sect. 2 presents background on SECO. Section 3 introduces SIG-P, our customized SIG [7]. Section 4 presents the context and design of our study. Section 5 presents the collected KDE practices and a preliminary analysis of their relation to KDE health. Section 6 presents findings, contributions and limitations of our work. Section 7 presents related work. Finally, Sect. 8 provides a brief description of future work and some concluding remarks.

2 Background

The concept of *software ecosystem health* was introduced by Iansiti and Levien as *the growing and continuity of the SECO remaining variable and productive over time* [11]. They argued that the performance of an organization also depends on its interactions with the whole ecosystem – not only on the relationship with competitors and stakeholders and on the organizational potential. Iansiti and Levien drew an analogy with biological ecosystems, and argued that SECO health should be assessed based on three aspects: robustness, productivity, and niche creation [11].

---

[1] https://www.kde.org/.

Robustness refers to the ability of the ecosystem to survive radical changes and problems resulting from these changes. The ecosystems should face and overcome all inevitable difficulties inherent in the evolutionary process. Productivity is related to the way in which the work is accomplished with the least waste of time and effort. The ecosystem should add value through innovation, management of resources and cost control. Lastly, niche creation represents SECO features that encourage and support diversity among the different species in the ecosystem. The ecosystem should provide the structure for creating new features over time, increasing the diversity among SECO members' products [11].

Campbell [5] introduces three views to classify the features of a SECO: technical, business and social. The Technical View presents the architecture and approaches to implementing software. The Business View captures business strategies at play in the ecosystem. In some cases, organizations will be in direct competition and making decisions on release dates and licensing in response to the actions of others within the ecosystem. The Social View captures relationships among humans: developers, users, managers and other participants.

SECO health should not be evaluated only by considering metrics. Practices also aid in understanding a project and its evolution with greater fidelity. They provide clear goals and forms to assess a good working performance to achieve a successful end [12]. For example, the practice *"Provide continuous integration tools to check code every day and report errors"* will impact several quality indicators as well as contribute to increasing productivity while avoiding rework.

3 The NFR Framework with Practices

The NFR framework [6,7] provides a systematic approach for defining and representing non-functional requirements (NFR) for software products. A set of goals represent NFR, design decisions and claims to support or not other goals. Goals are decomposed into subgoals and related with AND/OR relationships [7].

The term *softgoal* introduces the concept of *satisficing* [7]. Softgoals may contribute to some degree (positively (+, ++) or negatively (−, −−), fully or partially), in satisfying other softgoals. A Softgoal Interdependency Graph (SIG) models NFR and their interdependencies to achieve a softgoal (or desired quality). Design decisions are represented by operationalization softgoals. SIG diagrams provide a visual representation for SIG [7].

3.1 SIG with Practices (SIG-P)

SIG with Practices (SIG-P), our customized SIG, models SECO practices and their influence on SECO non-functional requirements. In SIG-P, each practice is modeled as a *satisficing technique* [7] and the degree of its influence on SECO health is documented.

Aspects of SECO health such as robustness, productivity, and niche creation [11] are modeled as *softgoals*. Each softgoal can be decomposed and refined

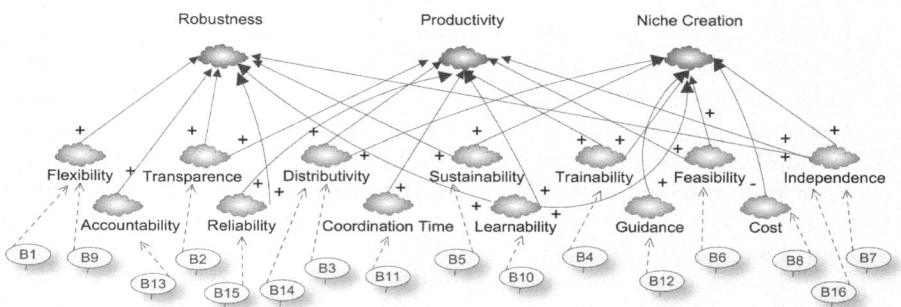

Fig. 1. SIG-P for business view

into mandatory and optional subgoals/NFR that influence directly the achievement of such aspects of SECO health. Practices are connected by interdependency links to NFR to indicate that they contribute to reach softgoals. Social, business and technical views [5] are presented in SIG-P diagrams.

SIG-P diagrams can be used to enhance general understanding about a SECO and its health. They provide a graphical representation for practices, their interdependencies and impacts on NFR and SECO aspects. Moreover, evaluators can build SIG-P models to reason and provide qualitative assessment on SECO health and use SIG-P diagrams to support discussions about correlations and trade offs among softgoals. Figure 1 presents an example of a SIG-P diagram. Details about this example are presented and discussed in Sect. 6.

3.2 SIG-P Construction

The construction of a SIG-P graph for an specific SECO view [5] starts with one or more ecosystem health aspects [11] and a set of practices used by some target SECO. A catalogue of documented NFR, such as the one provided in [7] is strongly recommended.

We defined three steps to guide the bottom-up construction of a SIG-P for each SECO view. Given a set of practices of a target SECO, a catalogue of NFR and SECO softgoals: (1) For each practice, identify a subset of NFR and consider its influence on each NFR; (2) For each identified NFR, analyze its influence on softgoals, considering ambiguities, trade offs and priorities; and (3) For each identified NFR, evaluate the impact (positive or negative) of NFR on softgoals.

These steps can be refined with many iterations considering the reasoning about NFR and their different alternatives. The SIG-P diagram from Fig. 1 illustrates a SIG-P for a business view.

4 Methodology

The KDE ecosystem[2] is an international community that provides a Free Open Source desktop environment for many Linux distributions. The KDE ecosystem has several initiatives to promote their projects around world. In Brazil, a branch of the global organization gathers a team of KDE supporters. The Brazilian group promotes LaKademy (Latin American Akademy), an annual event at which KDE users and contributors meet in person to exchange ideas about projects and discuss the future of KDE. At this event, attendees participate in a set of activities such as lectures, hackathon sessions, and meetings on specific topics.

Hackathons are events that produce working software in a limited period of time. They consist of strenuous and uninterrupted intervals of coding, and are very useful as social and educational events [14]. Komssi et al. stated that hackathons' participants can also learn new practices, technologies, and attitudes, which can be used in everyday work [14]. During KDE events, hackathons provide informal ways to meet new people and learn new technologies.

4.1 Research Method

In this study, research techniques commonly used in ethnographic studies were adopted to support the researcher in understanding the practices and communication strategies KDE uses to work collaboratively. Most of the work in the context of open source SECOs, including KDE, is performed by distributed teams and contributors. Therefore, LaKademy provided an appropriate setting for conducting an ethnographically-inspired [9,18], short term study about KDE. The researcher could observe and participate in LaKademy through in-person meetings and activities.

To address practical challenges faced when conducting ethnographic studies [16], we joined the KDE community to gain better access to the setting of the practices and the use of a common vocabulary. We also conducted our investigation without unnecessary formality, explaining our research, who we were and what we were doing, and trying not to interfere with the activities of LaKademy. Verbal consent was captured on audio recordings at the beginning of sessions. Furthermore, we were rigorous in data collection and analysis to avoid bias.

The first days of Lakademy hackathons are used to disseminate KDE practices and knowledge about the ecosystem. Then developers follow a plan to work hard and deliver planned features. Therefore even knowing that developers are not working in their natural setting, we assume that many practices can be transferred to everyday work of participants.

---

[2] http://www.kde.org/.

4.2 Data Collection and Analysis Procedures

On-site immersion and data collection took place at LaKademy 2015[3] event held in Salvador, from 3rd to 6th June, 2015. The event had 15 participants including students, professionals and KDE collaborators. During 4 days, we conducted semi-structured interviews, listened to lectures, analyzed KDE documents, and observed interactions of community members, mainly during hackathon sessions. Observations were documented in the form of field notes and audio records.

Interviews. Interviews were semi-structured, with 24 open-ended questions intended to understand the daily practices used in KDE ecosystem. Interviews were audio-recorded and later transcribed. We had interview sessions with 4 KDE members that have contributed actively to KDE for 6 years or more – three of them were members of KDE *e.V.* [3], a group that represents the KDE Community with respect to legal and financial issues. One of the interviewed KDE members is part of the KDE Board responsible for business management. We assumed that these people were heavily engaged and up to date regarding most of KDE decisions and practices. They also provided relevant information about the KDE community, contribution areas, financial issues and future plans. The questionnaire can be found at http://homes.dcc.ufba.br/~ssamorim/lakademy/.

Hackathons. During LaKademy 2015, the researcher joined two hackathon sessions for removing bugs from two KDE applications: Cantor, a mathematical application, and the Plasma Network Manager. These sessions provided a good opportunity to observe developers with different levels of experience performing tasks with their own style and ask questions about reasons behind their actions. Some practices, not identified during interviews, were collected during hackathon sessions.

Document Analysis. The researcher also gathered references to online KDE documents. The community maintains a rich website that describes various aspects of KDE ecosystem. We had access to international and Brazilian websites and their documents. Thus, we could explore in detail the dynamics of interactions of the entire KDE ecosystem.

5 Results and Analysis

5.1 Practices in KDE

We collected 68 practices used in KDE SECO. Although a practice could be associated to more than one SECO view (social, business, or technical), we linked it to a single view for which the practice seemed to be most influential. The collection of 68 practices was validated by two interviewees. Five practices (B14, T3, T21, T27, and T35) were not validated. We also asked the two interviewees to choose five important practices for each view.

---

[3] https://br.kde.org/lakademy-2015.

Table 1 presents 10 Social Practices, related to working together in the community, selected by two interviewees. Accordingly, Table 2 presents 10 Business Practices, related to aspects of management, strategic planning, and innovation, and organized activities such as marketing, making decisions, and so on. Finally, Table 3 presents 10 Technical Practices (out of 40 practices), related to product development (core and applications), technologies used, code rules, and others. Other practices are available at http://homes.dcc.ufba.br/~ssamorim/lakademy/.

Table 1. Social Practices

Id	Most important Social Practices	Id	Other Social Practices
S7	Conduct a general annual face to face meeting to discuss community issues	S12	Promote happy hours and dinners to facilitate social integration during events
S1	Create confidence in a member based on his work history. Based on this, provide different levels of responsibilities	S2	Require that at least two persons nominate a member to be promoted up the levels of responsibilities
S4	Promote networking in the work market	S3	Conduct annual meetings among translators by projects
S8	Perform elections to assign responsibility levels for new members	S5	Promote social relationships with members in other countries
S11	Use tools to support communication in the group such as: mailing lists, forums, IRCs, wikis, and blogs	S6	Create opportunities to practice another human language such as English

Table 2. Business Practices

Id	Most important Business Practices	Id	Other Business Practices
B5	Provide a nonprofit corporation to manage legal and financial issues	B6	Divide activities into working groups responsible for areas such as marketing, infrastructure, design, community to keep the group healthy
B8	Attract companies that will invest money to support the ecosystem	B1	Provide flexibility in translation schedule and negotiate deadlines
B11	Define a schedule of releases that will affect the work of the entire community	B2	Reach an agreement in the community on how to answer questions that are not addressed in tutorials or guidelines
B16	Assign a lead maintainer for each project for making technical decisions	B4	Provide lectures to teach how to translate and how to become a contributor
B3	Make decisions based on discussions in the mailing list	B7	Make technical decisions independently within each project

Table 3. Technical Practices

Id	Most important Technical Practices	Id	Other Technical Practices
T1	Each person chooses the work they desire to perform among available tasks in the ecosystem, e.g., file to translate, code to develop, applications to test, and so on	T11	Provide tools for code optimization, static analysis of code, code review, and test automation
T2	Review all code before accepting into the release.	T15	Provide a manifest which project must follow to be considered part of the ecosystem
T10	Provide a freeze period to stabilize the translation of a version before the launch of that version	T16	Require that all infrastructure must be under the control of the ecosystem and be based on technologies created by the ecosystem
T13	Provide continuous integration tools to check code every day and report errors	T25	Keep backward compatibility for a long time (around 6 years)
T23	Develop code to be extensible. The use of plug-ins and compilation is separated between the core and applications	T19	Use scripts to do an initial code review and catch errors

5.2 Analysis

We resorted to SIG-P diagrams to understand and analyze the effects of identified practices on KDE health. SIG-P diagrams were built, one for each SECO view, by following steps described previously (Sect. 3).

SIG-P diagram for KDE business view (Fig. 1, introduced in Sect. 3) supports the analysis of KDE business practices. For instance, practice B5 (*Provide a nonprofit corporation to manage legal and financial issues*) may influence **Sustainability** that, in turn, provides a positive influence on **Niche Creation**.

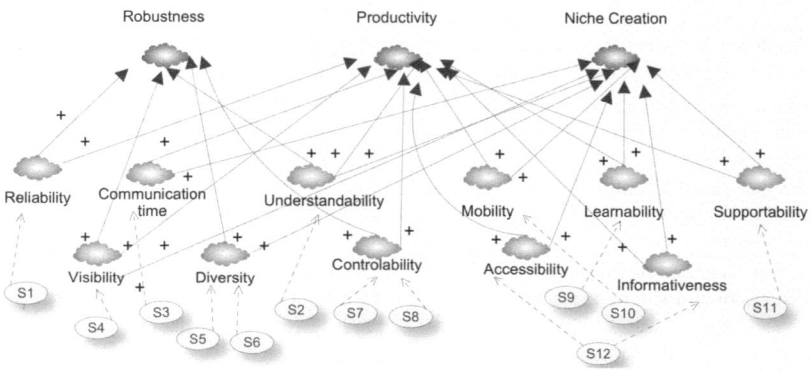

Fig. 2. SIG-P for Social View

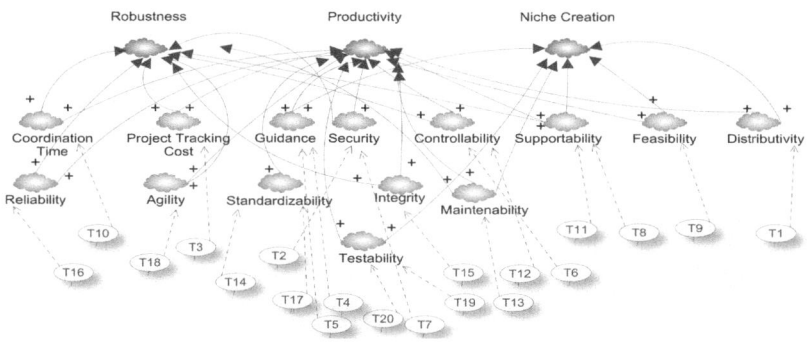

Fig. 3. SIG-P for Technical View

Fig. 2 presents a SIG-P diagram for KDE social view that is used to reason about KDE social practices. For instance, Practices S7 (*Conduct a general annual face to face meeting to discuss community issues*) and S8 (*Perform elections to assign responsibility levels for new members*) affect `Controllability`[4] that, in turn, provides a positive influence on `Robustness` and `Productivity`

Fig. 3 presents a SIG-P diagram for KDE technical view. For instance, Practice T16 (*Require that all infrastructure must be under the control of the ecosystem and be based on the technologies created by the ecosystem*) may influence `Reliability` that, in turn, provides a positive influence on `Robustness` and `Productivity`. At http://homes.dcc.ufba.br/~ssamorim/lakademy/ other SIG-P diagrams are available.

6 Discussion

6.1 Findings

This study allowed us to uncover implicit features of SECO practices and reveal the context in which they were immersed: (a) Many practices are not documented or standardized; (b) There is a great amount of tacit knowledge sharing during hackathon sessions – this highlights the importance of meeting people face-to-face to strengthen the community; and (c) Practices do have influence on KDE ecosystem health, which can be exploited later to support decision-taking processes.

6.2 Contributions

SECO participants can use the knowledge base of practices and related effects in situations such as: (a) SECO adoption, whenever an organization wants to adopt

---

[4] Controllability can be defined as a quality of ecosystems interested in keeping stable and pursuing sustainable development [15].

some ecosystem platform, the NFR with practices can be used to evaluate risks; (b) Getting involved, whenever an individual or team wants to contribute with an open source ecosystem, documented practices and their effects on SECO health can improve the learning curve; and (c) Partnership establishment, in scenarios of feasibility analysis, the NFR with practices can provide useful information to judge the feasibility of partnerships.

Researchers can use our results as input to new evaluation models and quality models for SECOs, and inspiration for performing additional qualitative studies on SECO health. So far additional studies and data are necessary to analyze which practices are more influential or the degree of their influence on SECO health. A deeper understanding on SECO practices will help us to further investigate factors that may contribute to balancing the trade-offs necessary for SECO health.

6.3 Limitations

The contributions of this study should be balanced against some limitations relating to the timing of the study, observer bias, and observed subject bias. Classical ethnographic studies are performed over a long period of time [10]. However, LaKademy provides a rare opportunity to meet people face-to-face in an ecosystem that carries out many online activities.

Additionally, there are limitations regarding practices not captured, variability of SIG-P configurations, and validation of the results. SIG-P models are supposed to support understanding and analysis of SECO practices with respect to their influence on NFR and different health aspects (robustness, productivity, and niche creation) of KDE. In this paper, we only show one combination for SIG-P, but many other combinations are possible including negative impacts. Moreover, we worked to avoid bias taking a rigorous approach to data collection and analysis. Nevertheless, we should perform more combination of practices and NFR and validate the results to produce a more comprehensive analysis.

7 Related Work

To our knowledge, there is no qualitative study in the context of SECO health that focuses on software practices. In this section, we outline related work that addresses ethnography and practices.

Sharp et al. [17] presented an ethnographic study to identify XP practices, conducted in a small company that developed web-based intelligent advertisements. Their findings included 5 characterizing themes within XP practice. The identified practices indicated that, in the XP culture, individuals and teams are respected, take responsibilities, and act to maintain the quality of working life. This work helped us in the identification of XP practices used by KDE.

Evangelista [8] in his PhD thesis investigated the Free Software Movement (FSM), with the overall goal of studying the relation between free software and topics such as culture, power, labor and ideology. To understand the FSM in the

Brazilian context, he conducted an ethnographic study during the 9th International Free Software Forum (FISL)[5]. His study reported several practices used in open source ecosystems. Furthermore, it inspired us to apply ethnography in our work, and provided guidance on observing and understanding practices used by KDE.

8 Conclusions and Future Work

SECOs have achieved success and attracted the attention of researchers. However, little is known about SECO practices and reasons for their success. In this paper, we presented an ethnographic-based study conducted during LaKademy 2015 to collect practices of the KDE ecosystem and understand how they affect ecosystem health. These practices were linked to non-functional requirements to provide a preliminary support to SECO health assessment.

This work provides a set of practices and a SIG-P catalogue of the analyses of the impact of practices on SECO health. These results are important steps for our ongoing research proposal of an assessment method for SECO health based on practices [4]. Our results can also support researchers in understanding operational aspects of open source SECOs.

Acknowledgments. We are thankful to Lakademy 2015 organizers and participants. John McGregor is partially funded by the NSF grant #ACI-1343033.

References

1. Success, Android's: by the Numbers. Information Week (2012). http://www.informationweek.com/mobile/mobile-devices/androids-success-by-the-numbers/d/d-id/1103058
2. Global Hadoop Market - industry analysis, size, share, growth, trends and forecast 2012–2018. Transparency Market Research - White Paper (2013). http://www.transparencymarketresearch.com/hadoop-market.html
3. Pintscher, L. (ed.): Years of KDE: Past, Present and Future (2016). http://20years.kde.org/book/20yearsofKDE.pdf
4. Amorim, S.S., Almeida, E.S., McGregor, J.D., Chavez, C.v.F.G.: Towards an evaluation method for software ecosystem practices. In: Proceeding of the 10th European Conference on Software Architecture Workshops, ECSAW 2016 (2016)
5. Campbell, P.R.J., Ahmed, F.: A three-dimensional view of software ecosystems. In: Proceeding of the Fourth European Conference on Software Architecture, ECSA 2010, pp. 81–84, August 2010
6. Chung, L., Mylopoulos, J., Nixon, B.: Representing and using nonfunctional requirements: a process-oriented approach. IEEE Trans. Softw. Eng. **18**, 483–497 (1992)
7. Chung, L., Nixon, B., Yu, E., Mylopoulos, J.: Non-Functional Requirements in Software Engineering. International Series in Software Engineering. Kluwer Academic Publishers, Boston (1999)

---

[5] http://softwarelivre.org/fisl17.

8. Evangelista, R.: Traidores do Movimento: política, cultura, ideologia e trabalho no Software Livre. Ph.D. thesis, University of Campinas, in Portuguese (2010)
9. Robinson, H., Segal, J., Sharp, H.: Ethnographically-informed empirical studies of software practice. Inf. Softw. Technol. **49**, 540–551 (2007)
10. Hammersley, M., Atkinson, P.: Ethnography: Principles in Practice. Routledge (2007)
11. Iansiti, M., Levien, R.: Keystones and dominators: Framing operating and technology strategy in a business ecosystem. Harvard Business School (03-061), November 2002
12. Jacobson, I., Ng, P.W., Spence, I.: Enough of processes - lets do practices. J. Object Technol. **6**(6), 41–66 (2007)
13. Jansen, S.: Measuring the health of open source software ecosystems: beyond the scope of project health. Inf. Softw. Technol. **56**, 1508–1519 (2014). Special Issue on Software Ecosystems
14. Komssi, M., Pichlis, D., Raatikainen, M., Kindström, K., Järvinen, J.: What are hackathons for? IEEE Softw. **32**, 60–67 (2015)
15. Mens, T., Claes, M., Grosjean, P.: ECOS: Ecological Studies of Open Source Software Ecosystems (2014). http://pdfs.semanticscholar.org/55d9/b45fbab62fbcb7ec09ef4495103361880419.pdf
16. Passos, C., Cruzes, D.S., Dybå, T., Mendonça-Neto, M.: Challenges of applying ethnography to study software practices. In: Proceeding of the ACM-IEEE International Symposium on Empirical Software Engineering and Measurement (ESEM), pp. 9–18, September 2012
17. Sharp, H., Robinson, H.: An ethnographic study of XP practice. Empirical Softw. Eng. **9**, 353–375 (2004)
18. Sharp, H., Dittrich, Y., de Souza, C.R.B.: The role of ethnographic studies in empirical software engineering. IEEE Trans. Softw. Eng. **42**(8), 786–804 (2016)

Open Access This chapter is licensed under the terms of the Creative Commons Attribution 4.0 International License (http://creativecommons.org/licenses/by/4.0/), which permits use, sharing, adaptation, distribution and reproduction in any medium or format, as long as you give appropriate credit to the original author(s) and the source, provide a link to the Creative Commons license and indicate if changes were made.

The images or other third party material in this chapter are included in the chapter's Creative Commons license, unless indicated otherwise in a credit line to the material. If material is not included in the chapter's Creative Commons license and your intended use is not permitted by statutory regulation or exceeds the permitted use, you will need to obtain permission directly from the copyright holder.

Challenges in Validating FLOSS Configuration

Markus Raab[1(✉)] and Gergö Barany[2]

[1] Institute of Computer Languages, Vienna University of Technology,
Vienna, Austria
markus.raab@complang.tuwien.ac.at
[2] Inria, Paris, France
gergo.barany@inria.fr

Abstract. Developers invest much effort into validating configuration during startup of free/libre and open source software (FLOSS) applications. Nevertheless, hardly any tools exist to validate configuration files to detect misconfigurations earlier. This paper aims at understanding the challenges to provide better tools for configuration validation. We use mixed methodology: (1) We analyzed 2,683 run-time configuration accesses in the source-code of 16 applications comprising 50 million lines of code. (2) We conducted a questionnaire survey with 162 FLOSS contributors completing the survey. We report our experiences about building up a FLOSS community that tackles the issues by unifying configuration validation with an external configuration access specification.

We discovered that information necessary for validation is often missing in the applications and FLOSS developers dislike dependencies on external packages for such validations.

1 Introduction

Configuration settings influence the behavior of software and are used ubiquitously today. *Configuration access* is done by the part of applications concerned with fetching configuration settings from configuration files, environment variables, etc. at run-time. *Configuration validation* detects configuration settings which do not fulfill the user's expectations, for example, setting a web browser's proxy to a server that is not reachable in the currently connected network.

While configuration access seems to be straightforward, system administrators experience many surprises on a daily basis. In the systems community the issue is well-known as *misconfiguration* [1,30,36,37]. Misconfigurations cause large-scale outages of Internet services [19]. Yin et al. [37] claim that *"a majority of misconfigurations (70.0%–85.5%) are due to mistakes in setting configuration"*.

Xu et al. argue that often configuration access code and not system administrators are to blame [35]. Often (38.1%–53.7%) misconfiguration is caused by illegal settings which clearly violate syntactic or semantic rules [37]. Thus most

---

Gergö Barany—This work was performed while the author was at CEA LIST Software Reliability Laboratory, France, and supported by the French National Research Agency (ANR), project AnaStaSec, ANR-14-CE28-0014.

© The Author(s) 2017
F. Balaguer et al. (Eds.): OSS 2017, IFIP AICT 496, pp. 101–114, 2017.
DOI: 10.1007/978-3-319-57735-7_11

errors could be caught with a consistency checker executed before configuration changes. Nevertheless, only in 7.2% to 15.5% cases do error messages pinpoint the error [37]. Free/libre and open source software (FLOSS) applications often do not validate their settings before startup or even later [34]. System administrators have to find their own ad-hoc ways [3,4,13,31,39].

Other factors also influence configuration settings. We will call validation that considers more than the settings of a single application *global validation*. Faulty global validation causes issues in 46.3%–61.9% of cases [37]. For example, when a web browser is started in a different network, previously working proxy settings will fail to work. Our holistic approach rejects misconfigurations early on.

These issues lead to our **research question**: Why do we lack tools for global validation, and how can we help developers provide them?

Our contributions are as follows:

- We showed that `getenv` is omnipresent and popular (Sect. 3).
- We unveiled challenges related to current configuration systems (Sect. 4).
- We implemented a tool implementing the unearthed requirements (Sect. 5).
- The tool is available as free software at https://www.libelektra.org.

2 Methodology

Our methodological foundation builds on *theory building from cases* [10,11]. In the present paper we will use two different methodologies embedded in a framework: source-code analysis and a questionnaire.

2.1 Source-Code Analysis

We study `getenv`, which is an application programming interface (API) to access environment variables. We chose it because it is the only widely standardized configuration access API (included in C, C++, and POSIX standards) and available in many programming languages. In earlier work [26], we showed that `getenv` is used at run-time ubiquitously. `getenv` is often combined with other techniques, for example, overriding configuration file settings. Furthermore, environment variables are not part of configuration settings dialogues, i.e., they are usually not validated before reaching the application.

We carefully selected 16 applications across different domains. We included large applications with a thriving community but also others for diversity. We used the versions of the applications as included in Debian 8 (Jessie) as shown later in Table 1. We downloaded package sources from http://snapshot.debian.org. To determine the code size we used Cloc 1.60 [7].

We manually counted all `getenv` occurrences for the version specified in Table 1. Then we categorized the resulting 2,683 code snippets around `getenv`. We looked if `getenv` occurrences *depend* on some other configuration. Such situations occur when configuration settings interact; for example, fallback chains of configuration access points depend on each other. Such fallback chains are hints to global configuration access, which we wanted to find. As our last experiment, we searched for places where global validation would be useful, and investigated how helpful the documentation of the `getenv` parameters is.

Threats to Validity: For evaluating usefulness (as only done in the last experiment), by nature, subjectivity is involved. In particular, it is possible that we overlooked dependences. We will report the numbers we found but we consider the experiment as exploratory and not as something that could be repeated with the same numbers as outcome. The individual examples, however, are insightful.

2.2 Questionnaire

We carefully prepared a questionnaire with FLOSS developers in mind. Then we conducted pilot surveys with developers, colleagues and experts for surveys. In the iterations we improved the questions and made the layout more appealing.

In order to reach the target group, we posted requests to fill out the survey in the respective FLOSS communication channels. To obtain a higher quality, we awarded non-anonymous answers with small donations to FLOSS-related projects. We used the non-anonymous answers to cross-check statistics.

We asked some personal questions about age, education, occupation, and FLOSS participation to have the important characteristics of our participants.

We used Limesurvey version 2.50+ for conducting the survey. We will report the percentages relative to the number of persons (n) who answered a particular question. We report means and standard deviations (s) of samples for $n \geq 95$. We used the Kolmogorov-Smirnov test [15] for smaller samples.

Threats to Validity: For the validity of our survey it is important that only FLOSS contributors participate. The donation might have persuaded some participants to fill out parts of the survey even though they had no particular experience. Thus we explicitly asked about contributions to specific projects.

The survey reflects the beliefs of participants. Thus we used other methods to distill facts about the applications. Because opinions help to understand goals and reasons, the survey is an important part of the overall study. It should be considered as supplement to the source-code analysis.

Demographics: The front page of the survey was shown to 672 persons, 286 gave at least one answer, 162 completed the questionnaire, and 116 persons entered their email addresses. The age of the population ($n = 220$) has a mean of 32 years ($s = 9$). The degrees in the population ($n = 244$) are: master (38%), bachelor (25%), student (18%), no degree (13%), or PhD (6%). As their occupation, 56% of the persons selected software developer, 21% system administrator, and 16% researcher (multiple choice question, $n = 287$). Participants reported work on up to five different FLOSS projects. For the first project, they estimated their participation with a mean of 5.3 years ($s = 5$, $n = 180$). 60% of them reported a second FLOSS project, 36% a third, 17% a fourth, and 9% a fifth.

Raw data and questions are available at https://rawdata.libelektra.org.

3 Configuration Access

Before we start exploring our research question, we need to validate that our evaluated configuration accesses are indeed relevant and popular. In this section we investigate which configuration access methods FLOSS developers use.

3.1 Which Methods for Configuration Access are Popular?

Finding 1_a: *We observed that* `getenv` *is omnipresent with 2,683 occurrences.*
The source code of the applications we analyzed has 4,650 textual `getenv` occurrences. 2,683 of them were actual `getenv` invocations, 1,967 were occurrences in comments, ChangeLog, build system, or similar. (See Table 1 for details.)

Finding 1_b: *Three kinds of configuration access are equally popular: Command-line arguments, environment variables, and configuration files. Developers are highly satisfied with them. Others are used less, and are more frustrating to use.*

Command-line arguments (92%, $n = 222$), environment variables (e.g., via `getenv`) (79%, $n = 218$), and configuration files (74%, $n = 218$) are the most popular ways to access configuration. Other systems, such as X/Q/GSettings, KConfig, dconf, plist, or Windows Registry, were used less ($\leq 13\%$, $n \geq 185$).

Participants rarely found it (very) frustrating to work with the popular systems: `getenv` (10%, $n = 198$), configuration files (6%, $n = 190$), and command-line options (4%, $n = 210$). Less-used systems frustrated more ($\geq 14\%$, $n \geq 27$).

3.2 What Is the Purpose of `getenv`?

Finding 1_c: *Like other configuration accesses,* `getenv` *is used to access configuration settings (57%). Sometimes it bypasses main configuration access.*

Of the 2,683 `getenv` invocations, 1,531, i.e., 57%, relate to run-time configuration settings and not debugging, build-system, or similar. Other investigations in this paper discuss these 1,531 `getenv` occurrences. (See Table 1 for details.)

We found occurrences where `getenv` obviously bypasses main configuration access, for example, to configure the location of configuration files.

Also in the survey we asked about the purpose of `getenv` ($n = 177$). The reasons to use it vary: in a multiple choice question 55% say they would use it for debugging/testing, 45% would use `getenv` to bypass the main configuration access, and 20% would use `getenv` if configuration were unlikely to be changed.

Finding 1_d: *In many cases* `getenv` *parameters are shared between applications.*
In the source code we investigated which parameters were passed to `getenv`. We found that 716 parameters were shareable parameters such as `PATH`. In the survey 53% say they use `getenv` for configuration integration ($n = 177$).

Finding 1_e: *Parameters of* `getenv` *are often undocumented.*
The function parameter passed to `getenv` invocations tells us which configuration setting is accessed. In an Internet search using the application's and `getenv`

parameter's name with https://startpage.com, we found documentation for only 283 of the non-shared `getenv` parameters but not for the 387 others.

The FLOSS projects deal with the missing documentation of `getenv` parameters in different ways. Most projects simply claim their `getenv` usage as internal, saying the environment should not be used for configuration by end users, even if there is no other way of achieving some goal. Often we miss a specification describing which parameters are available.

In other projects, the developers invest effort to create lists of available parameters. For example, in LibreOffice developers try to find `getenv` occurrences automatically with `grep`, which fails with `getenv` aliases[1].

Discussion: The `getenv` API has some severe limitations and is sometimes a second-class citizen. One limitation is that return values of `getenv` invocations cannot be updated by other processes. For example, `getenv("http_proxy")` within a running process will still return the old proxy, even if the user changed it elsewhere. Another limitation is that they do not support persistent changes by applications. Configuration files, however, are not easily shareable.

Implication: There is currently no satisfactory solution in FLOSS for global, shareable configuration settings. `getenv` supports all characteristics of configuration access and can be used to investigate challenges in configuration validation.

4 Configuration Validation

Having established which configuration accesses are popular (including, but not limited to, `getenv`), we will investigate challenges of configuration validation.

4.1 Which Are the Concerns Regarding Global Validation?

Finding 2_a: *Developers have concerns about adding dependencies for global validation (84%) and reducing configuration (30%) but desire good defaults (80%).*

Many persons (30%, $n = 150$) think that the number of configuration settings should *not* be reduced. But 43% said it should be reduced to prevent errors.

We got mixed answers ($n = 177$) to the question "Which effort do you think is worthwhile for providing better configuration experience?" Most persons (80%) agree that proper defaults are important. Most methods exceed the effort considered tolerable by the majority of participants: Only `getenv` would be used by the majority (53%). System APIs would be used by 44%. Fewer (30%) would use other OS-specific methods, such as reading `/proc`. Only 21% of the participants would use dedicated libraries, 19% would parse other's applications configuration files, and 16% would use external APIs that add new dependencies.

Discussion: To avoid dependencies, FLOSS developers currently expect users to configure their applications to be consistent with the global configuration.

---

[1] https://bugs.documentfoundation.org/show_bug.cgi?id=37338.

Implication: The results indicate demand for dependency injection to have global validation without direct dependencies.

4.2 Which Challenges Prevent Us from Supporting Validation?

Finding 2_b: *Present configuration validation is encoded in a way unusable for external validation or introspection tools.*

In none of the 16 applications was the validation code kept separately, e.g., in a library. Instead it was scattered around like other cross-cutting concerns.

Finding 2_c: *Developers are unable to support global validation, even if the problem is well-known and they put effort into it. We found out that information essential to check or fix constraints is not available within the applications.*

In Table 1 we present the list of applications we analyzed. The column *counted getenv* lists our manual count of all getenv invocations. The column *config getenv* shows getenv occurrences used for configuration as described in Finding 1_c. The column *depend getenv* presents manually counted getenv occurrences that depend on, or are used by, other configuration code. The last column *lines per getenv* shows how often manually counted getenv occurs in code.

Table 1. Manual count and classification of getenv occurrences.

Application	Version	1k lines of code	Counted getenv	Config getenv	Depend getenv	Lines per getenv
0ad	0.0.17	474	55	45	43	8,617
Akonadi	1.13.0	37	13	8	6	2,863
Chromium	45.0.2454	18,032	770	387	281	23,418
Curl	7.38.0	249	53	26	25	4,705
Eclipse	3.8.1	3,312	40	33	23	82,793
Evolution	3.12.9	673	23	13	5	29,252
Firefox	38.3.0esr	12,395	788	376	271	15,730
GCC	4.9.2	6,851	377	218	143	18,172
Gimp	2.8.14	902	56	27	21	16,102
Inkscape	0.48.5	480	19	16	13	25,255
Ipe	7.1.4	116	21	19	14	5,529
LibreOffice	4.3.3	5,482	284	207	143	19,304
Lynx	2.8.9dev1	192	89	79	66	2,157
Man	2.7.0.2	142	62	52	42	2,293
Smplayer	14.9.0~ds0	76	1	1	1	76,170
Wget	1.16	143	32	24	18	4,456
Total		49,556	2,683	1,531	1,115	18,470
Median		477	54	30	24	

Most of these places (1,115, i.e., 73%) were dependent on some other configuration. We found 204 places where some kind of configuration dependencies were forgotten. In 58 cases we found several hints, e.g., fallback chains with missing cases or complaints on the Internet about the not considered dependency.

We give a real-life example from the Eclipse source of how easily dependencies are forgotten. The missing dependencies lead to missing validation, which leads to frustrating user experience. If Eclipse wants to instantiate an internal web browser, some users get an error saying that MOZILLA_FIVE_HOME is not set. On GitHub alone, issues mentioning the variable were reported 71 times. The underlying issue usually is that the software package webkitgtk is missing[2]. The developers even considered the dependency (installation paths) for RPM-based systems by parsing gre.conf. But for other users on non-RPM-based systems the fallback is to query MOZILLA_FIVE_HOME which leads to the misleading error. In Eclipse the workarounds (including parsing gre.conf) needed 213 lines of code. Furthermore, most of the 9006 code snippets we found on GitHub referring to the variable are small wrappers trying to set MOZILLA_FIVE_HOME correctly.

Discussion: While the package managers easily answer where the missing files are located, within the application there is no reasonable way to find out. We found similar issues concerning network, firewall, hardware settings, etc.

Implication: Applications have a need to access global configuration settings.

5 Experience Report on Supporting Global Validation

Elektra is a library that aims at providing unified access to configuration settings as key/value pairs. It integrates a specification language for global validation. Here we will discuss how Elektra fulfills the requirements unearthed by the study before describing the challenges to adoption that Elektra faced in the past. We summarize requirements derived from the findings of Sects. 3 and 4.

5.1 Unify Configuration

Requirement 1_{a-c}: *Developers use different mechanisms for configuration accesses interchangeably or to bypass limitations of others.* To avoid the need for bypasses, Elektra bootstraps itself at startup, making it possible for configuration settings to describe the configuration access, for example, which configuration files should be used. To allow administrators to use all popular techniques, Elektra reads from different sources such as configuration files, system settings, and environment variables. Elektra integrates many different configuration file formats such as INI, XML, etc., and it supports notifications to always keep application's configuration settings in sync with the persistent configuration settings.

Requirement 1_d: *FLOSS developers demand a way to share configuration settings.* We implemented a layer similar to a virtual file system, which enables

---
[2] https://groups.google.com/forum/#!topic/xmind/5SjPTy0MmEo.

applications and system administrators to mount configuration files [29]. This technique facilitates applications to access configuration settings of any other application. Using links and transformations [22] one can even configure applications to use other settings without any support from the application itself.

Requirement 1_e: *There should be a way to document configuration settings.* Elektra introduces specifications for configuration settings [24]. These specifications should also include documentation. But even if they do not, users at least know which configuration settings exist, and which values are valid for them.

5.2 Validate Configuration

Requirement 2_a: *Dependencies exclusively needed for configuration settings should be avoided.* Elektra introduces plugins that enable a system-level dependency injection. Developers specify validations in specifications, without the need for their application to depend on additional external libraries. In plugins executed on configuration access, the settings get validated or default settings get calculated. Elektra only uses the C standard library and no other external dependencies [20]. Nevertheless, even the dependency on Elektra itself can be avoided. Elektra supports intercepting of library calls such as `getenv` [26,27]. Using this technique, applications think they use environment variables, while in reality they query Elektra.

Requirement 2_b: *Configuration settings and validations should be open to introspection.* Similarly to `getenv`, Elektra provides an API, but it aims to overcome the limitations of previous abstractions and interfaces. Elektra allows many configuration files to be integrated with a uniform key/value API. Even the specifications of accesses, dependencies, and validations are accessible via the same API. Thus system administrators and applications can use the API to introspect configuration settings. Elektra relies on file system permissions to restrict access to configuration files.

Requirement 2_c: *Global validation should be supported.* Elektra supports global validation through a range of different checker plugins. These plugins do not only check data for consistency but also check if configuration settings conflict with reality. For example, one plugin checks for presence of files or directories, while another plugin checks if a host name can be resolved. Checks are executed whenever Elektra's API is used for writing. This way also all administrator tools sitting on top of Elektra reject invalid configuration settings. Elektra also allows to integrate system information such as hardware settings via plugins.

5.3 Community Building

The *Elektra Initiative* is a community that started with the straightforward idea to have a single API for configuration access. Other projects watched how it progressed, but adoptions occurred rarely. Due to various grave issues in the first versions, the API needed several redesigns. Obviously, API changes are not very popular and Elektra lost most of its users at this time. Despite many marketing efforts to change the situation, it was predominantly companies and not FLOSS software that used Elektra. This slow adoption was unfortunate but an opportunity to continue making changes. Unfortunately, the changes were not done wisely, instead we introduced mostly unnecessary features. Here the Elektra Initiative had its low and turning-point.

Then the goals shifted towards a more technical solution: We avoid marketing campaigns to persuade everyone to use the API with arguments like "it will give benefits once everyone migrates". Instead it should offer immediate advantages previous APIs did not have. This meant Elektra went into a highly competitive market facing the difficulty of being better than any other configuration library. As a distinctive feature, we started to aim for global validation but without giving up compatibility to current configuration files. We avoid an API that forces our ideology, like our favourite configuration file format or validation, onto users.

These changes made the core more complicated, which led to a recruiting problem. The documentation was for a long time only a master thesis [20], which was a very unsatisfactory situation. The next efforts were to make the project community-friendly again. We started to improve quality by regression tests, fixing reports of code analysis tools, and adding code comments and assertions. Then we started overhauling documentation, writing tutorials, and created a website. Last but not least, we started releasing every two months with fixes and new features in every release. These changes led to more than a dozen contributors, Elektra being packaged for many distributions, and acceptance of a paper on Elektra in "The Journal of Open Source Software" [23].

6 Community Feedback and Future Work

The survey validated Elektra's goals: Many agreed (80%, $n = 153$) that a solution must be lightweight and efficient; and that a configuration library must be available anywhere and anytime (84%, $n = 153$). Many persons (70%, $n = 150$) consider it important that the community is supportive. Even more persons want bugs to be fixed promptly (88%, $n = 150$). Because 76% persons find it important that applications directly ship documentation ($n = 157$), external specifications should have documentation. Nearly everyone (96%, $n = 173$) agrees that configuration integration, such as global validation, would at least moderately improve user experience. Thus we will continue research in this area.

A participant said: *"Must be extensible/adaptable. If it is, users can take care of many of the above aspects themselves"*. We agree and continue to pioneer modularity. For example, many persons found readability of configurations important (65%, $n = 152$) but could not agree which formats are readable.

Another person wrote: *"It must offer a compelling reason to switch from e.g. gsettings. For example a killer feature that others don't have, etc. Otherwise, the status quo wins."* Elektra's "killer feature" can be global validation.

From our experience with Elektra, it was also clear that we need to put much more effort into API stability. Thus we avoid breaking changes to the API. We are about to provide easy-to-use high-level APIs for different use cases.

The 1.0 release of Elektra is still pending: (1) The specification language for validation/transformation/dependency injection is not completely defined. (2) The configuration parsers have limitations, e.g., they do not always preserve comments or order. (3) Elektra puts some unnecessary limitations on the plugins.

7 Related Work

Many other configuration libraries have validation capabilities, for example, Apache Commons Configuration. Unlike Elektra they do not have external specifications. Instead they require developers to hardcode them into the applications.

Other papers describe the technical details of Elektra [20,23,29]. In particular frontend code generation avoids errors in configuration access [21,28]. Other work describes Elektra's specification language [22,24] and how applications participate without code modifications [25,26].

Crowston et al. [6] created a survey of empirical research for FLOSS. Michlmayr et al. [16] investigated quality issues of FLOSS using interviews. We were able to confirm that documentation often is lacking. Barcomb et al. [2] used a questionnaire to investigate how developers acquire FLOSS skills.

PCheck [34] validates configuration files early. Unlike Elektra, it is not free software and does not support application-specific checks or plugins. Some work was done to automatically resolve misconfiguration [1,30,33,38]. These approaches aim at solving already manifested issues, Elektra aims at resolving them earlier. Xu et al. [36] surveyed further possibilities.

Nosál et al. [17,18] investigated similar abstractions but with a focus on language mapping. Denisov [8] collected requirements for configuration libraries.

Berger et al. [5] and Villela et al. [32] created a questionnaire that asks about variability modeling. Our survey focused on a different target group.

8 Conclusions

In this paper we examined challenges in configuration access and presented a solution. We addressed the research question: Why do we lack tools for global validation and how can we help developers provide them? The answer is that validations are encoded in the software in a way (1) unusable by external tools, and (2) incapable of using global knowledge of the system. The answer is backed up by both a questionnaire and a source analysis.

To overcome developers' configuration issues, we need to externalize configuration access specifications and use a unified configuration library. The empirical data backs up that this is possible and wanted. It is *possible*, because currently different configuration accesses are used interchangeably. It is *wanted*, because users stated that different forms of configuration access sources should be able to override each other.

Based on our survey we might have to rethink how to reduce the number of configuration settings because many developers do not agree with complete removal of less-used settings. The survey also showed that external dependencies in configuration access code are a contradictory topic: Developers want good defaults, but do not want to pay for them with dependencies. Elektra's way of implementing dependency injection and globally calculating default settings fulfills both goals. Because of the externalization of configuration access specifications, users can even introspect the (default) settings that applications receive.

Finally, we described FLOSS community efforts to improve on the issues. The results show that a dependency injection at the system level is feasible and practical. It has the potential to be accepted by developers if they perceive global integration and validation as "killer feature". The current status of the FLOSS project can be tracked at https://www.libelektra.org.

Acknowledgments. We thank the anonymous reviewers, Tianyin Xu, Franz Puntigam, Stefan Winter, Milan Nosál, and Harald Geyer for detailed reviews of this paper. Additionally, many thanks to all the people contributing to Elektra.

References

1. Attariyan, M., Flinn, J.: Automating configuration troubleshooting with dynamic information flow analysis. In: Proceedings of the 9th USENIX Conference on Operating Systems Design and Implementation, OSDI 2010, pp. 1–11. USENIX Association, Berkeley (2010)
2. Barcomb, A., Grottke, M., Stauffert, J.-P., Riehle, D., Jahn, S.: How developers acquire FLOSS skills. In: Damiani, E., Frati, F., Riehle, D., Wasserman, A.I. (eds.) OSS 2015. IAICT, vol. 451, pp. 23–32. Springer, Cham (2015). doi:10.1007/978-3-319-17837-0_3
3. Barrett, R., Chen, Y.Y.M., Maglio, P.P.: System administrators are users, too: designing workspaces for managing Internet-scale systems. In: CHI 2003 Extended Abstracts on Human Factors in Computing Systems, pp. 1068–1069. ACM (2003)
4. Barrett, R., Kandogan, E., Maglio, P.P., Haber, E.M., Takayama, L.A., Prabaker, M.: Field studies of computer system administrators: analysis of system management tools and practices. In: Proceedings of the 2004 ACM Conference on Computer Supported Cooperative Work, pp. 388–395. ACM (2004)
5. Berger, T., Rublack, R., Nair, D., Atlee, J.M., Becker, M., Czarnecki, K., Wąsowski, A.: A survey of variability modeling in industrial practice. In: Proceedings of the Seventh International Workshop on Variability Modelling of Software-intensive Systems, VaMoS 2013, pp. 7:1–7:8. ACM, New York (2013). http://doi.acm.org/10.1145/2430502.2430513
6. Crowston, K., Wei, K., Howison, J., Wiggins, A.: Free/libre open-source software development: what we know and what we do not know. ACM Comput. Surv. **44**(2), 7:1–7:35 (2008). http://dx.doi.org/10.1145/2089125.2089127
7. Danial, A.: Cloc-count lines of code (2017). https://github.com/AlDanial/cloc, Feb 2017
8. Denisov, V.S.: Functional requirements for a modern application configuration framework. Int. J. Open Inf. Technol. **10**, 6–10 (2015)
9. Di Cosmo, R., Zacchiroli, S., Trezentos, P.: Package upgrades in FOSS distributions: details and challenges. In: Proceedings of the 1st International Workshop on Hot Topics in Software Upgrades, HotSWUp 2008, pp. 7:1–7:5. ACM, New York (2008). http://dx.doi.org/10.1145/1490283.1490292

10. Easterbrook, S., Singer, J., Storey, M.A., Damian, D.: Selecting empirical methods for software engineering research. In: Shull, F., Singer, J., Sjøberg, D. (eds.) Guide to Advanced Empirical Software Engineering, pp. 285–311. Springer, London (2008)
11. Eisenhardt, K.M., Graebner, M.E.: Theory building from cases: opportunities and challenges. Acad. Manage. J. **50**(1), 25–32 (2007)
12. Ghosh, R.A., Glott, R., Krieger, B., Robles, G.: Free/libre and open source software: Survey and study. University of Maastricht, The Netherlands, International Institute of Infonomics (2002)
13. Haber, E.M., Bailey, J.: Design guidelines for system administration tools developed through ethnographic field studies. In: Proceedings of the 2007 Symposium on Computer Human Interaction for the Management of Information Technology, CHIMIT 2007. ACM, New York (2007). http://dx.doi.org/10.1145/1234772.1234774
14. Hammouda, I., Harsu, M.: Documenting maintenance tasks using maintenance patterns. In: Eighth European Conference on Software Maintenance and Reengineering, CSMR 2004, Proceedings, pp. 37–47, March 2004
15. Lilliefors, H.W.: On the Kolmogorov-Smirnov test for normality with mean and variance unknown. J. Am. Stat. Assoc. **62**(318), 399–402 (1967). http://amstat.tandfonline.com/doi/abs/10.1080/01621459.1967.10482916
16. Michlmayr, M., Hunt, F., Probert, D.: Quality practices and problems in free software projects. In: Proceedings of the First International Conference on Open Source Systems, pp. 24–28 (2005)
17. Nosál, M., Porubän, J.: Supporting multiple configuration sources using abstraction. Open Comput. Sci. **2**(3), 283–299 (2012)
18. Nosál, M., Porubän, J.: XML to annotations mapping definition with patterns. Comput. Sci. Inf. Syst. **11**(4), 1455–1477 (2014)
19. Oppenheimer, D., Ganapathi, A., Patterson, D.A.: Why do Internet services fail, and what can be done about it? In: USENIX Symposium on Internet Technologies and Systems, Seattle, WA, vol. 67 (2003)
20. Raab, M.: A modular approach to configuration storage. Master's thesis, Vienna University of Technology (2010)
21. Raab, M.: Global and thread-local activation of contextual program execution environments. In: Proceedings of the IEEE 18th International Symposium on Real-Time Distributed Computing Workshops (ISORCW/SEUS), pp. 34–41, April 2015
22. Raab, M.: Sharing software configuration via specified links and transformation rules. In: Technical report from KPS 2015, vol. 18. Vienna University of Technology, Complang Group (2015)
23. Raab, M.: Elektra: universal framework to access configuration parameters. J. Open Source Softw. **1**(8), 1–2 (2016). http://dx.doi.org/10.21105/joss.00044
24. Raab, M.: Improving system integration using a modular configuration specification language. In: Companion Proceedings of the 15th International Conference on Modularity, MODULARITY Companion 2016, pp. 152–157. ACM, New York (2016). http://dx.doi.org/10.1145/2892664.2892691
25. Raab, M.: Persistent contextual values as inter-process layers. In: Proceedings of the 1st International Workshop on Mobile Development, Mobile! 2016, pp. 9–16. ACM, New York (2016). http://dx.doi.org/10.1145/3001854.3001855
26. Raab, Markus: Unanticipated context awareness for software configuration access using the getenv API. In: Lee, Roger (ed.) Computer and Information Science. SCI, vol. 656, pp. 41–57. Springer, Cham (2016). doi:10.1007/978-3-319-40171-3_4

27. Raab, M., Barany, G.: Introducing context awareness in unmodified, context-unaware software. In: 12th International Conference on Evaluation of Novel Approaches to Software Engineering (ENASE) (2017, to appear)
28. Raab, M., Puntigam, F.: Program execution environments as contextual values. In: Proceedings of 6th International Workshop on Context-Oriented Programming, pp. 8:1–8:6. ACM, New York (2014). http://dx.doi.org/10.1145/2637066.2637074
29. Raab, M., Sabin, P.: Implementation of multiple key databases for shared configuration (2008). ftp://www.markus-raab.org/elektra.pdf, Accessed Feb 2014
30. Su, Y.Y., Attariyan, M., Flinn, J.: Autobash: improving configuration management with operating system causality analysis. ACM SIGOPS Operating Syst. Rev. **41**(6), 237–250 (2007)
31. Velasquez, N.F., Weisband, S., Durcikova, A.: Designing tools for system administrators: an empirical test of the integrated user satisfaction model. In: Proceedings of the 22nd Conference on Large Installation System Administration Conference, LISA 2008, pp. 1–8. USENIX Association, Berkeley (2008). http://dl.acm.org/citation.cfm?id=1496684.1496685
32. Villela, K., Silva, A., Vale, T., de Almeida, E.S.: A survey on software variability management approaches. In: Proceedings of the 18th International Software Product Line Conference, SPLC 2014, vol. 1, pp. 147–156. ACM, New York (2014). http://dx.doi.org/10.1145/2648511.2648527
33. Wang, H.J., Platt, J.C., Chen, Y., Zhang, R., Wang, Y.M.: Automatic misconfiguration troubleshooting with peerpressure. OSDI **4**, 245–257 (2004)
34. Xu, T., Jin, X., Huang, P., Zhou, Y., Lu, S., Jin, L., Pasupathy, S.: Early detection of configuration errors to reduce failure damage. In: Proceedings of the 12th USENIX Symposium on Operating Systems Design and Implementation (OSDI 2016), Savannah, GA, USA, November 2016
35. Xu, T., Zhang, J., Huang, P., Zheng, J., Sheng, T., Yuan, D., Zhou, Y., Pasupathy, S.: Do not blame users for misconfigurations. In: Proceedings of the Twenty-Fourth ACM Symposium on Operating Systems Principles, pp. 244–259. ACM (2013)
36. Xu, T., Zhou, Y.: Systems approaches to tackling configuration errors: a survey. ACM Comput. Surv. **47**(4), 70:1–70:41 (2015). http://dx.doi.org/10.1145/2791577
37. Yin, Z., Ma, X., Zheng, J., Zhou, Y., Bairavasundaram, L.N., Pasupathy, S.: An empirical study on configuration errors in commercial and open source systems. In: Proceedings of the Twenty-Third ACM Symposium on Operating Systems Principles, SOSP 2011, pp. 159–172. ACM, New York (2011)
38. Zhang, S., Ernst, M.D.: Automated diagnosis of software configuration errors. In: Proceedings of the 2013 International Conference on Software Engineering, ICSE 2013, pp. 312–321. IEEE Press, Piscataway (2013)
39. Zhang, S., Ernst, M.D.: Which configuration option should I change?. In: Proceedings of the 36th International Conference on Software Engineering. pp. 152–163. ICSE 2014, NY, USA (2014),. http://dx.doi.org/10.1145/2568225.2568251

Open Access This chapter is licensed under the terms of the Creative Commons Attribution 4.0 International License (http://creativecommons.org/licenses/by/4.0/), which permits use, sharing, adaptation, distribution and reproduction in any medium or format, as long as you give appropriate credit to the original author(s) and the source, provide a link to the Creative Commons license and indicate if changes were made.

The images or other third party material in this chapter are included in the chapter's Creative Commons license, unless indicated otherwise in a credit line to the material. If material is not included in the chapter's Creative Commons license and your intended use is not permitted by statutory regulation or exceeds the permitted use, you will need to obtain permission directly from the copyright holder.

Case Studies

Case Studies

Progression and Forecast of a Curated Web-of-Trust: A Study on the Debian Project's Cryptographic Keyring

Gunnar Wolf[1](✉) and Víctor González Quiroga[2]

[1] Instituto de Investigaciones Económicas,
Universidad Nacional Autónoma de México, Mexico City, Mexico
gwolf@gwolf.org
[2] Facultad de Ciencias, Universidad Nacional Autónoma de México,
Mexico City, Mexico

Abstract. The Debian project is one of the largest free software undertakings worldwide. It is geographically distributed, and participation in the project is done on a voluntary basis, without a single formal employee or directly funded person. As we will explain, due to the nature of the project, its authentication needs are very strict—User/password schemes are way surpassed, and centralized trust management schemes such as PKI are not compatible with its distributed and flat organization; fully decentralized schemes such as the PGP Web of Trust are insufficient by themselves. The Debian project has solved this need by using what we termed a "curated Web of Trust".

We will explain some lessons learned from a massive key migration process that was triggered in 2014. We will present the social insight we have found from examining the relationships expressed as signatures in this curated Web of Trust, some recommendations on personal key-signing policies, and a statistical study and forecast on aging, refreshment and survival of project participants stemming from an analysis on their key-handling.

Keywords: Trust management · Cryptography · Keyring · Survival · Aging · curated Web of Trust

1 Introduction

The Debian project is among the most veteran surviving free software projects; having been founded in August 1993 by Ian Murdock [5], it has grown to be one of the most popular Linux distributions by itself, as well as the technical base for literally hundreds of others. It is the only distribution that produces an integrated operating system capable of running on different operating system kernels – Although an overwhelming majority of Debian users use Linux, it hs been *ported* to the FreeBSD and GNU HURD kernels as well [15,16].

But besides all of its the technical characteristics, what makes Debian really stand out as a project is its social composition: It is, since its inception, a completely volunteer-driven, community-run project, with very big geographic dispersion [13].

Since Debian's early days, cryptographically strong identification was deemed necessary to guarantee the security guarantees Debian's users have; as the project grew, a viable trust management strategy had to be envised as well; we call it the *curated Web-of-Trust* model [20].

But cryptographic parameters that were deemed safe for long-term use in the mid nineties are now considered to be unsafe. By 2014, the Debian project underwent a large key migration to keep up with the security recommendations for the following years [14]. We described the full reasoning for this migration and an oveview of the process and its numeric impact in the project in [20].

The aforementioned migration prompted a study of the direct metrics of the keyring's health, such as those detailed by [19], as well as a more transdisciplinary analysis of the keyring as a social network. Throughout this work, we will present an overview of the *trust aging* that had started manifesting since around 2010, as well as its forceful re-convergence, and a statistical analysis on key survival expectations.

2 Trust Models in Public Key Cryptography

Besides encryption and signing, public key cryptography provides several models for identity assessment, called *trust models*. The most widespread model is the *Public Key Infrastructure* (PKI) model, a hierarchical model based on predetermined *roots of trust* and strictly vertical relationships (certificates) from *Certification Authorities* (CAs) to individuals. This model is mostly known for being the basis for secure communication between Web browsers and servers using the https protocol.

As we have presented [20], the Debian project, being geographically distributed and with no organizational hierarchy, bases its trust management upon the *Web of Trust* (WoT) model, with an extra step we have termed *curatorship*. The WoT model has been an integral part of OpenPGP since its inception [21]. For this model, there is no formal distinction between nodes in the trust network: All nodes can both receive and generate certificates (or, as they are rather called in the WoT model, *signatures*) to and from any other node, and trust is established between any two nodes that need to assert it by following a *trust path* that hopefully links them in the desired direction and within the defined tolerable distance [19].

Beside the aforementioned work, several other works have studied the information that can be gathered from the total keyring in the SKS keyserver network[1] [3]. The work we will present in this paper is restricted to a small subset

---

[1] For a WoT model to be able to scale beyond a small number of participants, *key servers* (systems that store and allow for retrieval of public key material) are needed. The *Synchronizing Key Server* (SKS) network is the largest network of OpenPGP key servers.

thereof—As of December 2016, the SKS network holds over 4 million keys, while the active Debian keyrings hold only around 1500.

2.1 Cryptographic Strength

Public key cryptography works by finding related values (typically, very large prime numbers). The relation between said numbers, thanks to mathematical problems that are *hard enough* to solve to be unfeasible to be attacked by brute force, translates to the strength of the value pair.

Said schemes' strength is directly related to the size of the numbers they build on. Back in the 1990s, when Internet connectivity boomed and they first became widely used [21], key sizes of 384 through 1024 bits were deemed enough; using longer keys demanded computing resources beyond what was practical at the time.

Of course, computers become more powerful constantly; cryptographic problems that were practically unsolvable 10 or 20 years ago are now within the reach of even small organizations [14, p. 11]. Cryptographic keys used for RSA and DSA algorithms should now be at least 2048 bits, with 4096 becoming the norm.

By 2009 (when the need to migrate to stronger keys was first widely discussed within the Debian project) the amount of 1024-bit keys was close to 90% of the total keyring; the upcoming need of migration was repeatedly discussed, and due to the threat of an attack becoming feasible for a medium-sized organization [14, pp. 30, 32], by July 2014 a hard cutoff line for expiring keys shorter than 2048 bits was set for January 2015, setting a six month period for key migration. We published a analysis on that migration process [20], which prompted the present work.

3 Trust Aging and Reestablishment

The work done for the described keyring migration, as well as the migration process itself, presented a great opportunity to understand the key migration as a social phenomenon as well, using the keyring as a way to measure social cohesion and vitality.

We prepared graphic representations of the keyring at its various points in time, in the hope to learn from it patterns about its growth and evolution that can warn about future issues. For the trust-mapping graphs, we use directed graphs, where each key is represented by a node and each signature by an edge from the signer to the signee. For starters, we were interested in asserting whether the characterstics observed on the whole OpenPGP WoT [19] repeated in the subset of it represented by the Debian keyrings. Of course, said work was done as a static analysis on the keyring back in 2011; back then, the whole OpenPGP keyring stood at 2.7 million keys; at the time of this writing there are 4.5 million keys, growing by 100 to 400 keys every day [17].

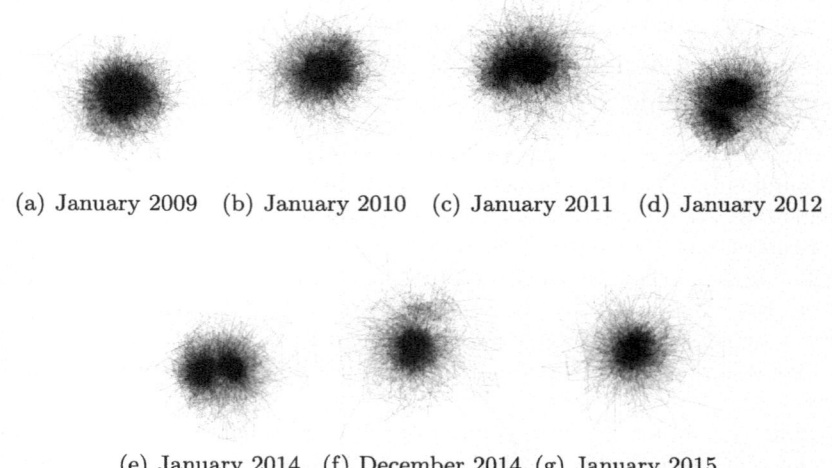

(a) January 2009   (b) January 2010   (c) January 2011   (d) January 2012

(e) January 2014   (f) December 2014   (g) January 2015

Fig. 1. Snapshots of the Debian keyring evolution at different points in time

Figure 1 presents seven snapshots of the main developers keyring, processed by *Graphviz* using the *neato* layout program, which implements the *spring* minimal energy model [6]. Of course, at the scale they are presented, each individual edge or node becomes irrelevant; there is too much density at the center, and the outlying nodes and edges appear as just noise. However, the *shape* of the strong set[2] does lend itself to analysis.

Figures 1(a), (b) and (g) present a regular shape, approximately following Ulrich's observations, that the strong set of the WoT exhibits scale-freen. Quoting [19, Sect. 4.3],

> Connectivity-wise, scale-free graphs are said to be robust against random removal of nodes, and vulnerable against the targeted removal of hubs (which leads to partitioning). This is usually explained by the hubs being the nodes that are primarily responsible for maintaining overall connectivity.

Ulrich notes that the WoT graph is *similar to a scale-free one and exhibits a hub structure, but is not scale-free in the strict sense.*

Something happened, however, in the course of 2010 that led to the WoT acquiring the shape shown in Fig. 1(c) by the end of the year – Instead of a seemingly uniform *blob*, there is a distinct protuberance. This horn grew throughout the following years, and by 2014, the keyring consisted of two roughly equivalent *blobs* somewhat weakly linked together, as Figs. 1(d) and (e) show.

We find this protuberance to be the portrait of a social migration: The project is often portrayed as unique among free software projects due to the close personal

---

[2] The strong set is defined as the largest set of keys such that for any two keys in the set, there is a path from one to the other [10].

ties among developers; its yearly developers' conference, *DebConf*, has a very high repeating attendance rate. However, given the project has lived for over 20 years, it is understandable many of the original members have grown inactive and moved on to other life endeavors; formal retirement is requested from developers, but many people reduce their engagement gradually, and just never formally retire.

While the geographical dispersion makes it quite hard for some developers to meet others and obtain new certificates, there is a tradition in Debian to announce travels in a (private, developers-only) mailing list, and active developers often will gladly meet people travelling to their region just for a key signature exchange.

Although the number of developers that by late 2010 had migrated to a stronger key was still quite small, the call for key migration was initially answered by those with most active key activity –hence, probably more conscious about the importance of this migration. Of course, although it was not a targetted removal, it was a socially self-selected one: Trust hubs were among the first to migrate to stronger keys. And even though they attempted to re-build their WoT relationships and cross-sign with other developers at gatherings such as DebConf, the group of developers that –as explained in Sect. 3– had drifted away from project activity didn't reconnect with them.

While the migration to keys longer than 1024 bits took much longer than originally expected, the initial push was not bad: During 2010, it reached from practicaly zero to close to 10% of the keys– But many of those keys were *hubs*, people long involved in the project, with many social bonds, and thus very central keys. When those people migrated to newer keys, the signatures linking their long-known fellow developers to the project were usually not updated, and several old keys could have even *become islands*, gradually losing connectivity to the strong set.

Given Debian's longstanding practices, rather than isolated, many such keys started *drifting apart* as a block, growing separated from the center of mass. This explains why the migration started as a *lump* to later become two large, still somewhat strongly connected bodies, mostly stable over the years. Of course, as more developers migrated to strong keys, by late 2014 the remaining group started losing cohesion, and by December 2014 (before it was completely removed), it is barely noticeable – All of its real *hubs* had migrated to the new center of mass, with many previously connected keys becoming isolated, as Fig. 1(f) shows.

In order to prove this hypothesis, we generated again the same graphs, but factoring in the *trust aging*: If individual signatures are colored by their age, it is possible to visually identify if a significant portion of the group's trust is aging – That is, if social bonds as reflected by intra-key signatures are over a given edge. The seven subfigures of Fig. 2 correspond with those of Fig. 1, but with color-coded edges (according to the image caption).[3]

---

[3] Some care should be taken interpreting the presented graphs. Particularly, chosen colors are not equally strong and visible against white background; mid-range (orange, yellow) signatures appear weaker than red or blue ones. Also, the drawing algorithm overlays lines, and in high density areas, only the top ones prevail. Still, we believe our observations to hold despite these caveats.

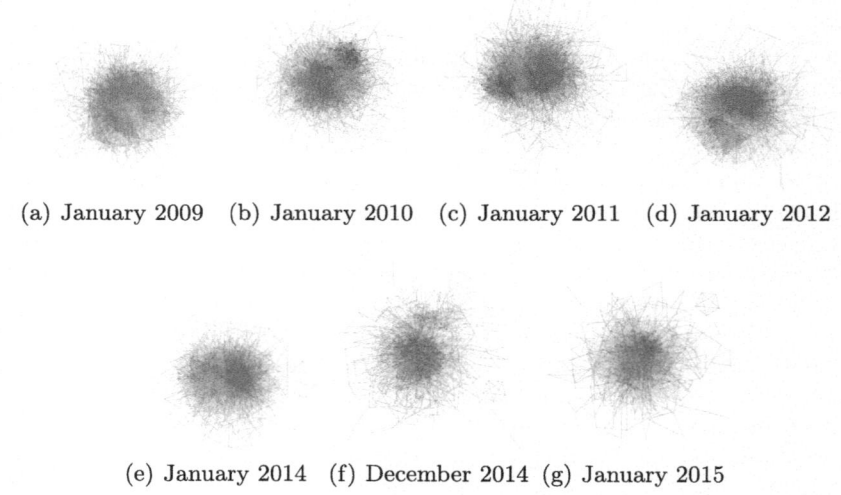

Fig. 2. Snapshots of the Debian keyring evolution at different points in time, showing signature age: Blue, ≤1 year; green, between 1 and 2 years; yellow, between 2 and 3 years; orange, between 3 and 4 years; red, ≥4 years. Signature coloring is relative to each of the snapshots: Blue edges in graph (a) represent signatures made throughout 2008. (Color figure online)

Surprisingly, even Fig. 2(b) shows a clear grouping of keys by signature age? But this grouping does not appear a year earlier, in Fig. 2(a). This can, again, be indicative that the first people to migrate to stronger keys, even before it altered the overall shape of the WoT, migrated during 2009; by early 2010, they might constitute te tight, new (blue) group still in the peripheria, that eventually became the core of the newer *blob*.

4 Expectations on Key Survival

Following from the same data set, we started a further statistical analysis; this section presents the preliminary results we gathered from applying survival analysis techniques.

The general focus of survival analysis is on the modeling the time it takes until a specific event occurs, in social sciences one often speaks of *event history* [18]. We have found interesting findings from studying how many people keeps participating in the Debian project throughout the time, that is, to model the time until departure from the Debian project. The main motivation comes from the need to understand keyring population along time. Our sampled data is defined by the PGP keys that make up the curated WoT from the Debian Developers keyring [20].

The analyzed data is treated as a longitudinal study. We point out that intervals are not of the same length in time: each data point is a *tag* in the keyring's Git history,[4] and the period of analysis spans between July 2008 and July 2016. During said period, 124 tags were recorded, averaging to 23.96 days each, with a standard deviation of 27.95, with a maximum of 69 days and a minimum of one day.

Given the way the keyring is structured, we used key the long key ID (the lowest 64 bits of its fingerprint, in hexadecimal representation) as a unique identifier for each key. For each tag and key we counted the number of signatures made to that key by counting the number of non-zero entries in the corresponding key column of an adjacency matrix at a specified tag.

We identified people's participation in Debian using their PGP key activity record (has the key stopped getting signatures?) and keyring membership (has the key stopped being part of the keyring of interest?) which makes our data is right-censored because no further information about keyring membership is known afterwards; right censoring scheme constitutes data where all that is known is that the individuals are still *alive* (the keys are still active) at a given time, [8].

For this analysis, we must highlight a drawback from our failure definition: in real life there's no 1-to-1 correspondence of a key-person pair; key migrations – regarding our current study logic– mean one key dies (leaves the keyring) and another key enters as a completely independent individual. This will be refined in further analysis.

We used the R programming language with its `survival`, `flexsurv` packges; unless otherwise stated, significance level is assumed to be 5%.

Our first line of approach was first to show through the survival function the proportion of remaining keys in the keyring along time, that is keyring permanency. Then using the cumulated hazard function we get the expected exits per key that remains in the keyring until the endtime (in perpetuity). Finally, for the hazard rate function, we get the departure rate from the keyring.

For the non-parametric or observed curves we used the Kaplan-Meier product limit estimator for the survival function, [7], the Nelson-Aalen moments estimator for the cumulated hazard function [1], and the kernel density estimator for the hazard rate function, [9].

A parametric estimation to see the *mortality law* fitting our data was made using a Generalised Gamma distribution through maximum-likelihood estimation [11]. The motivation for using the Gen. Gamma model is due to the closeness it has to the observed hazard rate function obtained non-parametrically. Proper justification for said model comes from the fact that it minimizes Akaike's Information Criterion when compared to the other models, making it a better model in terms of information loss, [2], while also rejecting other models using a log-likelihood test of −5790.042 at 3° of freedom, [12]. The estimated parameters found for our model

---

[4] Version control systems handle the concept of *tags* in a repository: Specific points of a project's development that are in some way relevant or significant; many projects use *tags* to mark their releases. This is the case of the Debian keyring maintainers' repository: Tags mark each keyring version that was put in production. The team attempts to put a new version in production roughly once a month.

were $\mu = 4.6808$, $\sigma = 0.1990$, $Q = 3.4078$, with standard errors of 0.0134, 0.123, 0.2205 respectively.

In the non-parametric plot of Fig. 3, we observe downward steps when at least one key stops getting signatures. The crosses represent the followup time for censored observations (for which no further information is known and thus the proportion of keys remains). This plot does reflect the fact that many keys were dropped during the 1024-bits key removal, at tag 107 (January 2015). Observed proportion of keys being above the theoretical model from tag 40 to tag 100 (around 4 years) suggests that after four years the keys wouldn't be much likely to leave; at least not until tag 95 where the probability of remaining afterwards is less than the 50% chance of heads in a coin flip.

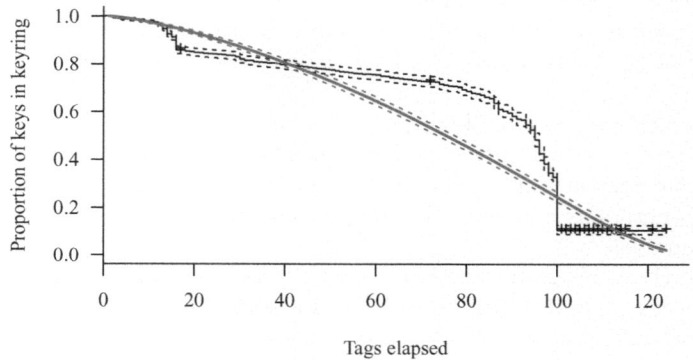

Fig. 3. Probability of key permanency. The black line follows observed (non-parametric) data from the keyring, with crosses representing the followup time for right-censored observations; the red line is the parametric estimation; dotted lines represent confidence bands. (Color figure online)

As we mentioned, due to the 1024-bit key migration, there is a clear skew that introduces a sharp drop around 100 tags; work is underway, as will be outlined in Sect. 5, to do a similar analysis based on personal identities instead of only key IDs.

Figure 4 shows the key exits given one key in perpetual risk, that is, if it is to remain in the keyring for all its time span. The increasing steps from the non-parameric exits is natural being the cumulated sum per tag of the exits over remaining keys ratios. The similarity from previous plot is expected since cumulated hazard is a logarithmic transformation from survival function. We see again that the observed plot lies below the theoretical model starting from tag 40 to 100 (about 4 years), quickly increasing afterwards more than expected. It is not until near tag 100 that a key is expected to leave, but if for any reason it didn't or inmediatly enters again afterwards, it would be expected to leave again shortly after 3 tags (about 2 months).

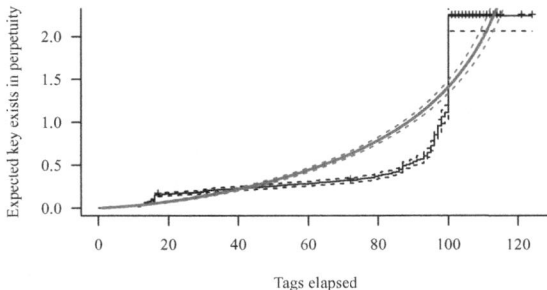

Fig. 4. Cumulated hazard of key exits. The black line follows observed (non-parametric) data from the keyring, with crosses representing the followup time for right-censored observations; the red line is the parametric estimation; dotted lines represent confidence bands. (Color figure online)

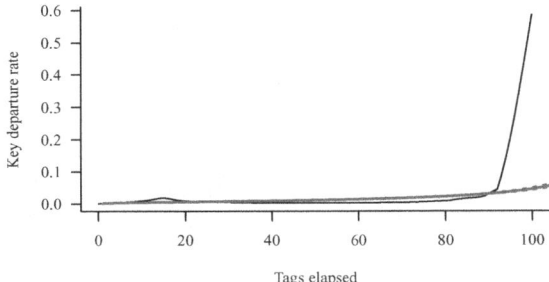

Fig. 5. Hazard rate of key exits. The black line follows observed (non-parametric) data from the keyring, the red line is the parametric estimation; dotted lines represent confidence bands. (Color figure online)

Figure 5 shows the departure rate is analogous to a *mortality* rate. The observed behaviour suggest that coming of age there's a sudden increase on the risk i.e. keys "wear out" to their age around tag 90 (close to 6 years). Yet the parametric departure rate being under the non-parametric rate at the final tags shows the dramatic effect from the 1024 removal. Another remarkably finding was that departure rate in general doesn't grow far from 0 giving empirical evidence to say that 5 out of 1000 keys will leave "any time now" (from the fact that hazard rate is the instantaneous probability of failure at a specified time) in a 8 year lapsus.

In general keys in the project will constantly remain for about 6 years, as long as they went through 4 years, which in turn suggests further confirmatory analysis. It is just after the six years where keys effectively don't survive until the end.

5 Conclusions and Future Work

The Debian keyring is a very peculiar subset of the whole OpenPGP Web of Trust analyzed in [19]. The work we present here provides data empirically supporting the theoretical observations, particularly regarding the robustness of what he defines as the LSCC (Largest Strongly Connected Component). The migration away from 1024-bit keys provided an opportunity to follow the progression of the connectivity in our WoT after several of its hubs were removed.

The preliminary results for this work have been shared with a group of Debian developers. Historically, the usual practice for key signing has been to generate non-expiring signatures; people that have already cross-signed their keys don't have an incentive to refresh their trust. There is an ongoing discussion as to whether this practice should change towards time-limited signatures, better modeling ongoing social relationships, or to stick to current practice.

As mentioned in Sect. 4, the survival study has so far been done around individual keys; work is underway so that a person's activity can be properly represented instead of following keys as separate individuals.

The resulting survival analysis can be used to generate cohort tables that further explain the keyring population for demographics, [4]. The outlined methodology can also be extended by introducing covariates such as the number of signatures received or network measures; this study was done only on the *Debian Developers* keyring, it would be interesting to compare with the more loosely connected *Debian Maintainers* keyring. We also want to further explain the keyrings by stratification. The survival analysis showcases good health of the *Debian Developers* keyring (which makes up the mass of Debian's WoT).

Finally, the methodology followed for this study could be applied to other free software projects, aiming to correlate with events and trends spanning a wider population than Debian's; the applicability of our work to other projects, however, depends on having a proper data set to base the work off. We are not aware of other projects having curated keyrings in a fashion that allows for analysis of their evolution over time.

Acknowledgments. We wish to thank GPLHost for donating the computing resources needed for this work.

References

1. Aalen, O.: Nonparametric inference for a family of counting processes. In: The Annals of Statistics, pp. 701–726 (1978)
2. Akaike, H.: A new look at the statistical model identification. IEEE Trans. Autom. Control **19**(6), 716–723 (1974). doi:10.1109/TAC.1974.1100705
3. Cederlöf, J.: Dissecting the leaf of trust (2004). http://wwwlysator.liu.se/~jc/wotsap/leafoftrust.html
4. Chiang, C.L.: Life table and its applications. In: Life Table and its Applications. Robert E. Krieger Publishing (1984)
5. Fernández-Sanguino, J., et al.: A Brief History of Debian (1997–2015). https://www.debian.org/doc/manuals/project-history/, Accessed 22 Dec 2016
6. Kamada, T., Kawai, S.: An algorithm for drawing general undirected graphs. Inf. Process. Lett. **31**(1), 7–15 (1989)
7. Kaplan, E.L., Meier, P.: Nonparametric estimation from incomplete observations. J. Am. Stat. Assoc. **53**(282), 457–481 (1958)

8. Klein, J.P., Moeschberger, M.L.: Survival Analysis: Statistical Methods for Censored and Truncated Data. Springer, New York (2003). doi:10.1007/b97377
9. Muller, H.-G., Wang, J.-L.: Hazard rate estimation under random censoring with varying kernels and bandwidths. In: Biometric, pp. 61–76 (1994). doi:10.2307/2533197
10. Penning, H.P.: Analysis of the strong set in the PGP web of trust (2015). http://pgp.cs.uu.nl/plot/
11. Prentice, R.L.: A log gamma model and its maximum likelihood estimation. Biometrika **61**(3), 539–544 (1974)
12. Prentice, R.L.: Discrimination among some parametric models. Biometrika **62**(3), 607–614 (1975)
13. Robles, G., Dueñas, S., Gonzalez-Barahona, J.M.: Corporate involvement of libre software: study of presence in Debian Code over time. In: Feller, J., Fitzgerald, B., Scacchi, W., Sillitti, A. (eds.) OSS 2007. ITIFIP, vol. 234, pp. 121–132. Springer, Boston, MA (2007). doi:10.1007/978-0-387-72486-7_10
14. Smart, N.: ECRYPT II Yearly Report on Algorithms and Keysizes (2011–2012). Technical report 7th Framework Programme, European Commission (2012). http://www.ecrypt.eu.org/ecrypt2/documents/D.SPA.20.pdf, Accessed 14 Jan 2016
15. SPI et al. Debian GNU/HURD (1997–2016). https://www.debian.org/ports/kfreebsd-gnu/, Accessed 22 Dec 2016
16. SPI et al. Debian GNU/kFreeBSD (1997–2016). https://www.debian.org/ports/kfreebsd-gnu/, Accessed 22 Dec 2016
17. Synchronizing Key Servers. SKS OpenPGP Keyserver statistics (2016). http://pool.sks-keyservers.net:11371/pks/lookup?op=stats, Accessed 31 Dec 2016
18. Tutz, G., Schmid, M.: Modeling Discrete Time-to-Event Data. Springer series in statistics. Springer, Cham (2016). doi:10.1007/978-3-319-28158-2
19. Ulrich, A., Holz, R., Hauck, P., Carle, G.: Investigating the OpenPGP web of trust. In: Atluri, V., Diaz, C. (eds.) ESORICS 2011. LNCS, vol. 6879, pp. 489–507. Springer, Heidelberg (2011). doi:10.1007/978-3-642-23822-2_27
20. Wolf, G., Gallegos-Garcí, G.: Strengthening a curated web of trust in a geographically distributed project. Cryptologia **41**, 1–16 (2017). http://www.tandfonline.com/doi/full/10.1080/01611194.2016.1238421
21. Zimmerman, P.R.: Why I Wrote PGP (1991). https://www.philzimmermann.com/EN/essays/WhyIWrotePGP.html

Open Access This chapter is licensed under the terms of the Creative Commons Attribution 4.0 International License (http://creativecommons.org/licenses/by/4.0/), which permits use, sharing, adaptation, distribution and reproduction in any medium or format, as long as you give appropriate credit to the original author(s) and the source, provide a link to the Creative Commons license and indicate if changes were made.

The images or other third party material in this chapter are included in the chapter's Creative Commons license, unless indicated otherwise in a credit line to the material. If material is not included in the chapter's Creative Commons license and your intended use is not permitted by statutory regulation or exceeds the permitted use, you will need to obtain permission directly from the copyright holder.

Understanding When to Adopt a Library: A Case Study on ASF Projects

Akinori Ihara[1(✉)], Daiki Fujibayashi[1], Hirohiko Suwa[1], Raula Gaikovina Kula[2], and Kenichi Matsumoto[1]

[1] Nara Institute of Science and Technology, Ikoma, Japan
{akinori-i,fujibayashi.daiki.eq3,h-suwa,matumoto}@is.naist.jp
[2] Osaka University, Suita, Japan
raula-k@ist.osaka-u.ac.jp

Abstract. Software libraries are widely used by both industrial and open source client projects. Ideally, a client user of a library should adopt the latest version that the library project releases. However, sometimes the latest version is not better than a previous version. This is because the latest version may include additional developer effort to test and integrate all changed features. In this study, our main goal is to better understand the relationship between adoption of library versions and its release cycle. Specifically, we conducted an empirical study of release cycles for 23 libraries and how they were adopted by 415 Apache Software Foundation (ASF) client projects. Our findings show that software projects are quicker to update earlier rapid-release libraries compared to library projects with a longer release cycle. Moreover, results suggest that software projects are more likely to adopt the latest version of a rapid-release library compared to libraries with a longer release cycles.

1 Introduction

A software library is a collection of reusable programs, used by both industrial and open software client projects to help achieve shorter development cycles and higher quality software [8]. Many of these libraries are open source software and are readily available through online repositories such as the GitHub[1] repository. To incorporate bug fixes and new features, open source library projects often release newer and improved versions of their libraries. Based on user feedback, libraries evolve faster to reach the market, making it difficult for client projects to keep up with the latest version.

Ideally, a client user of a library should adopt the latest version of that library. Therefore, it is recommended that a client project should upgrade their library version as soon as possible. However, the latest version is not always better than previous versions [5,9], as adoption of the latest version may include additional developer efforts to test and integrate changed features [7,10,13]. Developers of client projects may be especially wary of library projects that

---

[1] https://github.com.

© The Author(s) 2017

follow a rapid-release style of development, since such library projects are known to delay bug fixes [12]. Recent studies investigated the dependency relationships between evolving software systems and their libraries [5,6,15]. These tools makes it possible for developers to clarify and visualize these dependencies and aim to guide developers who are selecting possible candidate libraries for an upgrade.

In this study, our main goal is to better understand the relationship between the adoption of library versions and the library release cycle. Specifically, we conducted an empirical study of the release cycle of 23 libraries and how they were adopted by 415 Apache Software Foundation (ASF) client projects. These 23 libraries were used by over 50 software projects of our target ASF client projects. To guide our research, we address the following two research questions:

RQ1: Does the release cycle of a library project influence when it is adopted by a client project?
Recent studies [7,10,13] have found that open source software often has many issues soon after its release. Often these libraries are reactive in fixing issues based on user feedback. In other words, these software may be harmful in the early period after the release. Therefore, for RQ1, we would like to understand the effect of client project adoption on shorter release cycles.

RQ2: Does the release cycle of a library project influence whether the latest version is adopted by a client project?
Recent studies have shown that the newest version of a library is not always adopted by many client projects. For example, client projects may decide not to adopt the latest version to avoid untested bugs, especially if the library project has a shorter release cycle. Therefore, for RQ2, we would like to understand the effect of adopting the latest client project on shorter release cycles.

Our findings show that software projects are quicker to update earlier rapid-release libraries compared to library projects with a longer release cycle. Moreover, results suggest that software projects are more likely to adopt the latest version of a rapid-release library compared to libraries with a longer release cycles.

2 Background and Definitions

2.1 Motivation

Related work such as Almering et al. [1], Goel et al. [3] and Yamada et al. [14] all investigate when a software is ready to be used. These works use the Software Reliability Growth Model (SRGM) of the software evolution process to grasp the process of the convergence of defects discovered in software as the *'growth curve of the S-Shape (Sigmond curve)'*. Similarly, Mileva et al. [9] evaluated a library by its library usage by clients.

Building on this work, we conducted an exploratory investigation of when developers adopted versions of a library. Figure 1 shows the release date (broken lines) for the library log4j and the number of ASF projects (solid lines) which

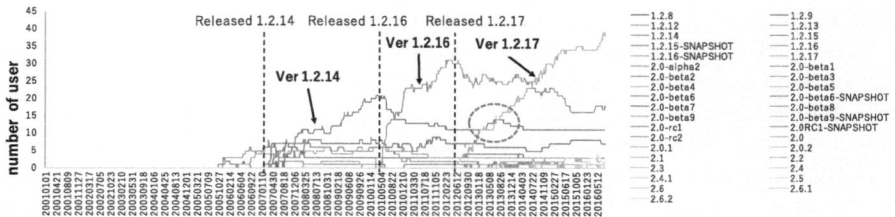

Fig. 1. Adoption trends based on client usage (Color figure online)

have adopted the new library version in a time series. The figure shows users of the popular log4j library, mined from 797 software projects. From this work, we highlight two points: (1) library adoption is not organized, with no clear patterns of migration and (2) in many cases the latest version is not always selected as the default option. For instance, in Fig. 1 we can see ver.1.2.14 is still being used by some client projects (red dotted circle), even though the latest version is ver.1.2.17.

In this paper, we define the *"release cycle"* as the time until a new version is released. As a cycle, usually a project will have a fixed release timing from as quickly as 1 day to a span of across several years. Due to agile development trends, we assume that the release cycles may become faster. For instance, the Google Chrome project and the Mozilla Firefox project are working on rapid release to develop a new version in 6 weeks [4]. A rapid-release cycle is beneficial in that it can fix a bug and make a new component quickly. Sometimes, these projects can be reactive in bug fixing, for example, projects can get feedback from users soon after their release [8]. However, this rapid release style creates an influx of releases, which is likely to further confuse users on when to adopt a new version. Therefore, our motivation is to investigate when and how software projects adopt a new library relative to their release.

2.2 Library Adoption and Release Timings

Figure 2 describes the evolution and adoption of a library during different release cycles. We use this figure to explain how we measure the timing of adoption relative to each release, including the relative definition of the latest release. This example shows a project S and two libraries (A, B). Library A has released versions $A1$ and $A2$, with $A2$ being the latest version. Similarly, Library B has released versions $B1$, $B2$, $B3$ and $B4$, with $B4$ being the latest version.

This example also shows library adoption. Specifically, we see that project version $S3$ imports the library $A1$, which is not the latest version at this point in time. This is because at this time, $A2$ was available for selection. $S3$ also imports library $B3$, which is the latest version at this time. However, we see that in the near future $B4$ will be released.

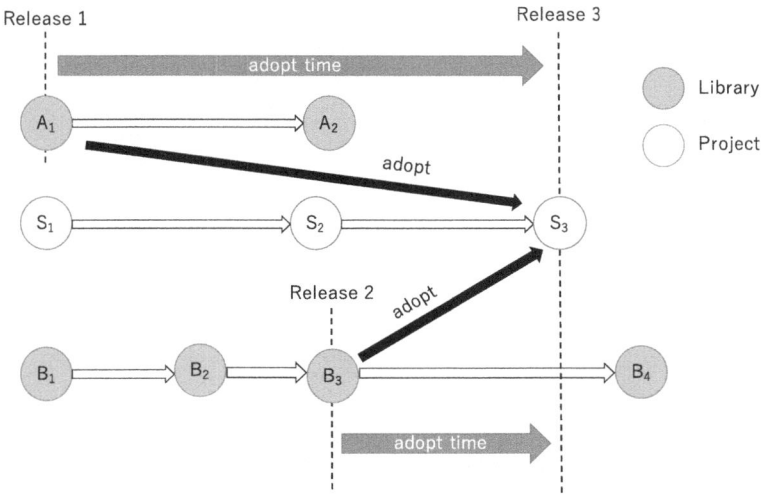

Fig. 2. Release cycle and adoption period

3 Empirical Study

Adopting the latest versions has the added benefits of new features, but adapting the latest version may also risk having untested bugs or removed features. Therefore, the goal of this study is to understand the impact of the release cycle on the developers decision whether to wait for the next library release or quickly adopt the latest version.

3.1 Data Preparation

Table 1 shows the top 23 of 4,815 libraries which the 415 software projects used. In total, these 23 libraries were used by over 50 software projects. These libraries were originally extracted from 415 projects of 797 ASF projects which are using MAVEN dependency tool on July 21, 2016. To analyze the library adoption and release timings, we extracted histories of library dependency information. Our dataset comprises of JAVA programs managed by the MAVEN dependency tool. MAVEN stores explicitly in meta information files (POM.xml). The meta information contains the libraries' names and the version number in which the software is adopted. By tracking the history of the POM.xml in a version control system, for any software, we can know when and which library version has been adopted.

3.2 Clustering Libraries by Release Cycle

In order to evaluate the impact of the release cycle, the rank and grouping of libraries based on their release cycles is needed. Hence, for each library, we

Table 1. Ranking of library users

Rank	Library	Num	Rank	Library	Num
1	junit	305	16	easymock	67
2	commons-logging	167	17	jackson-mapper-asl	60
3	log4j	153	18	commons-cli	55
4	slf4j-api	145	19	jackson-core-asl	53
5	commons-lang	130	20	mail	53
6	commons-io	122	21	velocity	52
7	slf4j-log4j12	109	22	jcl-over-slf4j	52
8	servlet-api	99	23	mockito-all	52
9	commons-collections	98			
10	commons-codec	96	.....	.....	....
11	commons-httpclient	83			
12	guava	81	.....	.....	....
13	ant	73			
14	xercesImpl	69	.....	.....	....
15	jetty-server	68	4815	axis2-transports	1

compute and assign a [2] variable importance score for each library. We then use the *Scott-Knott test* [11] to group libraries into statistically distinct ranks according to their release periods. The *Scott-Knott test* is a statistical multi-comparison procedure based on cluster analysis. The *Scott-Knott test* sorts the percentage of release periods for the different libraries. Then, it groups the factors into two different ranks that are separated based on their mean values (i.e., the mean value of the percentage of release periods for each library). If the two groups are statistically distinct, then the *Scott-Knott test* runs recursively to further find new groups, otherwise the factors are put in the same group. The final result of the *Scott-Knott test* is a grouping of factors into statistically distinct ranks.

Table 2 shows the 6 categories (i.e., C1, ..., C6) in which each of the 23 studied libraries were categorized. Based on these 6 groupings and the dataset, we are now able to address the research questions in our results.

4 Results

RQ1: Does the release cycle of a library project influence when it is adopted by a client project?
To answer RQ1, we use the clustered libraries groupings to compare release and adoption times. As a result, we make the following observations:

Observation1—All top frequent libraries are not released in one year.
The boxplot in Fig. 3 shows the distribution of the periods between releases in

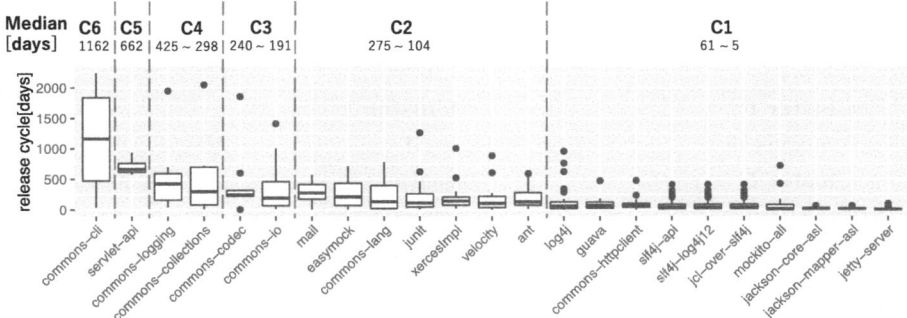

Fig. 3. The release cycle of each library by boxplot. The target libraries are sorted by clustering (broken lines) from C1 to C6. The top figure shows the clustering number and the median of the release cycle days.

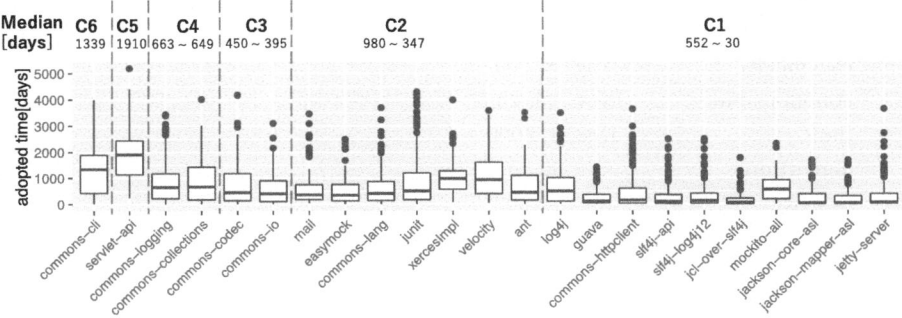

Fig. 4. The boxplot shows the adoption time of each library. The target libraries are sorted by clustering (broken lines) from C1 to C6. The top figure shows the clustering number and the median of the adoption time [days].

each library. The libraries are sorted by the number of adopted software projects. While some library projects (e.g., jetty-server, jackson-mapper-asl, mockito-all) often release new versions in one year, other library projects (e.g., commons-cli, servlet.api, commons-logging) often release new versions after more than one year. In particular, releases for the commons-cli project were delayed for a consideration time.

Observation2—While older and established projects often release new versions after more than one year, beginner projects often release new versions in three months. Through our analysis, we found the different features between quick-release projects and late-release projects. Table 2 shows the working period with GitHub for each library project. Traditional projects that have worked for 10 years often release new versions after more than one year.

Table 2. Clustering by library release cycle and each library start of the release date

Library	Date	Library	Date
Cluster 6		**Cluster 1**	
commons-cli	Nov. 6, 2002	log4j	May. 1, 2002
Cluster 5		guava	Sep. 15, 2009
servlet-api	Sep. 25, 2001	commons-httpclient	Aug. 31, 2001
Cluster 4		slf4j-api	Mar. 8, 2006
commons-logging	Aug. 13, 2002	slf4j-log4j12	Mar. 8, 2006
commons-collections	Apr. 2, 2002	jcl-over-slf4j	Mar. 8, 2006
Cluster 3		mockito-all	Feb. 28, 2008
commons-codec	Apr. 25, 2003	jackson-core-asl	Jan. 14, 2009
commons-io	Jul. 2, 2007	jackson-mapper-asl	Jan. 14, 2009
Cluster 2		xercesImpl	Mar. 29, 2009
mail	Feb. 22, 2000		
easymock	Aug. 8, 2001		
commons-lang	Nov. 25, 2002		
junit	Dec. 3, 2000		
xercesImpl	Jan. 30, 2002		
velocity	Jul. 7, 2002		
ant	Jul. 19, 2000		

Observation3—While software projects have adopted the quick-release libraries soon after the release, they have not adopted the late-release libraries as quickly. The boxplot in Fig. 4 shows the distribution of the adopted periods for our target projects in each library. We found that software projects have adopted the quick-release libraries (sixth group). In other words, they often adopt new versions soon after their release. On the other hand, software projects have adopted the late-release libraries (1st–2nd). This means that they do not adopt new versions quickly after the release.

In the group of the quick-release cycle, the adopted time of the `mockito-all` library is longer than the other libraries. To understand the reason, we analyzed software projects which adopted the `mockito-all` library. As we can see in Fig. 3, there are some outliers for `mockito-all`. Those are some versions which took a long time to release a new version. In particularly, version 1.9.0 was released approximately 1 year after releasing version 1.8.5. Also, version 1.10.0 was released approximately 2 years after releasing version 1.9.5. While waiting for the version 1.10.0, many software projects started using the `mockito-all` library just before releasing the version. In addition, although the `Velocity` library was adopted in a comparatively quick-release project, most software projects adopted the `Velocity` library a relatively long time after the release. The results show that many projects still started adopting the `Velocity` library after the project

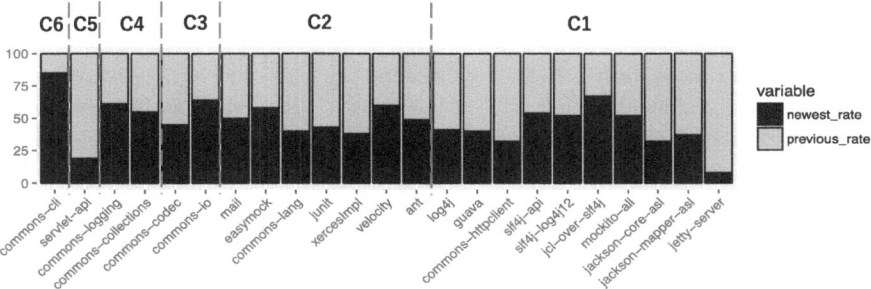

Fig. 5. Figure showing the adoption status rate of each library. The black bar means the adoption rate of newest version. The gray bar means the adoption rate of previous version. As showing by rate, the vertical axis means 100%

released the newest version on November 29th, 2010. Therefore, to answer RQ1, we find that:

> Software projects are more quickly updated than rapid release libraries compared to library projects with a longer release cycle.

RQ2: Does the release cycle of a library project influence whether the latest version is adopted by a client project?

To answer RQ2, we use the clustered libraries groupings to investigate whether the latest version of a library was adopted. As a result, we make the following observations:

Observation4—Software projects do not always adopt new library versions in their projects. Figure 5 shows the percentage of the newest or previous versions which software projects adopted from each library. The black and gray bars show the newest adopted version and the previous version applied to the software projects. We found 8%–85% of software projects adopted the new library versions. The `commons-cil` library often adopted the newest version to the software. On the other hand, the `jetty-server` library was often adopted the previous version to the software.

Observation5—While the quick-release library often adopts the newest version to the software, the late-release library often adopts the previous version to the software. 85% of the `commons-cli` library changes were applied to the newest version. This library project has released only 4 new versions during our target period (16 years). This number of releases is fewer than for the other library projects. Furthermore, one of the versions contained a new feature and maintenance bug fixes. The other two versions contained dozens of bug fixes. From this analysis, the project just maintained the initial a stable version.

On the other hand, only 19% of the `servlet.api` library changes were applied to the newest version although it is a late-release library. This library project has released only 7 new versions during our target period. To understand this strange result, we analyzed the history of applying the library. We found that version 2.5 is the majority even if the project released newer versions.

92% of the `jetty-server` library changes were applied to the previous version. This library project has released 267 new versions with most release intervals ranging from 0 to 20 days during our target period. 267 new versions show a clear contradiction to the `commons-cli` library and *servlet-api* library. Furthermore, we found that version 6.1.26 is the majority, even if the project released newer versions. In sum, to answer RQ2, we find that:

> Software projects are more likely to adopt the latest version of a rapid-release library compared to a library with a longer release cycles.

5 Conclusions and Future Work

In this study, we revealed the relationship between the release cycle and the time it takes to adopt a library. Our results suggests that the shorter the release cycle, the shorter the time to be adopted, and that the rapid-release library will be adopted faster even in the same release cycle. Also, for libraries with majority versions, it is difficult to adopt the latest version. We find that it is especially difficult to generalize the reason for adopting a previous version. We think that the reasons are clarified by analysis of the released version. In detail, we believe that reasons will be clarified by analyzing the number of bug fixes and the number of added functions to the released version. These factors are important when selecting a library although there are still many challenges in finding other factors.

In this study, we considered the adoption situation only by the adoption time and whether the version is the newest adoption or a previous adoption of the OSS library. We confirmed that the version was adopted, but we did not also consider the state after adoption. When downgrading a version, we think that the reason should be extracted from the commit log. Further research is needed to confirm this. Also, there are cases where users changed to a version whose adoption was skipped or a library with the same function. Future work will include how to analyze these cases and to clarify what influence what this has on library selection.

Acknowledgments. This work was supported by the JSPS Program for Advancing Strategic International Networks to Accelerate the Circulation of Talented Researchers: Interdisciplinary Global Networks for Accelerating Theory and Practice in Software Ecosystem and the Grant-in-Aid for Young Scientists (B) (No. 16K16037).

References

1. Almering, V., van Genuchten, M., Cloudt, G., Sonnemans, P.: Using software reliability growth models in practice. IEEE Softw. **24**(6), 82–88 (2007)
2. Breiman, L.: Machine Learning. Kluwer Academic Publishers, Hingham (2001)
3. Goel, A.L.: Software reliability models: assumptions, limitations, and applicability. IEEE Trans. Softw. Eng. **11**(12), 1411–1423 (1985)
4. Khomh, F., Dhaliwal, T., Zou, Y., Adams, B.: Do faster releases improve software quality?: an empirical case study of mozilla firefox. In: Proceedings of the 9th IEEE Working Conference on Mining Software Repositories, pp. 179–188 (2012)
5. Kula, R.G., German, D., Ishio, T., Inoue, K.: Trusting a library: a study of the latency to adopt the latest maven release. In: Proceedings of the 22nd IEEE International Conference on Software Analysis, Evolution, and Reengineering, pp. 520–524 (2015)
6. Kula, R.G., Roover, C.D., German, D., Ishio, T., Inoue, K.: Visualizing the evolution of systems and their library dependencies. In: Proceedings of the 2014 Second IEEE Working Conference on Software Visualization, pp. 127–136 (2014)
7. Mäntylä, M.V., Adams, B., Khomh, F., Engström, E., Petersen, K.: On rapid releases and software testing: a case study and a semi-systematic literature review. Empirical Softw. Eng. **20**(5), 1384–1425 (2015)
8. McCarey, F., Ó Cinnéide, M., Kushmerick, N.: Knowledge reuse for software reuse. Web Intell. Agent Syst. **6**(1), 59–81 (2008)
9. Mileva, Y.M., Dallmeier, V., Burger, M., Zeller, A.: Mining trends of library usage. In: Proceedings of the Joint International and Annual ERCIM Workshops on Principles of Software Evolution and Software Evolution Workshops (IWPSE-Evol), pp. 57–62 (2009)
10. Plate, H., E. Ponta, S.: Impact assessment for vulnerabilities in open-source software libraries. In: Proceedings of the International Conference on Software Maintenance and Evolution (ICSME), pp. 411–420 (2015)
11. Scott, A.J., Knott, M.: A cluster analysis method for grouping means in the analysis of variance, vol. 30. International Biometric Society (1974)
12. Tosin Daniel Oyetoyan, D.S.C., Thurmann-Nielsen, C.: A decision support system to refactor class cycles. In: 2015 IEEE 31st International Conference on Software Maintenance and Evolution (ICSME) (2015)
13. Tufano, M., Palomba, F., Bavota, G., Oliveto, R., Di Penta, M., De Lucia, A., Poshyvanyk, D.: When and why your code starts to smell bad. In: Proceedings of the 37th International Conference on Software Engineering (ICSE), pp. 403–414 (2015)
14. Yamada, S., Ohba, M., Osaki, S.: S-shaped reliability growth modeling for software error detection. IEEE Trans. Reliab. **32**(5), 475–484 (1983)
15. Yano, Y., Kula, R.G., Ishio, T., Inoue, K.: Verxcombo: an interactive data visualization of popular library version combinations. In: Proceedings of the IEEE 23rd International Conference on Program Comprehension, pp. 291–294 (2015)

Open Access This chapter is licensed under the terms of the Creative Commons Attribution 4.0 International License (http://creativecommons.org/licenses/by/4.0/), which permits use, sharing, adaptation, distribution and reproduction in any medium or format, as long as you give appropriate credit to the original author(s) and the source, provide a link to the Creative Commons license and indicate if changes were made.

The images or other third party material in this chapter are included in the chapter's Creative Commons license, unless indicated otherwise in a credit line to the material. If material is not included in the chapter's Creative Commons license and your intended use is not permitted by statutory regulation or exceeds the permitted use, you will need to obtain permission directly from the copyright holder.

Adoption of Academic Tools in Open Source Communities: The Debian Case Study

Pietro Abate[1]([✉]) and Roberto Di Cosmo[2]

[1] IRILL and INRIA, Paris, France
pietro.abate@inria.fr
[2] INRIA and University Paris Diderot, Paris, France
roberto@dicosmo.org

Abstract. Component repositories play a key role in the open software ecosystem. Managing the evolution of these repositories is a challenging task, and maintainers are confronted with a number of complex issues that need automatic tools to be adressed properly.

In this paper, we present an overview of 10 years of research in this field and the process leading to the adoption of our tools in a FOSS community. We focus on the Debian distribution and in particular we look at the issues arising during the distribution lifecycle: ensuring buildability of source packages, detecting packages that cannot be installed and bootstrapping the distribution on a new architecture. We present three tools, *distcheck*, *buildcheck* and *botch*, that we believe of general interest for other open source component repositories.

The lesson we have learned during this journey may provide useful guidance for researchers willing to see their tools broadly adopted by the community.

1 Introduction

In the last two decades, component repositories have played an important role in many areas, from software distributions to application development. All major Free and Open Source Software (FOSS) distributions are organized around large repositories of software components. Debian, one of the largest coordinated software collections in history [12], contains in its development branch more than 44'000 binary *packages*[1] generated from over 21'000 source packages; the Central Maven repository has a collection of 100'000 Java *libraries*; the Drupal web framework counts over 16'000 *modules*.

In Debian, components are developed independently by different communities and assembled in the main repository, giving raise to a small world dependency graph [15]. Apart from intrinsic coordination problems associated to this distributed development model, the number of dependencies in Debian distributions

---

Work partially performed at, and supported by IRILL http://www.irill.org.

[1] Debian software components are called packages.

poses new challenges for automation and quality assurance. During the last 10 years we have participated in the development and adoption of automatic tools for testing, integration and tracking of all components and aspects of a repository, in particular in the framework of the European project Mancoosi [1].

It is well known that achieving real world adoption of tools developed in academia and proposed by researchers is a painful and difficult process that only rarely succeeds [19]. After years of work, we managed to get almost all of our tools adopted in the Debian project.

We participated in extensive work performed by a team that spent 10 years of research in quality assurance, and package management, an area for which a comprehensive short survey is available elsewhere [8]. During this time, we had different collaborations with many other communities such as the Eclipse [16,17] and the OCaml [2] with different degrees of success.

In this article, we sum up and share the lessons we have learned in collaboration specifically with the Debian community, because of the direct involvement of a few members of our team, and because of the open and community driven bazaar-style development model. We truly believe that FOSS distribution and software collections alike can benefit from our experience and researcher should invest time and energy to work with developers in a proactive way and foster integration of modern and automatic QA (quality assurance) tools.

The rest of the paper is organised as follows: After a brief introduction, we present *distcheck* and *buildcheck*, the main tools developed by our team. Then we will discuss two examples in which our tools play an important role. The first one related to the distribution life cycle (from development to testing, to the stable release). The second is a tool (*botch*) that is used to bootstrap Debian for new hardware platforms. In the last part of the paper we summarize the lessons we have learned in the last 10 years and provide insights for researches and developer communities interested in embarking into a similar journey.

1.1 Packages in the Debian Distribution

Despite different terminologies, and a wide variety of concrete formats, software repositories use similar metadata to identify the components, their versions and their interdependencies. In general, packages have both *dependencies*, expressing what must be satisfied in order to allow for installation of the package, and *conflicts* that state which other packages must *not* be installed at the same time. As shown in Fig. 1, while conflicts are simply given by a list of offending packages, dependencies may be expressed using logical conjunction (written ',') and disjunctions ('|'). Furthermore, packages mentioned in inter-package relations may be qualified by constraints on package versions. Debian packages and come in two flavours: binary packages contain the files to be installed on the end user machine, and source packages that contain all of files needed to build these binary packages. Debian package meta-data describe a broad set of inter-package relationships: virtual-packages, dependencies, multi-architecture annotations, and many more, allow the Debian project to automatize tasks such as binary package recompilations, package life

```
Package: ant
Version: 1.9.7-2~bpo8+1
Installed-Size: 2197
Architecture: all
Depends: default-jre-headless | java5-runtime-headless | java6-runtime-headless
Recommends: ant-optional
Suggests: ant-doc, ant-gcj, default-jdk | java-compiler | java-sdk
Conflicts: libant1.6-java
Breaks: ant-doc (<= 1.6.5-1)
Description: Java based build tool like make
```

Fig. 1. Excerpt of Debian package metadata

cycle management among different releases, or bootstrapping the distribution on new architectures.

1.2 The Installability Problem

Finding a way to satisfy all the dependencies of a given package only using the components available in a repository, also known as the *installability problem*, is the key task for all component based repositories: all package managers need to tackle it, be it for Eclipse plugins, Drupal modules, or Debian packages.

And yet, it was not until 2006 that it was shown that this problem is NP-complete for the Debian distribution [7], and later on for a broad range of component repositories [4]. This result came as a kind of a surprise in the different engineering communities, that were using on a daily basis ad-hoc tools which were fast, but under closer scrutiny turned out to be incomplete [7].

Luckily, real world instances proved to be tractable, and it was possible to design and implement dependency solvers based on sound scientific basis, that could significantly outperform all the pre-existing tools: Jerôme Vouillon's early prototypes, `debcheck` and `rpmcheck`, originally developed in 2006, paved the way to modern dependency checking, and are nowadays at the core of the tools we describe in the rest of this paper.

1.3 The Edos and Mancoosi Research Projects

Edos and Mancoosi [1] are two research projects funded by the European Commission, that run respectively from 2004 to 2007 and from 2008 to 2011. They focused on the new research problems posed by the maintenance of free software distributions, and brought together industries and top research laboratories from over 10 countries. Besides publishing research articles, these projects produced several tools that significantly improved the state of the art, and that are now part of the Dose3 library, which has outlived the research projects and became over time a collection of all the algorithms and tools developed over more than a decade. Unlike what seems to often happen in these research areas [19], most of the tools that were developed have now been adopted, in particular in the Debian distribution, even if with varying degrees of delay and effort.

2 Our Tools

The first two tools produced by this research effort that were adopted in the Debian community are *distcheck* and *buildcheck*, which scan all the packages in a Debian distribution to identify installability issues. Both tools were developed to provide proof of concept prototypes to support our experiments but evolved, with the help of the Debian community, to production ready tools.

2.1 Distcheck and Buildcheck

The *distcheck* tool is a command line tool, capable of verifying the installability of all (or a selection of) components contained in a given repository. Internally, *distcheck* is designed as a pipeline, as shown in Fig. 2. The front-end on the left is a multiplexer parser that supports several formats for component metadata (Debian `Packages` files, RPM's synthesis or hdlist files, Eclipse OSGI metadata, etc.). After metadata parsing, component inter-relationships are converted in a data representation called CUDF (Common Upgradability Description Format), an extensible format, with rigorous semantics [22], designed to describe installability scenarios coming from diverse environments without making assumptions on specific component models, version schemas, or dependency formalisms. CUDF can be serialized as a compact plain text format, which makes it easy for humans to read component metadata, and which facilitates interoperability with other component managers that are not yet supported by *distcheck*.

The actual installability check work is performed by a specialized solver, that uses the SAT encoding [18] and employs an ad hoc customized Davis-Putnam SAT solver [9] by default instead of the many other standalone solvers now available for dependency solving like [6,10,13,14,20]. Since all computations are performed in-memory and some of the encoding work is shared between all packages, this solver performs significantly faster than a naive approach that would construct a separate SAT encoding for the installability of each package, and then run an off-the-shelf SAT solver on it. For instance, checking installability of all packages of the Debian main repository of the unstable suite (for 53696 packages[2]) takes just 30 s on a commodity 64 bit CPU laptop.

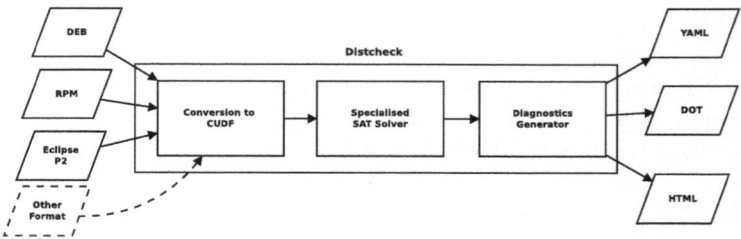

Fig. 2. *distcheck* architecture

---

[2] Snapshot of the Debian distribution 27/02/2017.

The final component of the pipeline takes the result from the solver and presents it in a variety of human and machine readable formats to the final user. An important feature of *distcheck* is its ability, in case a package is found not installable, to produce a concise human-readable explanation that points to the reasons of the issue in a machine-readable format.

The *buildcheck* tool follows the same pipeline philosophy of distcheck but it is aimed at source packages. It takes a list of source and binary packages and checks if the build dependencies of each source package can be satisfied with the given binary list. *buildcheck* is based on the same algorithm of *distcheck*, but because of different formats and metadata, packages are mangled behind the scenes in an ad-hoc CUDF that can be feed to the solver. The output, as for *distcheck*, is in YAML format and provides a human-readable explanation of the issue.

Adoption. *distcheck* has been adopted in the Debian project thanks to significant commitment on the side of the researchers. In particular, Ralf Treinen and Fabio Mancinelli, on occasion of the 2006 edition of DebConf (the annual meeting of the Debian project), worked on setting up a dedicated web page for use by the Debian Quality Assurance team. That quality dashboard was originally hosted on http://edos.debian.net and evolved over time, incorporating more tools developed later to detect outdated packages [3], and migrated in 2014 to the official Debian Quality Assurance infrastructure, that is now at qa.debian.org/dose/. Our tools are also part of their projects like *rebootstrap* and bootstrap.debian.net.

3 Enhancing the Debian Distribution Build Process

The Debian life cycle and evolution process is organised around three repositories: *stable*, which contains the latest official release and does not evolve any more (apart for security and critical updates); *testing*, a constantly evolving repository to which packages are added under stringent qualification conditions, and that will eventually be released as the new stable; and *unstable*, a repository in which additions, removals and modifications are allowed under very liberal conditions. A stringent set of requirements, which are formally defined, must be satisfied by packages coming from unstable to be accepted in testing (also known as package migration), and the repository maintainers have responsibility for enforcing them with the help of ad-hoc tools.

From their first release into the Debian repository, packages evolve over time following a well defined process. When a new version of a *source* package S is available, it is fist introduced in unstable (the only point of entry into the distribution), where the corresponding *binary* packages are gradually built. When a binary package is rebuilt, it replaces the previous version (if any), and when all binary packages associated to S are rebuilt, the old version of S is dropped. Building binary packages can be a long process because of compilation errors and broken dependencies. Moreover, because of the iterative nature of this process, it is sometimes possible to find in unstable several versions of the same source package, and a mixture of binary packages coming from these different versions of the same source.

In order to allow a smooth monitoring of the build process, to keep track of old and new packages in unstable and to handle the transition of packages from unstable to testing, Debian built a powerful internal infrastructure to automatically build and migrate packages from one repository to another.

3.1 Buildd, sbuildd, Dose-Tools

The Debian autobuilder network is a management system that allows Debian developers to easily add new source packages to the repository and compile all associated binary package for all architectures currently supported by Debian. This network is made up of several machines and uses a specific software package called *buildd* whose main function is to automatically build all binary packages, according to its metadata and multi-architecture annotations.

The build daemon, consists of a set of scripts (written in Perl and Python) that have evolved to help porters with various tasks. Over time, these scripts have become an integrated system that is able to keep Debian distributions up-to-date nearly automatically. The build infrastructure is composed of three main components, first *wanna-build* is a tool to collect and keep track of all package metadata. The *buildd* is the multiplexer that selects which builder for each architecture must be invoked for each package, and finally *sbuild* is the actual builder to automatically recompile the package. *buildcheck* and *distcheck* are integrated in different components of the Debian build daemon.

buildcheck is used in the *wanna-build* daemon to check if a all the build dependencies of a given source package are available. This step allows one to catch dependency problems before even allowing the package to enter the build queue, hence saving considerable resources and space. *buildcheck* is fed with the metadata of the current source package, and the metadata of all available packages in the archive at one moment in time. By using different options, *buildcheck* is able to check, for each architecture, if the all dependencies are available and if this is not the case, to provide a human readable explanation for the package maintainer. This tool is also available to the package maintainer and it can be run independently on a personal machine.

distcheck is used in *sbuildd* to provide better explanations to the package maintainer in case of failure. Depending on the solver (by default aspcud [11]), the dose3 explainer might report a dependency situation as satisfiable even if the apt-get found it to be unsatisfiable. This is a consequence of the fact that the default Debian resolver (apt-get) employs an algorithm that is, albeit very fast, incomplete. Having a sound and complete dependency solver for Debian helped developers in many occasions. The same solver is also available to the final user via apt-get, where the user can choose to select an external solver while installing a binary package on their machine. Before the introduction of *distcheck* packages where tested for broken dependencies using apt, that because of its nature, it was less adapted to this task.

Adoption. *buildcheck* and *distcheck* have also been adopted in the Debian project thanks to significant commitment on the side of the researchers: in particular, after a common presentation with Ralf Treinen in DebConf 2008 [21], Stefano Zacchiroli gave another presentation in DebConf 2009 that motivated the swift integration of the Dose tools in `wanna-build`. This was highly facilitated by the fact that the Dose tools were already properly packaged for Debian, after the work done by Ralf Treinen, and that they had started to be known in the Debian community thanks to the regular participation of the researchers to these events.

4 Bootstrapping Debian on a New Architecture

With new hardware architectures and custom co-processor extensions being introduced to the market on a regular basis, porting Debian to a new architecture not only involves adapting the low-level software layer for a different hardware, but also considering the inter-dependencies among different components and how these can affect the compilation and packaging process. Binary packages and source packages use meta-data to describe their relationships to other components. Bootstrapping a distribution to a new architecture deals with the problem of customizing the software (source packages) for a specific architecture and to instantiate a new set of binary packages that is consistent with the constraints imposed by the new hardware.

Bootstrapping a distribution is the process by which software is compiled, assembled into packages and installed on a new device/architecture without the aid of any other pre-installed software.

The method routinely used in Debian consists in first, the creation (by cross compilation) of a minimal build system, and later the creation of the final set of binary packages on the new device (by native compilation). Cross compiling a small subset of source packages is necessary because an initial minimal set of binary packages must exist in order to compile a larger set of source packages natively. Once a sufficient number of source packages is cross compiled (we call the set of binary packages produced by them a minimal system) new source packages can be compiled natively on the target system. The minimal system is composed of a coherent set of binary packages that is able to boot on the new hardware and to provide a minimal working OS. This minimal set of binary packages contains at the very least an operating system, a user shell and a compiler. This initial selection is generally provided by distribution architects.

4.1 Botch

Botch is a set of tools designed to help porters to refine and complete this selection in a semi-automatic way and to build the rest of the distribution on top of it [5]. Botch is based on the Dose3 library and re-uses many of its components. The main contribution of botch is the ability of providing a compilation order of source packages to gradually rebuild the entire archive. The goal is to break compilation loops by pruning build dependencies according to special metadata describing compilation *stages*. At each iteration/stage, new binary packages are added to the repository that in turn will allow new source packages to be build.

The development of botch started with an academic collaboration with Johannes Schauer, a student that participated in a Google Summer of Code co-organised with Debian in 2012 [23]. Slowly, from prototype and thanks for the personal investment of the main developer of botch, it evolved from an academic project into an industry-strength tool.

Adoption. Before botch, porting Debian to a new architecture was a long manual process based on the intuition and personal experience. Because of the complex dependency network and inherent recursive nature of the problem (in order to compile a package we need to compile first all the source packages that will generate its build dependencies), it was also particularly error prone.

Hence it came as no surprise to see that it was adopted pretty swiftly: it was not just a matter of improving quality of a distribution, but of saving weeks of hard work. Botch is now referenced in the Debian official page on bootstrapping https://wiki.debian.org/DebianBootstrap and is used regularly.

5 The Technology Transfer Problem

The adoption path of the tools we have surveyed required significant effort and lasted several years. To understand why this was the case, it is important to take a step back and look at the basic principles governing both the FOSS community and the research community.

5.1 Community vs. Academia

The evolution of Debian has imposed the adoption of many different automated tools to handle the continually growing number of packages, developers and users. Historically, all tools belonging today to the Debian infrastructure have evolved independently, often in competition to each other. Because of the Debian governance model, where no central authority takes technical decisions, the adoption of a specific tool has always been left to the so called *do-ocracy*: if you want a particular tool to be used, you need to show its usefulness, integrate it in the infrastructure yourself, and convince others to use it.

As a consequence, the development and acceptance of these tools has always been quite slow because of the *human factor* and often not because of technical objections: once a developer has spent significant time and energy getting his own tool adopted, it is quite natural that they expect high returns in term of their own image in the project. Hence he will not be particularly open to admit that there is an interest in adopting new, more advanced technologies, and one can observe in the debate surprising arguments, like "that's surely a great tool, but you need to rewrite it using programming language A for it to be accepted", where A is a programming language different from the one used in the new tool.

This attitude has often been one of the first reaction we encountered and often the most difficult to overcome.

On the academic side, researchers face a publication pressure that seldom allows them to invest the time required to gain enough traction within this kind of communities. With these constraints, researchers often focus on one community while simply do not have the time to engage others. On top of that, to convince the infrastructure developers to see the "greater good" associated to adapt and use proved and stable solutions spin-off from research projects, one needs to actually produce a tool that is going to work in real-world situations, and not just in the small test cases often used as validation test-beds for academic publication.

Our approach over the year has been to adapt our way of doing research to match the real-world, following "ante litteram" the path highlighted in [19]. Therefore we invested a considerable amount of time to create tools that were able to work with real data, and at the same time use these data as empirical support in our publications. This approach kept us motivated and at the same time proved to be a good return of investment in the long run.

5.2 The Communication Gap

While approaching the Debian community, we faced issues that were sometimes technical in nature, sometimes political, and sometimes even personal. Moreover, after realizing the communication gap between our academic approach and the FOSS communities, we had to learn to speak a new language, and engage the community on their own ground. Researchers often focus exclusively on the effectiveness and correctness on their approach, while forgetting the cost in terms of integration time and learning curve.

The FOSS community is large and diverse. And while everybody has some technical knowledge, adopting a lingo that is too complex to understand can be counter productive. Hackers are more concerned about the results than the mathematics behind a tool, they are concerned about the ease of use, more than the expressive power of a new language. Providing something the community can readily understand, use and modify, in terms of programming language used, development tools, following de-facto standards, can greatly speed up the time of adoption of a new solution.

In our experience, bridging the academia-community gap has been possible only by actively engaging with the community. This involved, on one side, a significant effort to participate in online forums and live conferences: during the years covered in this article, we presented our work in a major European Developer conference (FOSDEM), and invited lead developers to work with us. We greatly benefit from having few members of our research team personally involved in the Community. While this is not always possible and largely dependent on the personal motivation of each team member, having deep ties within Debian helped us greatly to gain trust and respect. We also hosted hacking sprints and provide support for several events. By meeting the community, we tried to reduce this gap and to engage a fruitful and long-standing collaboration.

5.3 Community Driven Open Development

Our next step was to fully open up our development process and welcome different developers from different communities to contribute to our tools. We started this by funding students interested in FOSS and interacting with other researchers that are already active members of the community. The Dose3 library, which has consolidate most of our research work outcomes, has now an active community of developers, it is packaged for all major FOSS distributions and is currently maintained by the first author. To gain acceptance with the community we followed the unix philosophy, providing a lean and powerful command line tool, and an easily parse-able output. We also provided documentation and examples for other languages such as python or perl to foster interoperability and simplify the integration into existing frameworks. During the years we attracted several students interested to work on the project. Two of them developed important components of the library and one of the has now become one of the main contributors.

Finally, we consider that our commitment to handle real-world case studies, with direct applicability in the field, instead of the usual toy examples, proved to be a real important element of success.

5.4 Lesson Learned

From our experience, we can draw the following recommendations for colleges from academia that want to see their tools adopted.

Be proactive. Do not wait for the community to reach out to you for help. It is your task to engage developers and publicize your work.
Communication. Attending conferences and learning how to frame our work for a specific community is essential.
Engagement. Seeking collaboration, hosting events and participating to the development process of a distribution is essential to build trust and ease acceptance.
The extra mile. Provide tools and documentation accessible to a wide audience. Make it easy for your tools to be integrated in the existing framework, do not expect others to do it in your place.
Hiring interns, PhD students or post-docs that are interested in free software is a great way of creating connections between the two worlds, and establishing trust.

6 Conclusion

The take-away from this paper is that developing amazing and efficient tools behind the high walls of academia is only the starting point, and much more is needed to achieve impact in the real world.

Acknowledgements. The work described in this article has been performed over a very long span of time, in collaboration with many researchers, that contributed in different periods, and to varying degrees, to some or all of the tools that we mention. Roberto Di Cosmo, Fabio Mancinelli, Ralf Treinen and Jerôme Vouillon were actively involved in the EDOS project, with Fabio Mancinelli leaving after that period. In the MANCOOSI project, that was set up and coordinated by Roberto Di Cosmo, Ralf Treinen and Jerôme Vouillon were joined by Pietro Abate, Jaap Boender and Stefano Zacchiroli.

References

1. The mancoosi project (2011). http://www.mancoosi.org
2. Abate, P., Cosmo, R.D., Gesbert, L., Fessant, F.L., Treinen, R., Zacchiroli, S.: Mining component repositories for installability issues. In: 12th IEEE/ACM Working Conference on Mining Software Repositories (MSR 2015), Florence, Italy, 16–17 May 2015, pp. 24–33 (2015)
3. Abate, P., Cosmo, R.D., Treinen, R., Zacchiroli, S.: Learning from the future of component repositories. Sci. Comput. Program. **90**, 93–115 (2014)
4. Abate, P., Di Cosmo, R., Treinen, R., Zacchiroli, S.: Dependency solving: a separate concern in component evolution management. J. Syst. Softw. **85**(10), 2228–2240 (2012)
5. Abate, P., Schauer, J.: Bootstrapping software distributions. In: Proceedings of International Symposium of Component Based Software Engineering (CBSE) (2013)
6. Argelich, J., Le Berre, D., Lynce, I., Marques-Silva, J., Rapicault, P.: Solving Linux upgradeability problems using boolean optimization. In: LoCoCo: Logics for Component Configuration, vol. 29 of EPTCS (2010)
7. Di Cosmo, R., Mancinelli, F., Boender, J., Vouillon, J., Durak, B., Leroy, X., Pinheiro, D., Trezentos, P., Morgado, M., Milo, T., Zur, T., Suarez, R., Lijour, M., Treinen, R.: Report on formal mangement of software dependencies. Technical report, EDOS (2006)
8. Cosmo, R., Treinen, R., Zacchiroli, S.: Formal aspects of free and open source software components. In: Giachino, E., Hähnle, R., Boer, F.S., Bonsangue, M.M. (eds.) FMCO 2012. LNCS, vol. 7866, pp. 216–239. Springer, Heidelberg (2013). doi:10.1007/978-3-642-40615-7_8
9. Eén, N., Sörensson, N.: An extensible SAT-solver. In: Giunchiglia, E., Tacchella, A. (eds.) SAT 2003. LNCS, vol. 2919, pp. 502–518. Springer, Heidelberg (2004). doi:10.1007/978-3-540-24605-3_37
10. Galindo, J.A., Benavides, D., Segura, S.: Debian packages repositories as software product line models. Towards automated analysis. In: Proceedings of the 1st International Workshop on Automated Configuration and Tailoring of Applications. CEUR-WS.org (2010)
11. Gebser, M., Kaminski, R., Schaub, T.: aspcud: a Linux package configuration tool based on answer set programming. In: Drescher, C., Lynce, I., Treinen, R., (eds.) Proceedings Logics for Component Configuration. LoCoCo (2011)
12. Gonzalez-Barahona, J., Robles, G., Michlmayr, M., Amor, J., German, D.: Macro-level software evolution: a case study of a large software compilation. Empir. Softw. Eng. **14**(3), 262–285 (2009)
13. Janota, M.: Do sat solvers make good configurators? In: SPLC: Software Product Lines Conference, vol. 2 (2008)

14. Jenson, G., Dietrich, J., Guesgen, H.W.: An empirical study of the component dependency resolution search space. In: Grunske, L., Reussner, R., Plasil, F. (eds.) CBSE 2010. LNCS, vol. 6092, pp. 182–199. Springer, Heidelberg (2010). doi:10.1007/978-3-642-13238-4_11
15. LaBelle, N., Wallingford, E.: Inter-package dependency networks in open-source software. CoRR, cs.SE/0411096 (2004)
16. Le Berre, D., Parrain, A.: On SAT technologies for dependency management and beyond. In: SPLC 2008: Software Product Lines Conference, vol. 2 (2008)
17. Le Berre, D., Rapicault, P.: Dependency management for the Eclipse ecosystem. In: IWOCE 2009: International Workshop on Open Component Ecosystems. ACM (2009)
18. Mancinelli, F., Boender, J., Di Cosmo, R., Vouillon, J., Durak, B., Leroy, X., Treinen, R.: Managing the complexity of large free and open source package-based software distributions. In: ASE 2006: Automated Software Engineering. IEEE (2006)
19. Marinescu, R.: Confessions of a worldly software miner. In: 2015 IEEE/ACM 12th Working Conference on Mining Software Repositories, May 2015
20. Michel, C., Rueher, M.: Handling software upgradeability problems with MILP solvers. In: LoCoCo 2010: Logics for Component Configuration, vol. 29 of EPTCS (2010)
21. Treinen, R., Zacchiroli, S.: Solving package dependencies: from EDOS to Mancoosi. In: DebConf 8: Proceedings of the 9th Conference of the Debian Project (2008)
22. Treinen, R., Zacchiroli, S.: Common upgradeability description format (CUDF) 2.0. Technical report 3, The Mancoosi Project, November 2009
23. Wookey, Abate, P.: Google summer of code on debian bootstrap (2012)

Open Access This chapter is licensed under the terms of the Creative Commons Attribution 4.0 International License (http://creativecommons.org/licenses/by/4.0/), which permits use, sharing, adaptation, distribution and reproduction in any medium or format, as long as you give appropriate credit to the original author(s) and the source, provide a link to the Creative Commons license and indicate if changes were made.

The images or other third party material in this chapter are included in the chapter's Creative Commons license, unless indicated otherwise in a credit line to the material. If material is not included in the chapter's Creative Commons license and your intended use is not permitted by statutory regulation or exceeds the permitted use, you will need to obtain permission directly from the copyright holder.

Assessing Code Authorship: The Case of the Linux Kernel

Guilherme Avelino[1,2], Leonardo Passos[3], Andre Hora[1], and Marco Tulio Valente[1(✉)]

[1] Federal University of Minas Gerais (UFMG), Belo Horizonte, Brazil
{gaa,hora,mtov}@dcc.ufmg.br
[2] Federal University of Piauí (UFPI), Teresina, Brazil
[3] University of Waterloo, Waterloo, Canada
lpassos@gsd.uwaterloo.ca

Abstract. Code authorship is a key information in large-scale open-source systems. Among others, it allows maintainers to assess division of work and identify key collaborators. Interestingly, open-source communities lack guidelines on how to manage authorship. This could be mitigated by setting to build an empirical body of knowledge on how authorship-related measures evolve in successful open-source communities. Towards that direction, we perform a case study on the Linux kernel. Our results show that: (a) only a small portion of developers (26%) makes significant contributions to the code base; (b) the distribution of the number of files per author is highly skewed—a small group of top-authors (3%) is responsible for hundreds of files, while most authors (75%) are responsible for at most 11 files; (c) most authors (62%) have a specialist profile; (d) authors with a high number of co-authorship connections tend to collaborate with others with less connections.

Keywords: Code authorship · Linux kernel · Developer networks

1 Introduction

Collaborative work and modularization are key players in software development, specially in the context of open-source systems [14,23,27]. In a collaborative setup imposed by open-source development, code authorship allows developers to identify which project members to contact upon maintaining existing parts of the code base. Additionally, authorship information allows maintainers to assess overall division of work among project members (e.g., to seek better working balance) and identify profiles within the team (e.g., specialists versus generalists).

Our notion of authorship is broader than the English definition of the word. In the context of code, authorship relates to those who make significant changes to a target file. This may include the original file creator, as well as those who subsequently change it. Hence, different from authorship in books and scientific papers, code authorship is inherently dynamic as a software evolves.

Problem Statement. Currently, open-source communities lack guidance on how to organize and manage code authorship among its contributors.

Research Goal. We argue that the stated problem could be mitigated by setting to build an empirical body of knowledge on how authorship-related measures evolve in successful open-source communities. In that direction, we investigate authorship in a large and long-lived system—the Linux kernel. Our goal is to identify authorship parameters from the Linux kernel evolution history, as well as interpret why they appear as such. We also check whether those parameters apply to the subsystem level, allowing us to assess their generality across different parts of the kernel. Our analysis accounts for 56 stable releases (v2.6.12–v4.7), spanning a period of over 11 years of development (June, 2005–July, 2016).

Research Questions. When investigating the Linux kernel authorship history, we follow three research questions:

RQ1: What is the distribution of the number of files per author?

<u>Motivation:</u> Answering such a question provides us with a measure of the work overload and the concentration of knowledge within team members, as well as how that evolves over time.

RQ2: How specialized is the work of Linux authors?

<u>Motivation:</u> Following the Linux kernel architectural decomposition, we seek to understand the proportion of developers who have a narrower understanding of the system (specialists), versus those with a broader knowledge (generalists). Specialist developers author files in a single subsystem; generalists, in turn, author files in different subsystems. Answering our research question seeks to assess how effective the Linux kernel architectural decomposition is in fostering specialized work, a benefit usually expected from a good modularization design [3,30].

RQ3: What are the properties of the Linux co-authorship network?

<u>Motivation:</u> The authorship metric we use enables identifying multiple authors per file, evidencing a co-authorship collaboration among developers [20]. Such collaborations form a network—vertices denote authors and edges connect authors sharing common authored files. This question seeks to identify collaboration properties in the Linux kernel co-authorship network.

Contributions. From the investigation we conduct, we claim two major contributions: (a) an in-depth investigation of authorship in a large, successful, and long-lived open-source community, backed up by several authorship measures when answering each of our research questions. The findings we report also serve researchers, allowing them to contrast the authorship in the Linux kernel with those of other communities; (b) the definition of several authorship-centric concepts, such as authors and specialists/generalists, that others may use as a common ground to study the social organization of software systems.

In Sect. 2, we provide a description of our study design. Section 3 details our results. Sections 4 and 5 discuss threats to validity and related work, respectively. Section 6 concludes the paper, also outlining future work.

2 Study Design

2.1 Author Identification

At the core of our study lies the ability to identify and quantify authorship at the source code level. To identify file authors, as required by our three research questions, we employ a normalized version of the *degree-of-authorship* (DOA) metric [9,10]. The metric is originally defined in absolute terms:

$$DOA_A(d, f) = 3.293 + 1.098 * FA + 0.164 * DL - 0.321 * \ln(1 + AC)$$

From the provided formula, the absolute degree of authorship of a developer d in a file f depends on three factors: first authorship (FA), number of deliveries (DL), and number of acceptances (AC). If d is the creator of f, *FA* is 1; otherwise it is 0; *DL* is the number of changes in f made by d; and AC is the number of changes in f made by other developers. DOA_A assumes that FA is by far the strongest predictor of file authorship. Further changes by d (DL) also contributes positively to his authorship, but with less importance. Finally, changes by other developers (AC) contribute to decrease someone's DOA_A, but at a slower rate. The weights we choose stem from an experiment with professional Java developers [9]. We reuse such thresholds without further modification.

The normalized DOA (DOA_N) is as given in [2]:

$$DOA_N(d, f) = DOA_A(d, f)/max(\{DOA_A(d', f) \mid d' \in changed(f)\})$$

In the above equation, *changed(f)* denotes the set of developers who edited a file f up to a snapshot of interest (e.g., release). This includes the developer who creates f, as well as all those who later modify the file. $DOA_N \in [0..1]$: 1 is granted to the developer(s) with the highest absolute DOA among those changing f; in other cases, DOA_N is less than one.

Lastly, the set of authors of a file f is given by:

$$authors(f) = \cup\{d \mid d \in changed(f) \wedge DOA_N(d, f) > 0.75 \wedge DOA_A(d, f) \geq 3.293\}$$

The authors identification depends on specific thresholds—0.75 and 3.293. Those stem from a calibration setup when applying DOA_N to a large corpus of open-source systems. For full details, we refer readers to [2].

2.2 Linux Kernel Architectural Decomposition

Investigating authorship at the subsystem level requires a reference architecture of the Linux kernel. Structurally, the Linux kernel architectural decomposition comprises seven major subsystems [8]: *Arch* (architecture dependent code), *Core*

Table 1. Linux subsystems size and authors proportion

Subsystem	Files		Authors proportion			
			Last release (v4.7)			All releases
	#	%	Developers	Authors	Proportion	Avg ± Std Dev
Driver	22,943	42%	10,771	2,604	24%	25.00 ± 0.80%
Arch	17,069	32%	3,613	1,145	32%	33.10 ± 1.28%
Misc	6,621	12%	644	78	12%	14.85 ± 2.69%
Core	3,840	7%	4,165	1,083	26%	25.77 ± 1.56%
Net	1,957	4%	2,161	269	13%	13.63 ± 0.90%
Fs	1,809	3%	1,777	175	10%	12.61 ± 1.95%
Firmware	151	0%	–	–	–	–
All	54,400	100%	13,436	3,459	26%	26.86 ± 0.83%

(scheduler, IPC, memory management, etc.), *Driver* (device drivers), *Firmware* (firmware required by device drivers), *Fs* (file systems), *Net* (network stack implementation), and *Misc* (miscellaneous files, including documentation, samples, scripts, etc.). To map files in each subsystem, we rely on mapping rules set by G. Kroah-Hartman, one of the main Linux kernel developers.[1] Table 1 shows the number of files in each kernel subsystem as mapped by using the expert rules.

2.3 Data Collection

We study 56 stable releases of the Linux kernel, obtained from LINUS/TORVALDS GitHub repository. A stable release is any named tag snapshot whose identifier does not have a $-rc$ suffix. To define the *authors* set of a file f in a given release r, we calculate DOA_N from the first commit up to r. It happens, however, that the Linux kernel history is not fully stored under Git, as explained by Linus Torvalds in the first commit message.[2] Therefore, we use `git graft` to join the history of all releases prior to v2.6.12 (the first release recorded in Git) with those already controlled by Git. After join, we increment the Linux kernel Git history with 64,468 additional commits.

Given the entire development history, we check out each stable release at a time, listing its files, and calculating their DOA_N. In the latter case, we rely on `git log --no-merges` to discard merge commits and retrieve all the changes to a given file prior to the release under investigation. To compute the DOA_N, we only consider the author of each commit, not its committer (Git repositories store both) [6]. It is worth noting that prior to calculate DOA_N, we map possible aliases among developers, as well as eliminate unrelated source code files. As

---
[1] https://github.com/gregkh/kernel-history/blob/master/scripts/stats.pl
[2] https://github.com/torvalds/linux/commit/1da177e4c3f41524e886b7f1b8a0c1fc7321cac2.

example, the *Firmware* subsystem was removed because most of its files are binary blobs. To perform these steps, we adopt the procedures described in [2].

Table 1 shows the proportion of authors in each Linux subsystem. In the last release, Linux kernel has 13,436 developers, but only 3,459 (26%) are authors of at least one file. Throughout the kernel development, the proportion of authors is nearly constant (*Std dev* = ±0.83%). Thus, the heavy-load Linux kernel maintenance has been kept in the hands of less than a third of all developers.

Using custom-made scripts, we fully automate authorship identification, as well as the collection of supporting data for the claims we make. Our infrastructure is publicly available on GitHub.[3] We encourage others to use it as means to independently replicate/validate our results.

3 Results

(RQ.1) Distribution of the Number of Files per Author

What is the distribution of the number of files per author?

The number of files per author is highly skewed. Figure 1 presents the boxplots of files per author across the Linux kernel releases (adjusted for skewness—see [15]). To simplify the visualization of the results, we present the boxplots at each two releases. With exception of one release (v2.6.24), 50% of the authors responds to at most three files (median); for 75% of the authors, the number of files ranges from 11 to 16. Outliers follow from the skewed distribution. Still, the number of authors with more than 100 files is always lower than 7% of the authors, ranging from 7% in the first release to 3% in the last one. Similar behavior is observed at the subsystem level. In the last release (v4.7), for instance, the number of files per author up to the 75% percentile in *Fs*, *Arch*, and *Driver* closely resemble one-another and the global distribution as a whole—all share the same median (three). *Core* and *Misc*, however, have less variability than the other subsystems, as well as lower median values (two and one, respectively).

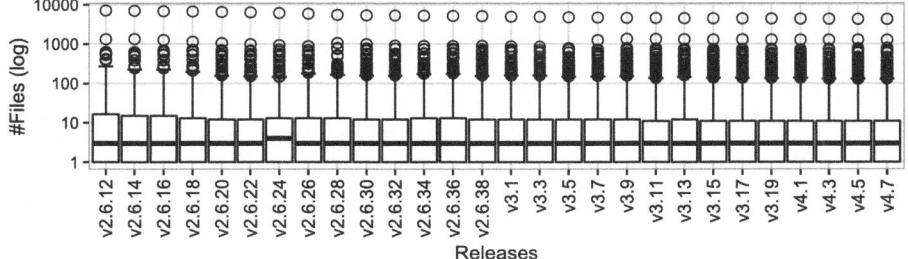

Fig. 1. Distribution of the number of files per author in each release

---

[3] https://github.com/gavelino/data_oss17.

It is interesting to note that file authorship follows a pyramid-like shape of increasing authority; at the top, Linus Torvalds acts as a "dictator", centralizing authorship of most of the files (after all, he did create the kernel!). Bellow him lies his hand-picked "lieutenants", often chosen on the basis of merit. Such organization directly reflects the Linux kernel contribution dynamics, which is itself a pyramid [4]. However, as the kernel evolves, we see that Torvalds is becoming more "benevolent". As Fig. 2 shows, the percentage of files authored by him has reduced from 45% (first release) to 10% in v4.7. Currently, he spends more time verifying and integrating patches than writing code [7]. Similar behavior is observed downwards the authorship pyramid. The percentage of files in the hand of the next top-9 Linux kernel authors (bars) is consistently decreasing. This suggests that authorship is increasing at lower levels of the pyramid, becoming more decentralized. This is indeed expected and to an extent required to allow the Linux kernel evolves at the pace it does.

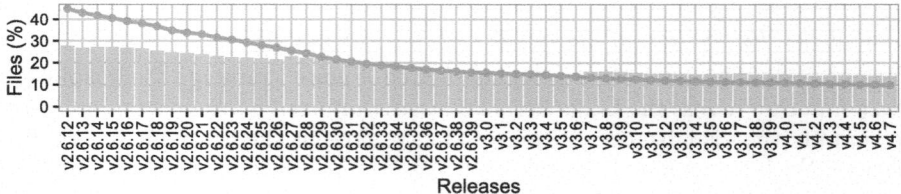

Fig. 2. Percentage of files authored by the top-10 authors over time. The line represents Linus Torvalds (top-1) and the bars represent the accumulated number of files of the next top-9 authors

We also apply the Gini coefficients [12] to analyze the distribution of the number of files per author (Fig. 3). In all releases, the coefficient is high, confirming skewness. However, we notice a decreasing trend, ranging from 0.88 in the first release to 0.78 (v4.7). Such a trend further strengthens our notion that authorship in the Linux kernel is becoming less centralized.

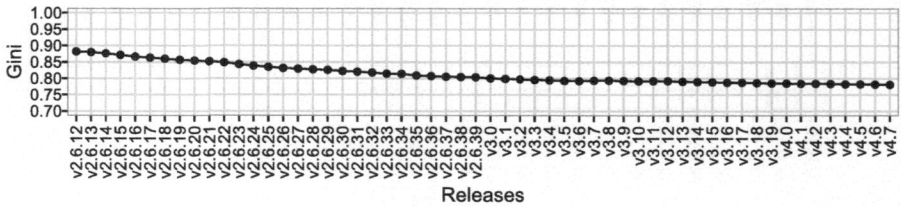

Fig. 3. Gini coefficients. It ranges from 0 (perfect equality) to 1 (perfect inequality).

(RQ.2) Work Specialization

How specialized is the work of Linux authors?

To assess work specialization, we introduce two author profiles. We call authors *specialists* if they author files in a single subsystem. *Generalists*, in turn, author files in at least two subsystems. As Fig. 4 shows, the number of specialists dominates the amount of generalists. In the Linux kernel (All), any given release has at least 61% of specialist authors, with a maximum of 64%; at all times, 39% of the authors are generalists. Moreover, the proportion of generalists and specialists appears to be fairly stable across the entire kernel (All) and its constituent subsystems (except for *Misc*).

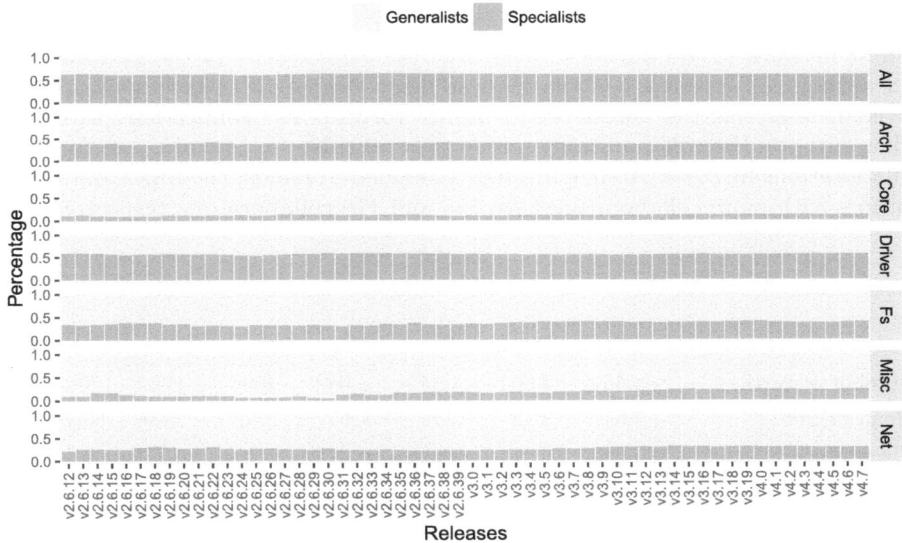

Fig. 4. Percentage of specialists and generalists

Looking at the work specialization in each subsystem also provides a means to assess how much the Linux kernel architectural decomposition fosters specialized work. The architectural decomposition plays a key role in fostering specialists inside the *Driver* subsystem (more than 50% of specialists), but less so elsewhere. The reason it occurs so extensively inside *Driver* follows from the plug-in interface of the latter and its relative high independence to other subsystems [8,28]. In contrast, *Core* and *Misc* have the lowest percentage of specialized workers. More than 75% of their authors own files in more than one subsystem. Specifically, *Core* is the subsystem with the lowest percentage of specialized workers (13%). This is also expected since *Core* developers tend to have expertise on Linux's central features, which allows them to also work on other subsystems.

(RQ.3) Co-authorship Properties

What are the properties of the Linux co-authorship network?

Many files in the Linux kernel result from the work of different authors. As such, we set to investigate such collaboration by means of the properties of the Linux kernel *co-authorship network*. We model the latter as follows: vertices stand for Linux kernel authors; an edge connects two authors v_i and v_j if $\exists f$ such that $\{v_i, v_j\} \subseteq authors(f)$. In other words, an edge represents a *collaboration*.

To answer our research question, we initially analyze the latest co-authorship network, as given in release v4.7 (Table 2).[4] The number of vertices (authors) determines the size of a co-authorship network. The mean degree network, in turn, inspects the number of co-authors that a given author connects to. In the system level (All), the mean vertex degree is 3.64, i.e., on average, a Linux author collaborates with 3.64 other authors. At the subsystem level, *Driver* forms the largest network (2,604 authors, 75%), whereas *Misc* results in the smallest one (78 authors, 2%). *Arch* has the highest mean degree (3.14 collaborators per author); *Misc* has the lowest (0.79). Linus Torvalds has connections with 215 other authors. His collaborations spread over all subsystems and range from 92 collaborations in *Driver* to five in *Misc*. Excluded Torvalds, the top-2 and top-3 authors with more collaborators have 156 and 118 collaborators, respectively.

Table 2. Co-authorship network properties (release v4.7)

	All	Driver	Arch	Core	Net	Fs	Misc
Number of vertices	3,459	2,604	1,145	1,083	269	175	78
Mean degree	3.64	2.74	3.14	1.67	2.57	2.59	0.79
Clustering coefficient	0.080	0.074	0.128	0.074	0.205	0.175	0.188
Assortativity coefficient	−0.070	−0.115	−0.060	−0.072	−0.003	−0.146	−0.062

The third property, *clustering coefficient*, reveals the degree to which adjacent vertices of a given vertex tend to be connected [31]. In a co-authorship network, the coefficient gives the probability that two authors who have a co-author in common are also co-authors themselves. A high coefficient indicates that the vertices tend to form high density clusters. The clustering coefficient of the Linux kernel is small (0.080). Nonetheless, *Net*, *Misc*, and *Fs* exhibit a higher tendency to form density clusters (0.205, 0.188, and 0.175, respectively) in comparison to other subsystems. The three subsystems are the smallest we analyze, a factor that influences the development of collaboration clusters [1].

Last, but not least, we compute the *assortativity coefficient*, which correlates the number of co-authors of an author (i.e., its vertex degree) with the number of co-authors of the authors it is connected to [26]. Ranging from −1 to 1, the coefficient shows whether authors with many co-authors tend to collaborate with

---

[4] We use the R *igraph* (version 1.0.1) to calculate all measures.

other highly-connected authors (positive correlation). In v4.7, all subsystems have negative assortativity coefficients, ranging from -0.134 in *Fs* to -0.029 in *Net* subsystem. This result diverges from the one commonly observed in scientific communities [25]. Essentially, this suggests that Linux kernel developers often divide work among experts who help less expert ones. These experts (i.e., highly-connected vertices), in turn, usually do not collaborate among themselves (i.e., the networks have negative *assortative coefficients*).

We identify in the co-authorship networks a relevant amount of *solitary authors*—authors that do not have co-authorship with any other developer. In total, 20% (699) of Linux kernel developers are solitary. Although there is a high percentage of solitary authors, only 9% of them have more than three files. Additionally, 66% of them work in the *Driver* subsystem. The latter is likely to follow from the high proportion of specialists within that subsystem (see RQ.2).

Evolution of Co-authorship network properties. We set to investigate how the co-authorship properties evolved to those in release v4.7. Figure 5 displays the corresponding graphics. Although we can observe a small decrease in some intermediate releases, by looking at the first and last releases, the mean degree has little variation, ranging from 3.61 to 3.64. Clustering coefficient, in turn, varies from 0.099 (first release) to 0.080 (v4.7). Since the mean degree does not vary considerably, we interpret such decrease as an effect of the growth of the number of authors (network vertices). The latter creates new opportunities of collaboration, but these new connections do not increase the density of the already existing clusters. A similar behavior is common in other networks, as described by Albert and Barabási [1]. Finally, we observe a relevant variation in the evolution of assortativity coefficients. Measurements range from -0.25 in the first release to -0.07 in v4.7. Such a trend aligns with the decrease of the percentage of files authored by Linus Torvalds and the other top authors (refer to RQ.1). With less files, these authors are missing some of their connections and becoming more similar (in terms of vertex degree) to their co-authors.

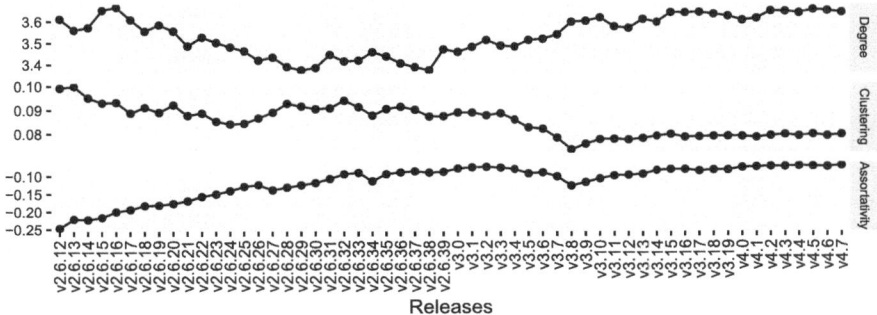

Fig. 5. Co-authorship network properties over time

4 Threats to Validity

Construct Validity. Our results depend on the accuracy of DOA calculations. Currently, we compute DOA values using weights from the analysis of other systems [9,10]. Although the authors of the absolute DOA claim their weights are general, we cannot fully eliminate the threat that the choice of weights pose to our results. Still, we have previously applied them when analyzing different open-source systems, obtaining positive feedback from developers [2].

Internal Validity. We measure authorship considering only the commit history of the official Linux kernel Git repository. Hence, we do not consider forks that are not merged into the mainstream development. Although these changes might be relevant to some (e.g., studies about integration activities [11]), they are not relevant when measuring authorship of the official Linux kernel codebase. We also consider that all commits have the same importance. As such, we do not account for the granularity of changes (number of lines of code affected) nor their semantics (e.g., bug fixes, new features, refactoring, etc.).

External Validity. The metrics we use can be applied to any software repository under a version control system. Still, our findings are very specific to the Linux kernel development. Thus, we cannot assume that the findings about workload, specialization, and collaboration are general. Nonetheless, we pave the road for further studies to validate our findings in the context of other systems.

5 Related Work

Code Authorship. McDonald and Ackerman propose the "Line 10 Rule", one of the first and most used heuristics for expertise recommendation [19]. The heuristic considers that the last person who changes a file is most likely to be "the" expert. Expertise Browser [24] and Emergent Expertise Locator [22] are alternative implementations to the "Line 10 Rule". The former uses the concept of experience atoms (EA) to give the value for each developer's activity and takes into account the amount of EAs to quantify expertise. The latter refines the Expertise Browser approach by considering the relationship between files that change together. Fine-grained algorithms that assign expertise based on the percentage of lines a developer has last touched are used by Girba et al. [13] and by Rahman and Devanbu [29].

Social Network Analysis (SNA). Research in this area use information from source code repositories to build a social network, adopting different strategies to create the links between developers. Fernández et al. [18] apply SNA, linking developers that perform commits to the same module, to study their relationship and collaboration patterns. Others rely on fine-grained relations, building networks connecting developers that change the same file [5,16,21,32]. Joblin et al. [17] propose an even more fine-grained approach, connecting developers that change the same function in a source code. They claim that file-based links result in dense networks, which obscures important network properties. Our approach, although centered on file-level information, does not produce dense networks, as authorship requires that developers make significant contributions to a file.

6 Conclusion

In this paper, we extract and analyze authorship parameters from a successful case: the Linux kernel. By mining over 11 years of the Linux kernel commit history, we investigate how authorship changes over time, deriving measures that other communities mirroring the Linux kernel evolution could directly replicate. Moreover, our study provides the grounds for further analyses—we define authorship concepts setting basic terminology and operationalization, in addition to providing a dataset of a large case study that others may use as a comparison baseline. As future work, we seek to validate our findings directly with Linux kernel developers. Moreover, we plan to study authorship in other systems.

Acknowledgment. This study is supported by grants from FAPEMIG, CAPES, CNPq, and UFPI.

References

1. Albert, R., Barabási, A.L.: Statistical mechanics of complex networks. Rev. Modern Phys. **74**, 47–97 (2002)
2. Avelino, G., Passos, L., Hora, A.C., Valente, M.T.: A novel approach for estimating truck factors. In: 24th International Conference on Program Comprehension (ICPC), pp. 1–10 (2016)
3. Baldwin, C.Y., Clark, K.B.: Design Rules: The Power of Modularity. MIT Press, Cambridge (1999)
4. Bettenburg, N., Hassan, A.E., Adams, B., German, D.M.: Management of community contributions. Empir. Softw. Eng. **20**(1), 252–289 (2015)
5. Bird, C., Nagappan, N., Murphy, B., Gall, H., Devanbu, P.: Don't touch my code! In: 19th International Symposium on Foundations of Software Engineering (FSE), pp. 4–14 (2011)
6. Chacon, S., Straub, B.: Pro Git. Expert's voice in software development, 2nd edn. Apress, New York (2014)
7. Corbet, J., Kroah-Hartman, G., McPherson, A.: Who writes Linux: Linux kernel development: how fast it is going, who is doing it, what they are doing, and who is sponsoring it. Technical report, Linux Foundation (2013). http://www.linuxfoundation.org/publications/linux-foundation/who-writes-linux-2013
8. Corbet, J., Rubini, A., Kroah-Hartman, G.: Linux Device Drivers, 3rd edn. O'Reilly, Sebastopol (2005)
9. Fritz, T., Murphy, G.C., Murphy-Hill, E., Ou, J., Hill, E.: Degree-of-knowledge: modeling a developer's knowledge of code. ACM Trans. Softw. Eng. Methodol. **23**(2), 14:1–14:42 (2014)
10. Fritz, T., Ou, J., Murphy, G.C., Murphy-Hill, E.: A degree-of-knowledge model to capture source code familiarity. In: 32nd International Conference on Software Engineering (ICSE), pp. 385–394 (2010)

11. German, D.M., Adams, B., Hassan, A.E.: Continuously mining distributed version control systems: an empirical study of how Linux uses Git. Empir. Softw. Eng. **21**, 260–299 (2015)
12. Gini, C.: Measurement of inequality of incomes. Econ. J. **31**(121), 124–126 (1921)
13. Girba, T., Kuhn, A., Seeberger, M., Ducasse, S.: How developers drive software evolution. In: 8th International Workshop on Principles of Software Evolution (IWPSE), pp. 113–122 (2005)
14. Herbsleb, J.D.: Global software engineering: the future of socio-technical coordination. In: 2007 Future of Software Engineering (FOSE), pp. 188–198 (2007)
15. Hubert, M., Vandervieren, E.: An adjusted boxplot for skewed distributions. Comput. Stat. Data Anal. **52**(12), 5186–5201 (2008)
16. Jermakovics, A., Sillitti, A., Succi, G.: Mining and visualizing developer networks from version control systems. In: 4th International Workshop on Cooperative and Human Aspects of Software Engineering (CHASE), pp. 24–31 (2011)
17. Joblin, M., Mauerer, W., Apel, S., Siegmund, J., Riehle, D.: From developer networks to verified communities: a fine-grained approach. In: 37th International Conference on Software Engineering (ICSE), pp. 563–573 (2015)
18. López-Fernández, L., Robles, G., Gonzalez-Barahona, J.M., Herraiz, I.: Applying social network analysis techniques to community-driven libre software projects. Int. J. Inf. Technol. Web Eng. **1**(3), 27–48 (2006)
19. McDonald, D.W., Ackerman, M.S.: Expertise recommender: a flexible recommendation system and architecture. In: Conference on Computer Supported Cooperative Work (CSCW), pp. 231–240 (2000)
20. Meneely, A., Williams, L.: Socio-technical developer networks: should we trust our measurements? In: 33rd International Conference on Software Engineering (ICSE), pp. 281–290 (2011)
21. Meneely, A., Williams, L., Snipes, W., Osborne, J.: Predicting failures with developer networks and social network analysis. In: 16th International Symposium on Foundations of Software Engineering (FSE), pp. 13–23 (2008)
22. Minto, S., Murphy, G.C.: Recommending emergent teams. In: 4th Workshop on Mining Software Repositories (MSR), p. 5 (2007)
23. Mistrík, I., van der Hoek, A., Whitehead, J.: Collaborative software engineering: challenges and prospects. In: Mistrik, I., Grundy, J., Hoek, A., Whitehead, J. (eds.) Collaborative Software Engineering, 4th edn, pp. 389–403. Springer, Heidelberg (2010)
24. Mockus, A., Herbsleb, J.D.: Expertise browser: a quantitative approach to identifying expertise. In: 24th International Conference on Software Engineering (ICSE), pp. 503–512 (2002)
25. Newman, M.E.J.: Coauthorship networks and patterns of scientific collaboration. Proc. Natl. Acad. Sci. **101**, 5200–5205 (2004)
26. Newman, M.E.J.: Mixing patterns in networks. Phys. Rev. E **67**, 026126 (2003)
27. Parnas, D.L.: On the criteria to be used in decomposing systems into modules. Commun. ACM **15**(12), 1053–1058 (1972)
28. Passos, L., Padilla, J., Berger, T., Apel, S., Czarnecki, K., Valente, M.T.: Feature scattering in the large: a longitudinal study of Linux kernel device drivers. In: 14th International Conference on Modularity, pp. 81–92 (2015)
29. Rahman, F., Devanbu, P.: Ownership, experience and defects. In: 33rd International Conference on Software Engineering (ICSE), pp. 491–500 (2011)

30. Sullivan, K.J., Griswold, W.G., Cai, Y., Hallen, B.: The structure and value of modularity in software design. In: 9th International Symposium on Foundations of Software Engineering (FSE), pp. 99–108 (2001)
31. Watts, D.J., Strogatz, S.H.: Collective dynamics of small-world networks. Nature **393**, 440–442 (1998)
32. Yang, X.: Social network analysis in open source software peer review. In: 22nd International Symposium on Foundations of Software Engineering (FSE), pp. 820–822 (2014)

Open Access This chapter is licensed under the terms of the Creative Commons Attribution 4.0 International License (http://creativecommons.org/licenses/by/4.0/), which permits use, sharing, adaptation, distribution and reproduction in any medium or format, as long as you give appropriate credit to the original author(s) and the source, provide a link to the Creative Commons license and indicate if changes were made.

The images or other third party material in this chapter are included in the chapter's Creative Commons license, unless indicated otherwise in a credit line to the material. If material is not included in the chapter's Creative Commons license and your intended use is not permitted by statutory regulation or exceeds the permitted use, you will need to obtain permission directly from the copyright holder.

Project Management, Development and Evaluation

Release Early, Release Often and Release on Time. An Empirical Case Study of Release Management

Jose Teixeira[1,2(✉)]

[1] Åbo Akademi, Turku, Finland
jose.teixeira@abo.fi
[2] Turku Centre for Computer Science (TUCS), Turku, Finland
http://www.jteixeira.eu

Abstract. The dictum of "Release early, release often." by Eric Raymond as the Linux modus operandi highlights the importance of release management in open source software development. Nevertheless, there are very few empirical studies addressing release management in open source software development. It is already known that most open source software communities adopt either feature-based or time-based release strategies. Each of these has its advantages and disadvantages that are context-specific. Recent research reported that many prominent open source software projects have moved from feature-based to time-based releases. In this longitudinal case study, we narrate how OpenStack shifted towards a liberal six-month release cycle. If prior research discussed why projects should adopt time-based releases and how they can adopt such a strategy, we discuss how OpenStack adapted its software development processes, its organizational design and its tools toward a hybrid release management strategy — a strive for balancing the benefits and drawbacks of feature-based and time-based release strategies.

Keywords: Open-Source · OSS · FLOSS · Release management · OpenStack

1 Introduction

The dictum of "Release early, release often." by Eric Raymond as the Linux modus operandi [1,2] highlights the importance of release management in open source software development (see [3–5]). Across disciplines, release management was acknowledged as a very complex process that raises many issues among the producers and users of software [6–9]. Nevertheless, there are very few empirical studies addressing release management in open source software development [5,10]. This is unfortunate since many lessons can be learned from open source software communities [11–13]. After all, the freedom to study socio-technical aspect of software development contrasts open source software from the proprietary model where access to the software development team is only granted to a few.

Given such scarcity of empirical work addressing release management in the context of open source software [5,10], we address how a particularly large, complex and high-networked open source software ecosystem implemented a time-based release strategy. Taking the case of OpenStack, a fast growing cloud computing platform that is attracting great scholarly attention recently (e.g., [14–18]), we explore a 'time-based release management strategy' implementation in practice by looking at the release management process *per se* as well as to the organizational design and the tools supporting it.

2 Prior Related Work

Within the open source context, it is known that release management affects both producers of software and its users. In one side, prior research suggested that community activity increases when the scheduled release date gets closer [19]. On the user side, new releases result in spikes of downloads [20]. After all, as noted by the early work of Martin Michlmayr that focused on release management in open source software (see [21]), release management is concerned with the delivery of products to end-users. Is therefore not surprising that some recently saw release management as a process that supports value co-creation among suppliers and consumers of software (see [6]).

As pointed out by three recent doctoral dissertations addressing release management in the context of open-source software [10,21,22], most open source software communities adopt either feature-based or time-based release strategies. Many prominent open source software projects start with sporadic releases in which developers announce the newly developed features[1]. However, as many of this projects grown in size and complexity, they start adopting time-based release strategies[2]. An early empirical study that mined the repository of a project while it adopted a time-based release strategy (i.e., the Evolution e-mail client), suggested that the adoption of a time-based released boosted the development in general terms over time in comparison to feature-based release management [23]. More recent research, based on interviews with key members of seven prominent volunteer-based open source projects, point out that many of the problems associated with release-based strategies can be overcome by employing a time-based release strategy [5]. It is getting generally accepted that when a open-source software project grows in size and complexity, a time-based release strategy should be considered.

Time-based release strategies encompass meeting a schedule, an agenda, a deadline – either a strict or more liberal ones. To enforce that software is released on time, the use of freezes (such as code freezes), will set a clear deadline to the

---

[1] See the historical newsgroup news: comp.os.linux.announce where developers announced new releases of open-source software for Linux with a strong emphasis on the implemented features.
[2] See https://www.kernel.org/category/releases.html and https://www.debian.org/releases/ for information on the releases of Linux (2–3 months release cycle) and Debian (with a two years release cycle).

software development team. If open source developers have much freedom to self-manage their own software development efforts (when comparing with traditional proprietary paradigms), the use of freezes acts in the opposite way, it constrains the developers. If new features are not implemented before the next freeze, they will not be included in the next release. Consequently, when developers realize that a set of new features will bot be ready before the next freeze, the development of such features is either canceled, put on hold or developed at the side to be integrated later on future software releases.

Such freezes, that occur before the scheduled time-based release, act as control mechanisms that slowly halt the production of the development core code (see [13,24]). In large and complex open source software projects involving a modular architecture in which many components integrate with each other, such freeze forces developers to (1) fix and release the individual components upstream, (2) integrate the different components and test the integrated core.

As earlier reported (see [13]) such freeze categories can include:

feature freeze "no new functionality can be added, the focus should is on removing defects;"
string freeze "no messages displayed by the program, such as error messages, can be changed — this allows translating as many messages as possible before the release;"[3]
code freeze "permission is required to make any change, even to fix bugs."

3 Empirical Background

The cloud computing business is dominated by a small number of players (e.g., Amazon, Google and Microsoft). The leading players do not sell cloud infrastructure products. Instead, they provide bundled computing services. If there would be no alternatives, all cloud computation would run in hardware and software infrastructures controlled by very few players with increased customer lock-in (see [16]).

Competing with the providers of such services, the leading product alternatives are not commercial but rather four open source projects (i.e., OpenStack, CloudStack, OpenNebula, and Eucalyptus). While the commercial cloud computing services are developed and tightly controlled by a single organization, the open source products are more inclusive and networked — multiple firms participate in its development as well as multiple firms attempt to capture value from it.

Our empirical unit of analysis, OpenStack is an open source software cloud computing infrastructure capable of handling big data. It is primarily deployed as an "Infrastructure as a Service" (IaaS) solution. It started as a joint project of Rackspace, an established IT web hosting company, and NASA, the well-known U.S. governmental agency responsible for the civilian space program, aeronautics

---

[3] Here we add that many automated user-interface testing tools and techniques depend on the 'steadiness' of certain strings (see [25,26]).

and aerospace research. The project attracted much attention from the industry. By the end of 2016, OpenStack counted with more than 67000 contributors, 649 supporting companies. Furthermore, more than 20 millions lines of code were contributed from 169 countries[4].

Both private companies (e.g., AT&T, AMD, Canonical, Cisco, Dell, EMC, Ericsson, HP, IBM, Intel, and NEC, among many others) and public entities (e.g., NASA, CERN, Johns Hopkins University, Instituto de Telecomunicações, Universidade Federal de Campina Grande, and Kungliga Tekniska Högskolan, among others) work together with independent, non-affiliated developers in a scenario of pooled R&D in an open source way (i.e., emphasizing development transparency while giving up intellectual property rights). Paradoxically, even if OpenStack emphasizes collaboration in the joint-development of a large open source ecosystem, there are many firms directly competing with each other within the community. Among others, there is competition among providers of public cloud services based on OpenStack (e.g., HP, Canonical, and Rackspace), among providers of specialized hardware complementing OpenStack (e.g., HP, IBM, and Nebula), and among providers of complementary commercial software plug-ins complementing OpenStack (e.g., VMware, Citrix, and Cisco) (see [16,27]).

We decided to address OpenStack due to its perceived novelty, its high internetworked nature (i.e., an "ecosystem" involving many firms and individual contributors), its heterogeneity (i.e., an ecosystem involving both startups and high-tech corporate giants), its market-size ($1.7 bn, by 2016[5]), its complexity (i.e., involving different programming languages, different operating systems, different hardware configurations) and size (20 millions lines of code contributed by more than 67000 developers).

From the early beginnings, and while OpenStack was growing (e.g., in terms of the number of contributors, its code-base, and adoption among other sociotechnical indicators), it adopted a six-month, time-based release cycle with frequent development milestones that raised much discussion among its developers. We found it an interesting case to study release management within the overlap of open source software, software ecosystems, and complex software systems.

4 Methodological Design

This empirical case study was guided by the broad research question on "How OpenStack implemented a time-based release strategy". A particular emphasis was given to the release management process *per se* as well as to the organizational design and the tools supporting it.

Our efforts were built on top of publicly-available and naturally-occurring archival data derived from the OpenStack project. Such data are not a consequence of our own actions as researcher, but are created and maintained by the OpenStack community in their own pursuits of developing a cloud computing

---

[4] See http://www.openstack.org/ for the official website.
[5] See http://451research.com/report-short?entityId=82593.

infrastructure. We took into account many methodological notes in case study research that legitimate the use of archival data when studying a case [28–32].

We started by digesting many websites officially related to OpenStack (e.g., https://www.openstack.org/, https://wiki.openstack.org and http://docs.openstack.org/) expanding later to other websites. The selection of the initial sources (i.e., departure points) took in consideration key guidelines on how to conduct qualitative empirical research online [33,34]. From the initial sources, we were forced to follow many links to collect further information related to release management in OpenStack — we often landed in blogs maintained by organizations and individuals that recurrently contribute to OpenStack. Relevant data was meticulously organized withing a database for later analysis [35, pp. 94–98].

From our initial screening of qualitative data, we were able to: (1) make sense of the industrial background in which Openstack is embedded, (2) make sense of the complex software development processes that steer the project evolution, (3) survey complex inter organizational arrangements within the project, and (4) understand the role of many of the software tools that support software development processes.

After getting familiar with many social-technical issues within OpenStack, we analyzed the collected data from the lenses of extant knowledge in release management and open source software. Given the lack of empirical knowledge addressing release management in open source software [5, 10], we explored a 'time-based release management strategy' in practice. Our rich description on how OpenStack implemented its six-month, time-based release cycle with frequent development milestones should increase our ability to understand and explain release management within the context of complex open source software ecosystems. To enhances the validity of our description on how OpenStack implemented its time-based release strategy, we asked four OpenStack developers (two of them with release management responsibilities) to early read and comment our Sect. 5.1 in advance — we reduced then possible misinterpretations of the collected natural occurring data.

5 Results

Although our research is still at preliminary stage, we believe that some of our preliminary results can already contribute towards a better understanding of release management within complex open source software ecosystems. After all, release management is an under-researched area in which many lessons can be learned from open source software [13]. Our description of the implementation of a 'time-based release management strategy' in the particular case of OpenStack is organized as a complex socio-technological process and as a complex inter-organizational arrangement supported by different tools and systems.

5.1 Release Management at OpenStack

OpenStack was first launched by Rackspace and NASA in July 2010 as an "open-source cloud-software initiative". The first release, code-named 'Austin', appeared four months later, with plans to release regular updates of the software every few months. 'Austin' was already a sizable release as it inherited the code-base from NASA's Nebula platform as well as the code-base from Rackspace's Cloud Files platform. Firms such as Canonical, SUSE, Debian and Red Hat — all with a recognized role in the open software world were among the first organizations engaging with OpenStack. On the other side, Citrix, HP, and IBM were among the first high-tech giants that contributed to development of the project.

As OpenStack increased both in size and complexity, the forthcoming releases code-named 'Bexar', 'Cactus', and 'Diablo' came at irregular periods that ranged from three to five months[6]. As captured by the following quote, the 'Diablo' was the first of many forthcoming releases launched within a six months release cycle.

> "This release marks the first six month release cycle of OpenStack. The next release, Essex, will also be a six month release cycle and development is now officially underway. While Diablo includes over 70 new features, the theme is scalability, availability, and stability." — Devin Carlen, 29 September 2011[7].

OpenStack is so far orchestrated by the Git distributed version control system (aka repository) and the Gerrit revision control system (aka code review tool). Its source-code is hosted across dozens of repositories[8]. Due to the inherent complexity of a large-scale project developed by dozens of firms and hundred of developers, keeping everything within a single repository would raise issues on "when and where are bugs introduced" or "tracing longitudinally the development of features". Moreover, by using a multiple-repository approach access-control could be customized to each individual repository, new developers would not spend so much time learning the structure of a large source-code tree, and small changes across the multiple projects would not bother so much the other projects. Additionally, OpenStack also attempted a modular architecture with various components, each repository was then managed by the project team responsible by each component[9]. Some components, such as the OpenStack Compute (aka Nova and the computing fabric controller), are core components in which many other components rely on. To be able to integrate with such components, modular designs and much cross-project coordination is required.

> "We started this five-year mission with two projects: Nova (Compute) and Shift (Object Store) and over time, the number of projects in OpenStack grew. Some of

---

[6] See historical information on the exact release dates at https://releases.openstack.org/.

[7] See https://www.openstack.org/blog/2011/09/openstack-announces-diablo-release/.

[8] For an exhaustive list of OpenStack repositories see http://git.openstack.org/cgit.

[9] We acknowledge that some OpenStack components are also hosted in multiple repositories (e.g., Neutron the "network connectivity as a service"component. They are however exceptional cases.

this where parts of the existing projects that split out to have their own separate teams and become little more modular. Other things were good new ideas that people had that fit within the realm of OpenStack — Like interesting things that you would want to do in or with a cloud. Over time, we built a process around that to deal with the fact that there were so many of this projects coming in." — Sean Dague, 15 May 2015[10]

OpenStack keeps refining its release management process but always committed to a six-month release cycle. Each release cycle encompasses: planning (1 month), implementation (3 months), and integration where most pre-release critical bugs should be fixed (2 months). During the earlier release phase, the 'coding' efforts are much driven by discussion and specifications, while in a later release phase (i.e., stabilization of release candidates) the development turns into the bug-fixing mode (as reported in other open source projects [5,19,23]). At each release, developers start by implementing the discussed and/or specified key features while, by the end of the release, there is a peak of bug-fixing activities. To sum up, each release cycle starts in a specification and discussion driven way and ends in a bug-tracker oriented way.

The 'planning stage' is at the start of a cycle, just after the previous release. After a period of much stress to make the quality of the previous release acceptable, the community steps back and focus on what should be done for the next release. This phase usually lasts four weeks and runs in parallel with the OpenStack Design Summit on the third week (in a mixture of virtual and face-to-face collaboration). The community discusses among peers while gathering feedback and comments. In most cases, specification documents are proposed via an infrastructure system[11] that should precisely describe what should be done. Contributors may propose new specs at any moment in the cycle, not just during the planning stage. However doing so during the planning stage is preferred, so that contributors can benefit from the Design Summit discussion and the elected Project Team Leads (PTLs) can include those features into their cycle roadmap. Once a specification is approved by the corresponding project leadership, implementation is tracked in a blueprint[12], where a priority is set and a target milestone is defined, communicating when in the cycle the feature is likely to go live — At this stage, the process reflects the principles of agile methods.

The 'implementation stage' is when contributors actually write the code (or produce documentation, test cases among other software-related artifacts) mapping the defined blueprints. This phase is characterized by milestone iterations (once again a characteristic of agile software development methods). Once developers perceive their work as ready to be proposed for merging into the master

---

[10] Transcribed from video, see [1:26–2:06] https://www.openstack.org/summit/vancouver-2015/summit-videos/presentation/the-big-tent-a-look-at-the-new-openstack-projects-governance.
[11] See http://specs.openstack.org/ for intra-project and cross-project specifications.
[12] See https://wiki.openstack.org/wiki/Blueprints for blueprints that track each features implementation.

branch, it is pushed to OpenStack's Gerrit review system for public review[13]. It is important to remark that in order to be reviewed in time for a milestone, the change should be proposed a few weeks before the targeted milestone publication date. An open source software collaboration platform[14] is used to track blueprints in the 'implementation stage'. In a more open-source way and not to discourage contributors, it is worth remarking that not all "features" have to go through the blueprints tracking: contributors are free to submit any *ad hoc* patch. Both specifications and blueprints are tools supporting the discussion, design, and progress-tracking of the major features in a release. Even if the *big* corporate contributors are naturally more influential in the election of Project Team Leads (PTLs) steering the tracking process, it should not prevent other contributors from pushing code and fixes into OpenStack. Development milestones are tagged directly on the master branch during a two-day window (typically between the Tuesday and the Thursday of a milestone week). At this stage, heavy infrastructure tools that continuously integrate and test the new code play a very important role[15].

At the last development milestone OpenStack applies three feature freezes (i.e., *FeatureFreeze*, *SoftStringFreeze* and *HardStringFreeze* as described in Table 1. At this point, the project stops accepting new features or other disruptive changes. It concentrates on stabilization, packaging, and translation. The project turns then into a 'pre-release stage' (termed as 'release candidates dance'[16]). Contributors are encouraged to turn most of their attention to testing the result of the development efforts and fix release-critical bugs. Critical missing features, dubious features, and bugs are documented, filed and prioritized. Contributors are advised to turn their heads to the quality of the software and its documentation. The development becomes mainly bug-fixing oriented and a set of norms and tools guide this last product-stabilization phase[17]. Between the last milestone and the publication of the first release candidate, contributors are incited to stop adding features and concentrate on bug fixes. Only changes that fix bugs and do not introduce new features should be allowed to enter the master branch during this period. Any change proposed for the master branch should at least reference one bug on the bug tracking system. Once all the release-critical bugs are fixed, OpenStack produces the first release candidate for that project

---

[13] For more information on the OpenStack code-review activities, see http://docs.openstack.org/infra/manual/developers.html#code-review.

[14] See https://launchpad.net/ for more information on the adopted software collaboration platform as well as https://launchpad.net/openstack for more information on how OpenStack uses it.

[15] See http://docs.openstack.org/infra/jenkins-job-builder/ for more information on continuous upstream unit testing as well as http://docs.openstack.org/infra/zuul/ and http://docs.openstack.org/developer/tempest/ for more information on continuous upstream integration testing across interrelated projects and repositories.

[16] See http://docs.openstack.org/project-team-guide/release-management.html for more information on the release cycles.

[17] See https://wiki.openstack.org/wiki/BugTriage and https://wiki.openstack.org/wiki/Bugs for more information on bug-fixing activities.

(named RC1). Across this last stage, the repository version control system (i.e., Git) plays an important role in alleviating the interruption caused by the freezes — freeze applies only to the stable branch so that developers can continue their work on other the development branches (i.e., the trunk). New features should be committed to other branches, discussed at the 'planning stage', and merged into the stable branch at the next 'implementation stage'.

Table 1. The three feature freezes of OpenStack

Freeze	Description
FeatureFreeze	Project teams are requested to stop merging code adding new features, new dependencies, new configuration options, database schema changes, changes in strings ... all things that make the work of packagers, documenters or testers more difficult
SoftStringFreeze	After the FeatureFreeze, translators start to translate the strings. To aid their work, any changed of existing strings is avoided, as this will invalidate some of their translation work. New strings are allowed for things like new log messages, as in many cases leaving those strings untranslated is better than not having any message at all
HardStringFreezee	10 days after the SoftStringFreeze, any string changes after RC1 should be discussed with the translation team

The OpenStack release team is empowered during this last phase. It creates a `stable/*` branch from the current state of the *master branch* and uses access control list (ACL) mechanisms to introduces any new release-critical fix discovered until the release day. In other words, further changes at this stage require permission from the release team – in the words of OpenStack, they will be treated as feature freeze exceptions (FFE). Between the RC1 and the final release, OpenStack looks for regression and integration issues. RC1 may be used *as is* for the final release unless new release-critical issues are found that warrant an RC respinning. If this happens, a new milestone will be open (RC2), with bugs attached to it. Those RC bug fixes need to be merged in the *master branch* before they are allowed to land in the `stable/*` branch. Once all release-critical bugs are fixed, the new RC is published. This process is repeated as many times as necessary before the final release. As it gets closer to the final release date, to avoid introducing last-minute regressions, the release team limits the number of changes and their impact: only extremely critical and non-invasive bug fixes can get merged. All the other bugs are documented as known issues in the Release Notes instead.

On the release day, the last published Release Candidate of each integrated project is collected and the result is published collectively as the OpenStack release for this cycle. OpenStack should by then be stable enough for real industrial deployments. But once the version is released, a new cycle will commence within OpenStack; the *master branch* switches to the next development cycle, new features can be freely merged again, and the process starts again. After the release and a period of much stress that required much coordination, most of the community shifts again to the 'planning stage' and many will attend the Design Summit. A new branch was opened already to accommodate new developments. Even so, the launched release needs to be maintained and further stabilized until its end of life (EOL) when it is no longer officially supported by the community. OpenStack might release "bugfix updates" on top of previously announced releases with fixed bugs and resolved security issues, actions that might distract developers working on newer stuff.

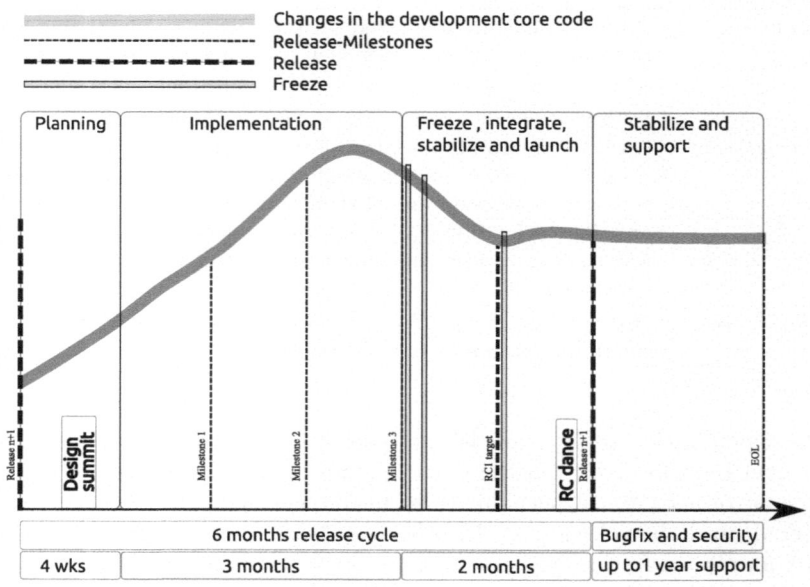

Fig. 1. Overview of the OpenStack standard release cycles.

The overall release management process, as illustrated in Fig. 1, follows a 'plan, implement, freeze, stabilize and launch' cycle between releases. Each release is then re-stabilized with *a posteriori* release-updates to fix bugs and security issues. Nevertheless, the process described so far is just the most recurrent pattern within OpenStack – the default *modus operandi*. The described process is actually quite open and liberal. It acts as a 'recommendation' for the different teams so that whatever is developed is then later more smoothly integrated, stabilized and released in a coordinated fashion.

Since the October 2016 (affecting the 'Newton' release), OpenStack actually recommends its project teams to opt from four different release management models: *Common cycle with development milestones*, *Common cycle with intermediary releases*, *Trailing the common cycle* and *Independent release model* as following described. Most of this models follow a common six-month development cycle, some release intermediary releases within the six-months cycle and others are allowed to manage their own release strategy[18].

Common cycle with development milestones. The official and default time-based model followed by most teams. It results in a single release at the end of the development cycle and includes three development milestones (as in Fig. 1).

Common cycle with intermediary releases. For project teams which want to do a formal release more often, but still want to coordinate a release at the end of the cycle from which to maintain a stable branch. Recommended for libraries, and to more stable components which add a limited set of new features and do not plan to go through large architectural changes.

Trailing the common cycle. For project teams that rely on the completeness of other components (e.g., packaging, translation, and UI testing) and may not publish their final release at the same time the other projects. For example, teams packaging and deploying OpenStack components need the final releases of many other components to be available before they can run their own final tests. Cycle-trailing project teams are given an extra two weeks after the official release date to request the publication of their own releases. They may otherwise use intermediary releases or development milestones.

Independent release model. For project teams that do not benefit from a coordinated release or from stable branches. They may opt to follow a completely independent release model. Suitable for instance for the OpenStack own infrastructural systems (e.g., the ones supporting upstream testing and integration) as well for components with little dependence on the overall Openstack core architecture.

"We still have a coordinated release at the end of the six months for projects that are willing to those deadlines and milestones, but the main change is that we will move from managing most of them to refine processes and tools for each project to be able to produce those releases easier. The development cycle will still be using a six months development cycle, even if some projects might do intermediary releases where it makes sense, but will still organize almost everything under a six months development cycle between design summits." — Thierry Carrez, 15 May 2015[19]

6 Discussion

Prior work had already inquired on OpenStack release management issues (see [16, pp. 10–11] for work pointing up collaboration issues and [10, pp. 80–82] for work pointing up communication issues). However and to the best of our

---

[18] See http://docs.openstack.org/project-team-guide/release-management.html for the details of each release management model.

[19] Transcribed from video, see [6:34–7:00] https://www.openstack.org/summit/vancouver-2015/summit-videos/presentation/the-big-tent-a-look-at-the-new-openstack-projects-governance.

knowledge, this is the first paper that is explicitly aimed at describing how a large and complex open-source software ecosystem implemented a liberal time-based release strategy. As this point, we are not attempting to evaluate, appraise or compare it — we are just describing it. Future research could contrast the processual practices of release management across multiple cases (see [5,10]). Digital trace data generated by the upstream integration processes, the source-code repository and the bug tracker could be used to triangulate the authenticity of the conceptual release management models.

Our results confirm the pivotal role of freezes within the release management process (cf. [13,24]). In our case, the use of freezes forces developers that want to see their work in the next release to make three big shifts in the focus of the production: (1) from the individual component level to the overall integration as a whole, (2) from developing new features to ensuring its landing, integration and stabilization, and (3) from individual work, or collaboration within smaller teams, to coordination across the overall community.

Finally, in the light of prior work, the liberal release management process of OpenStack can be considered a hybrid of feature-based and time-based release management (see [22, pp. 23]). This as OpenStack encourages regular releases (every six months) but also attempts to plan the introduction of new features at each regular release. Leaders of each project team choose a set of features for the next release at the planning stage. However, if these features are not stable enough to be included in the next release, they will be left out by the cross-project release management team. As pointed out recently, release management constrains the evolution of the integrated whole [10, p. 4].

7 Conclusion

OpenStack implemented a time-based release strategy on a six-month release cycle. Each cycle comprehended a 'planning stage', an 'implementation stage' and 'freeze, stabilize and launch' stage. At the middle of each release cycle, the community relies upon three freezes (i.e., "FeatureFreeze", "SoftStringFreeze" and "HardStringFreezee") that encourages developers to change their production focus from the development of components to the overall upstream integration and stabilization of components as a whole — thus affecting much the work and communication patterns of the community. The implemented release cycle is quite liberal (i.e., flexible to adaptation), in particular contexts, different project teams across the community are allowed adapt the 'default' six months release cycle. Moreover, the implemented release management process exhibits hybrid characteristics of both feature-based and time-based release management strategies as the process is both feature and time oriented.

In the case of large and complex open-source software ecosystem, the implementation of a time-based release strategy, as a complex process that intertwines with many other software development processes, requires the support of a well suited organizational design as much coordination is needed. Moreover, the process constrains the evolution of integrated core and depends heavily on many software tools that make it possible (e.g., version control, revision control, continuous upstream integration, continuous upstream testing, and configuration management). Besides its acknowledged benefits, the implementation of a time-based release strategy is a challenging cooperative task involving multiple people and technology.

References

1. Raymond, E.: The Cathedral and the Bazaar. Knowl. Technol. Policy **12**(3), 23–49 (1999)
2. Raymond, E.: The Cathedral & the Bazaar: Musings on Linux and Open Source by an Accidental Revolutionary. O'Reilly Media, Sebastopol (2001)
3. Zhao, L., Elbaum, S.: A survey on quality related activities in open source. SIGSOFT Softw. Eng. Notes **25**(3), 54–57 (2000)
4. Aberdour, M.: Achieving quality in open-source software. IEEE Softw. **24**(1), 58–64 (2007)
5. Michlmayr, M., Fitzgerald, B., Stol, K.J.: Why and how should open source projects adopt time-based releases? IEEE Softw. **32**(2), 55–63 (2015)
6. Barqawi, N., Syed, K., Mathiassen, L.: Applying service-dominant logic to recurrent release of software: an action research study. J. Bus. Ind. Market. **31**(7), 928–940 (2016)
7. Khomh, F., Adams, B., Dhaliwal, T., Zou, Y.: Understanding the impact of rapid releases on software quality. Empir. Softw. Eng. **20**(2), 336–373 (2015)
8. Choudhary, V., Zhang, Z.: Research note-patching the cloud: the impact of saas on patching strategy and the timing of software release. Inf. Syst. Res. **26**(4), 845–858 (2015)
9. Wright, H.K., Perry, D.E.: Release engineering practices and pitfalls. In: 2012 34th International Conference on Software Engineering (ICSE). pp. 1281–1284, June 2012
10. Poo-Caamaño, G.: Release management in free and open source software ecosystems. Ph.D. thesis, University of Victoria, Canada (2016)
11. O'Reilly, T.: Lessons from open-source software development. Commun. ACM **42**(4), 32–37 (1999)
12. Spinellis, D., Szyperski, C.: How is open source affecting software development? IEEE Softw. **21**(1), 28 (2004)
13. Fitzgerald, B.: Open source software: lessons from and for software engineering. Computer **44**(10), 25–30 (2011)
14. Wuhib, F., Stadler, R., Lindgren, H.: Dynamic resource allocation with management objectives-implementation for an openstack cloud. In: 2012 8th International Conference on Network and Service Management (CNSM) and 2012 Workshop on Systems Virtualiztion Management (SVM), pp. 309–315. IEEE (2012)
15. Corradi, A., Fanelli, M., Foschini, L.: VM consolidation: a real case based on openstack cloud. Futur. Gener. Comput. Syst. **32**, 118–127 (2014)
16. Teixeira, J., Robles, G., González-Barahona, J.M.: Lessons learned from applying social network analysis on an industrial free/libre/open source software ecosystem. J. Internet Serv. Appl. **6**(1), 14 (2015)
17. Ge, X., Liu, Y., Du, D.H., Zhang, L., Guan, H., Chen, J., Zhao, Y., Hu, X.: OpenANFV: Accelerating network function virtualization with a consolidated framework in openstack. ACM SIGCOMM Comput. Commun. Rev. **44**(4), 353–354 (2015)

18. Malik, A., Ahmed, J., Qadir, J., Ilyas, M.U.: A measurement study of open source SDN layers in openstack under network perturbation. Comput. Commun. (2017)
19. Rossi, B., Russo, B., Succi, G.: Analysis of open source software development iterations by means of burst detection techniques. In: Boldyreff, C., Crowston, K., Lundell, B., Wasserman, A.I. (eds.) OSS 2009. IFIPAICT, vol. 299, pp. 83–93. Springer, Heidelberg (2009)
20. Wiggins, A., Howison, J., Crowston, K.: Heartbeat: measuring active user base and potential user interest in FLOSS projects. In: Boldyreff, C., Crowston, K., Lundell, B., Wasserman, A.I. (eds.) OSS 2009. IFIPAICT, vol. 299, pp. 94–104. Springer, Heidelberg (2009)
21. Michlmayr, M.: Quality improvement in volunteer free and open source software projects - exploring the impact of release management. Ph.D. thesis, University of Cambridge (2007)
22. Wright, H.K.: Release engineering processes, their faults and failures. Ph.D. thesis, University of Texas (2012)
23. Martinez-Romo, J., Robles, G., Gonzalez-Barahona, J.M., Ortuño-Perez, M.: Using social network analysis techniques to study collaboration between a floss community and a company. In: Russo, B., Damiani, E., Hissam, S., Lundell, B., Succi, G. (eds.) OSS 2008. IFIPAICT, vol. 275, pp. 171–186. Springer, Boston (2008)
24. Anand, A., Bhatt, N., Aggrawal, D., Papic, L.: Software reliability modeling with impact of beta testing on release decision. In: Ram, M., Davim, J.P. (eds.) Advances in Reliability and System Engineering. Management and Industrial Engineering, pp. 121–138. Springer, Cham (2017)
25. Mesbah, A., Van Deursen, A.: Invariant-based automatic testing of AJAX user interfaces. In: IEEE 31st International Conference on Software Engineering, 2009. ICSE 2009, pp. 210–220. IEEE (2009)
26. Artzi, S., Dolby, J., Jensen, S.H., Moller, A., Tip, F.: A framework for automated testing of Javascript web applications. In: 2011 33rd International Conference on Software Engineering (ICSE), pp. 571–580. IEEE (2011)
27. Teixeira, J., Mian, S., Hytti, U.: Cooperation among competitors in the open-source arena: the case of openstack. In: Proceedings of the International Conference on Information Systems (ICIS 2016). Association for Information Systems (2016)
28. Runeson, P., Höst, M.: Guidelines for conducting and reporting case study research in software engineering. Empir. Softw. Eng. **14**(2), 131–164 (2008)
29. Easterbrook, S., Singer, J., Storey, M.A., Damian, D.: Selecting empirical methods for software engineering research. In: Shull, F., Singer, J., Sjøberg, D.I.K. (eds.) Guide to Advanced Empirical Software Engineering, pp. 285–311. Springer, London (2008)
30. Yin, R.K.: Applications of Case Study Research. Sage, London (2011)
31. Eisenhardt, K.M.: Building theories from case study research. Acad. Manag. Rev. **14**(4), 532–550 (1989)
32. Flynn, B.B., Sakakibara, S., Schroeder, R.G., Bates, K.A., Flynn, E.J.: Empirical research methods in operations management. J. Oper. Manag. **9**(2), 250–284 (1990)
33. Kozinets, R.V.: The field behind the screen: using netnography for marketing research in online communities. J. Market. Res. **39**, 61–72 (2002)
34. Kozinets, R.V.: Netnography: Doing Ethnographic Research Online. Sage Publications Limited, London (2009)
35. Yin, R.: Case Study Research: Design and Methods. Applied Social Research Methods Series. Sage Publications, London (1994)

Open Access This chapter is licensed under the terms of the Creative Commons Attribution 4.0 International License (http://creativecommons.org/licenses/by/4.0/), which permits use, sharing, adaptation, distribution and reproduction in any medium or format, as long as you give appropriate credit to the original author(s) and the source, provide a link to the Creative Commons license and indicate if changes were made.

The images or other third party material in this chapter are included in the chapter's Creative Commons license, unless indicated otherwise in a credit line to the material. If material is not included in the chapter's Creative Commons license and your intended use is not permitted by statutory regulation or exceeds the permitted use, you will need to obtain permission directly from the copyright holder.

Technical Lag in Software Compilations: Measuring How Outdated a Software Deployment Is

Jesus M. Gonzalez-Barahona[1], Paul Sherwood[2], Gregorio Robles[1(✉)], and Daniel Izquierdo[3]

[1] Universidad Rey Juan Carlos, Madrid, Spain
grex@gsyc.urjc.es
[2] Codethink, Manchester, UK
[3] Bitergia, Madrid, Spain

Abstract. Large software compilations based on free, open source software (FOSS) packages are the basis for many software systems. When they are deployed in production, specific versions of the packages in the compilation are selected for installation. Over time, those versions become outdated with respect to the *upstream* software from which they are produced, and from the components available in the compilations as well. The fact that deployed components are outdated is not a problem in itself, but there is a price to pay for not being "as much updated as reasonable". This includes bug fixes and new features that could, at least potentially, be interesting for the deployed system. Therefore, a balance has to be maintained between "being up-to-date" and "keeping the good old working versions". This paper proposes a theoretical model (the "technical lag") for measuring how outdated a system is, with the aim of assisting in the decisions about upgrading in production. The paper explores several ways in which technical lag can be implemented, depending on requirements. As an illustration, it presents as well some specific cases in which the evolution of technical lag is computed.

1 From Upstream to Deployment

Many production systems are deployed as collections of FOSS (free, open source software) components. All of them are based on the software produced by the corresponding FOSS projects. And usually, as time passes, those projects deliver new releases with more functionality, more fixed bugs, and in many cases, more overall stability and performance [1]. We will use the term "upstream project" for referring to the project originally producing a FOSS component. Upstream projects release, from time to time, versions of the FOSS components they produce and maintain. This release may be continuous, each time a change is done to the code, or discrete, at specific points in time, when the project considers it convenient [2]. In fact, many projects release in both ways: they release continuously in their source code management system (one release per commit), but they also offer "official" tagged discrete releases. In any case, we will consider the released component as the "upstream released package".

But it is unusual that upstream packages are directly deployed in production systems. Instead of that, packages coming from software compilations, usually referred to as "distributions", are used for deployment. We will refer to the packages released as a part of a software compilation as "distribution packages" (to avoid using "compilation packages", which could be easily mistaken for "package produced as the result of compiling some software"). Distribution packages are produced by adapting upstream packages to the policies and mechanisms defined by the software compilation. That usually makes the deployment of components easier, more coordinated with other components, and in general more uniform. This adaption usually includes changes to the code, with respect to upstream. For example, Debian packages include certain files with information on how to build (produce a binary version from the source code) and install the package, and may include changes to improve or adapt it to the distribution [3].

We propose the following model for the process from the production of a FOSS component to its deployment in production:

- The upstream project produces an upstream package. This will be a new upstream release of the FOSS component. This can be just a commit in a Git repository, or a curated official tagged release.
- That new upstream package is used by a software compilation as the basis for a new release of their corresponding distribution package. For producing it, upstream code is used, maybe with some patches applied, and some extra files.
- Deployers use a certain release of the distribution package to deploy the FOSS component in production.

A real deployment may include hundreds or thousands of FOSS components, each corresponding to a certain release of the corresponding upstream package.

This model can be applied to deployments in many scenarios, such as: a collection of Debian packages in a virtual machine or container, providing some cloud-based service; a collection of JavaScript libraries used by a web app, installed from npm.org; or a collection of Python packages (or Ruby gems) installed in a certain machine to run a Python (or Ruby) program; a certain Yocto-based distribution deployed in a certain car (Yocto is a Linux-based distribution oriented towards embedded systems); etc.

2 Technical Debt and Technical Lag

Each deployment scenario has different requirements with respect to their "ideal" relationship with upstream. But in all cases, if no updating action is performed, they stay static, "frozen in the past", while upstream evolves, fixing bugs and adding new functionality. The same happens with software compilations with respect to upstream, if they do not release new updated packages for their components.

Depending on the requirements of the final system, and the resources to maintain it, lags of deployed systems with respect to their software compilations, and to the latest upstream packages, can be larger or shorter. For example, in deployments with a large number of components and high stability requirements, updating even a single new package can be a challenge: the whole system has to be tested, since the updated package could break something, specially if it is a dependency to many other packages [4]. Even if upstream developers and compilation maintainers did their own thoughtful testing, some integration bug could be triggered when deployed. A significant amount of effort has to be devoted to upgrading, and tracking the behavior of the system after the upgrade. Besides, in some cases the new version could break some assumption about how it works, affecting the overall functionality or performance. Therefore, every new version has to be carefully examined before it can be deployed.

As time passes, if deployed components are not upgraded, the system misses more and more new functionality and bug fixes: it is not "as good as it could be". This situation is akin to the one described as "technical debt" for software development. The metaphor of "technical debt" introduced in 1992, tries to capture the problems caused for not writing the best possible code, but code that could (and should) be improved later on [5]. The difference between code "as it should be" and code "as it is" is a kind of debt for the developing team. If technical debt increases, code becomes more difficult to maintain. A similar concept is "design debt", which translates the concept to the design of software components [6].

In the case we are considering in this paper, we are not exactly in a technical debt scenario, although the concept could be easily extended to include it. The main differences are:

– The concept does not try to capture that deployment is not done "as it should be done". On the contrary, the system "degrades" just with the passing of time, and not because some code needed to be improved when deployed.
– Software development is not really involved, since it only happens upstream, and to a certain extent, in software compilations. Only deployment decisions are considered.
– The metaphor of the debt is difficult to understand in this case, since it is not some "debt" being acquired at some spot, which has to be returned later. Our case could be more comparable to a tax, paid for not being updated, in the form of less functionality and more bugs that we could have if updating.

To recognize the differences, we are coining a new term, "technical lag", which refers to the increasing lag between upstream development and the deployed system if no corrective actions are taken. Deployers need to balance the technical lag their systems acquire as time passes, with the effort and problems caused by upgrading activities.

3   Computing Technical Lag for a Deployment

When measuring technical lag, the first problem is to decide what is the "gold standard" with which to compare. Depending on requirements and needs, the comparison may focus on stability, functionality, performance, or something else.

For example, if there is interest in calculating the technical lag of a Debian-based distribution, with a specific interest in stability, we need to find the standard for stability for Debian-based distributions. One choice could be Debian *stable* (the Debian release which is currently considered "stable"[1]). In a different case, a system could be interested in being as much up-to-date as possible with respect to upstream, because they are interested in having as much functionality and bugs fixed as possible. In this case, the standard would be the latest checkout for each upstream package.

Once the gold standard is defined, we still need to find out the function to compute the lag between the component in the standard compilation and the deployed component. For example, if the focus is on security, the lag function could be the number of security issues fixed in the standard which have not been fixed in the deployed system. If the focus is functionality, the function could be the number of features implemented in the standard which have not been implemented in the deployed component. Some other interesting lag functions could be the differences in lines of source code between standard and deployed components, or the number of commits of difference between them, if both cases correspond to upstream checkouts.

Therefore, when defining the technical lag for a system, it is not enough to just define the deployment to consider. The standard to compare (or the requirements of the ideal deployment) and the function to calculate the lag between versions of the component need to be defined as well.

4   Formal Definition of Technical Lag

Assume we have a **deployment** D composed of a set of certain **components** C, deployed as packages of a certain software collection, and a certain **standard distribution** S, composed by the same set of components, but packaged for that distribution. We denote d_i as a package in distribution D corresponding to component i, while s_i denotes a package in the standard distribution S corresponding to the same component i:

$$D = \{d_i : i \in C\} \quad S = \{s_i : i \in C\} \tag{1}$$

We define the **lag function for packages** corresponding to a component, $Lag(d_i, s_i)$, as the function computing the lag between packages $d_i \in D$ and $s_i \in S$, for a given component $i \in C$. Lag is defined for all pairs (d_i, s_i), as long as s_i is more up-to-date than d_i, and zero in other cases. Lag has the

---

[1] See https://www.debian.org/releases/ for a description of the different Debian releases.

following properties, which result in the technical lag of a deployment being a non-negative real number. For *Lag* to be useful, it should fulfill the "lagging condition": computing a larger value for distribution packages "lagging behind". That is, the more distant d_i is from s_i, for some lag requirements, the larger $Lag(d_i, s_i)$ should be.

We define the **lag aggregation function**, *LagAgg*, as the function used to aggregate the package lags for a set of components.

Finally, we define the **technical lag** for the deployment D with respect to the standard distribution S as the aggregation of the lags between the deployed and the standard distribution packages:

$$TechLag(D, S) = LagAgg(Lag(d_i, s_i) \forall i \in C) \qquad (2)$$

When the aggregation function is summation, technical lag is defined as:

$$TechLag(D, S) = \sum_{i \in C} Lag(d_i, s_i) \qquad (3)$$

This definition captures how technical lag depends on:

- the distribution selected as the standard distribution to compare
- the function used to calculate the lag for each of the components in the deployment
- the aggregation function for the lags of the deployed components

5   Calculating Lag Between Packages

After the formal definition of the concept, this section will illustrate with an example how the lag can be computed for a certain component, how results differ depending on the distribution selected as the gold standard, and how they however make sense from a practical point of view. For simplicity, we will work with packages for which upstream is working openly in a Git repository. This allows us to model upstream as following a continuous release process, with each commit in the master branch of the Git repository being a release.

We selected components packaged for Debian, because it is a very popular distribution, basis for many other popular distributions, such as Ubuntu. It is common to find Debian or Ubuntu packages in real deployments, both of cloud and embedded systems, to mention just two domain areas. Debian provides the Debian Snapshot Archive[2], which offers for each component a very complete collection of all packages that have been in Debian distributions in the past. This collection includes not only packages in Debian stable releases, but also in Debian unstable and Debian testing, that –because of their nature– may include many interim versions. For each package in the Debian Snapshot archive, its version tag and the date of its release are available. This allows for easy plotting of the evolution of the technical lag of those packages, either just over time, or grouping by releases, as will be shown in the figures in this section.

---

[2] http://snapshot.debian.org/.

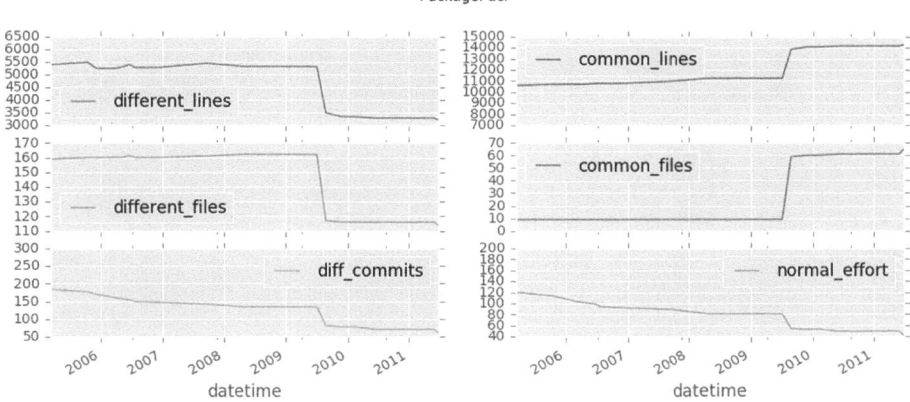

Fig. 1. Lag functions applied to Debian acl package releases, by release date

The selected illustrative cases are the acl and Git packages. In the case of acl, we have found 24 packages in the Debian archive (released from 2005 to 2012), while for Git we have found 192 (from 2005 to 2016). Only since 2010 Debian Git packages correspond to the "current" Git package, the popular source code management system. Before 2010, there were 7 packages which corresponded to GNU Interactive Tools, a set of tools for extending the shell. Therefore, only data since 2010 is really relevant, and we consider 185 Debian Git packages.

To estimate the technical lag of each Debian package, we will assume that it is deployed as such, and compared with the current upstream master HEAD checkout at the time of the study (Oct. 2016). Therefore, following the notation in the previous section: d_i is each of the Debian packages considered; s_i is the latest upstream continuous release (defined as the HEAD of the master branch in the upstream Git repository); and *LagAgg* is summation.

As *Lag*, we computed four different functions, to offer different lagging criteria[3]:

- different_lines and different_files: number of different lines or files, including those that are present only in d_i or s_i.
- diff_commits: number of commits, following the master branch of the upstream Git repository, needed to go from the most likely upstream commit corresponding to d_i to the commit corresponding to s_i.
- normal_effort: total normalized effort for the commits identified when computing diff_commits. We define normalized effort (in days) for an author as the number of days with at least one commit between the dates corresponding to two commits in the master branch. We define total normalized effort (in days) as the sum of normalized effort for all the authors active during the period between two commits.

---

[3] For computing different and common lines and files, we used the Python3 *difflib* module.

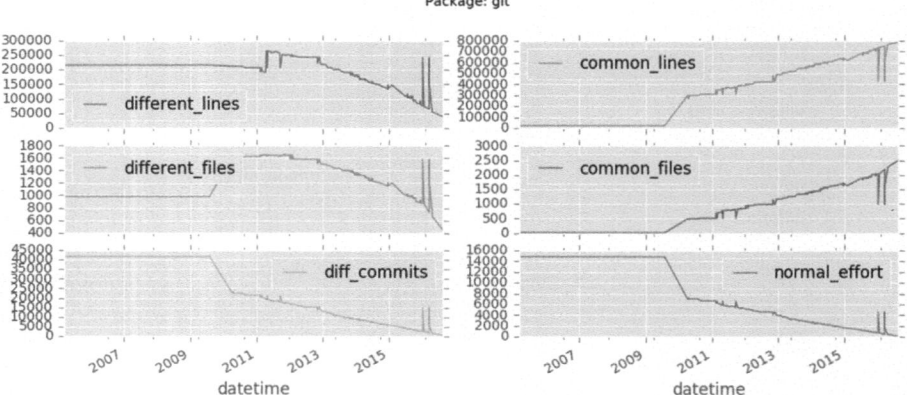

Fig. 2. Lag functions applied to Debian Git package releases, by release date

The first two lag functions capture how different is the deployed component is from the component in the standard distribution (in our case, the most recent commit upstream). The last two functions capture how many changes (or, to some extent, effort in changing) were applied to the component in the standard distribution since the upstream release used to build the deployed package.

To provide some context, we computed as well common_lines and common_files, which is the number of lines an files in common between D_i and C_i (lines exactly the same). Those are not really *Lag* functions, since they do not fulfill the lagging condition: both grew larger when d_i and s_i were closer.

Figures 1 and 2 show the evolution of the lag over time, considering the release time of Debian packages. Each chart shows the value of lag (using one of the lag functions mentioned above) for the release time of each Debian package. For all the four "Lag" functions, it can be seen that they are almost monotonically decreasing over time, clearly converging to zero as time approaches the release time of s_i (the rightmost values). For acl, there is a clear step in 2009, which corresponds to major changes in the component, as will be shown later. For Git the change around 2010 is due to the different packages being tracked (see above, that means that only the data from 2010 onwards is really meaningful). After that point there are some spikes and steps, notably two large spikes in late 2015 and early 2016. But in general, the trend in all charts is clearly decreasingly monotonic.

Figures 3 and 4 are more revealing, because they have into account two common practices in Debian: labeling package releases (in part) with upstream version tags, and releasing slightly modified versions for stable distributions.

The first is observed by the different colors and lines in the charts: all Debian packages corresponding to the same major release have been depicted in the same color, and linked with lines. Now, when we look at the charts for acl in Fig. 3, we see how the step in 2009 corresponds to a change in version (from pink to red), which did a major refactoring of the code. That is clearly appreciated in the

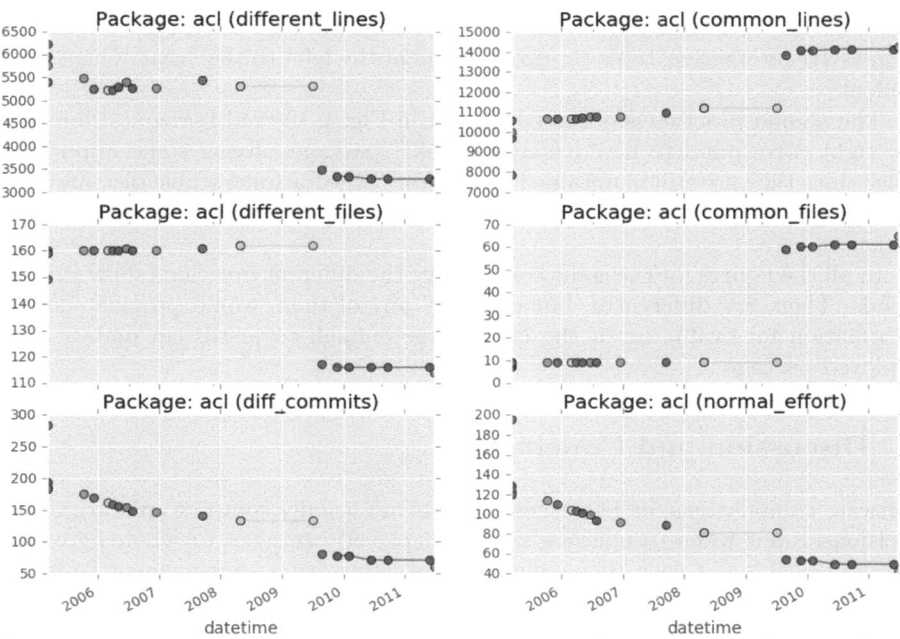

Fig. 3. Lag functions applied to all releases of the Debian acl package, by release date, organized by version (Color figure online)

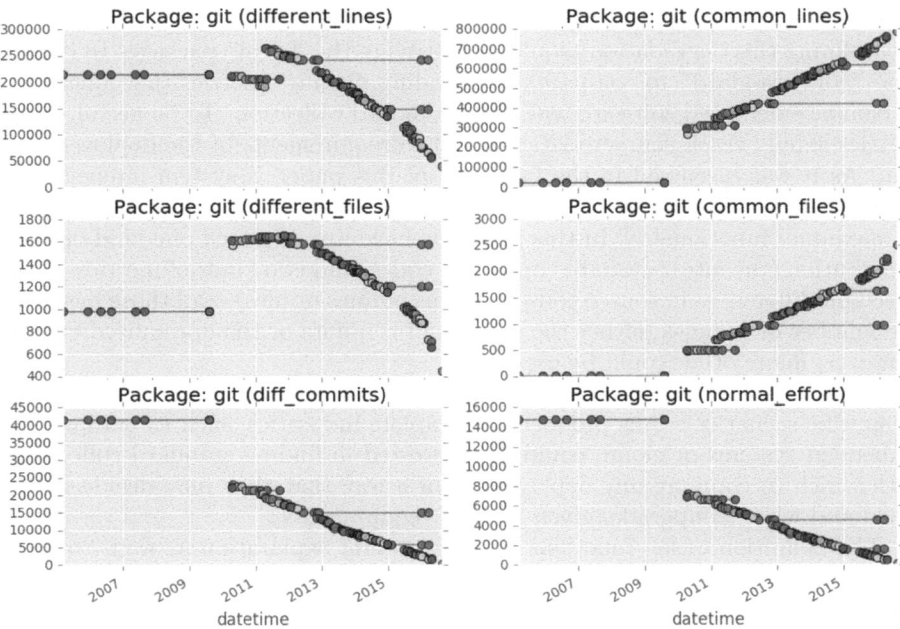

Fig. 4. Lag functions applied to all releases of the Debian Git package, by release date, organized by version (Color figure online)

functions showing common and different lines. In the case of Git, the transition from GNU Interactive Tools (horizontal line in the left) to the "real" Git is now evident.

The second practice is observed for Git in Fig. 4: the red horizontal lines on the right correspond to new releases of "old" packages, fixing some important bugs, since they are still maintained after a long time for some stable distribution. That helps to explain the spikes we saw in Fig. 2: those d_i are really "out of order" packages.

In all the figures for the same component, the different functions show similar trends. There are differences, but probably any of them would provide enough information for evaluating if the lag is large enough to justify an update of a deployed package.

6 Discussion and Conclusions

Software compilations for FOSS components are usually complex and large, and decisions about when to upgrade specific deployed packages, or whole deployed distributions, is not easy. The complexity of dependency management [7–9], or their significant evolution over time [3] are reasons both to delay upgrading (because of the potential problems), and to consider it (because of the added functionality and improved code). The same way that the complexity in dependencies, or the some parameters of their evolution [10] can be measured, we are exploring the concept of technical lag to measure their "degradation" over time with respect to some "ideal" gold standard.

Defining this degradation requires identifying the "ideal" packages to deploy (the "gold standard" to compare), and finding distance metrics (lag functions) to compare deployed software with that standard collection. To be useful, these metrics should track characteristics linked to requirements of the deployed system. As it was discussed in the first part of this paper, a system interested in stability may define very different metrics and gold standard than one interested in maximum functionality. In this paper we have just explored one kind of ideal distribution (the latest available upstream code), and two kinds of metrics: those based on differences in source code (in terms of lines or files), and those based on the number of changes (either the number of commits or the normalized effort). However, many other could be explored.

In particular, the exploration of criteria to define "gold standards" for general or specific scenarios seems promising. Complete industries, such as automotive, embedded systems or cloud, could be interested in finding standard collections with which to compare any deployment, in a way that they may decide better when and what to upgrade, given a set of requirements.

The definition of lag functions requires careful exploration as well. Some of them may be difficult, because the needed information may be heterogeneous, and distributed. But some seem feasible: the number of bugs fixed, or security advisories addressed; the number of new features implemented; improvements in performance, etc. (obviously, when there are ways of collecting that information).

This makes us think that there is a lot of work to do in this area, and that we have not even collected all the low hanging fruits.

In this paper, we have considered that distribution packages are directly deployed in production, and therefore make no real difference between the packages in a distribution, and those packages when deployed. In the real world, packages may be deployed with some differences with respect to the distribution packages used. For example, some patches could be applied to fix known bugs. However, this does not make the model less general: the patched packages can be modeled as a new distribution, based on the "original" one, and all the above considerations will apply.

As a kind of a conclusion, we propose technical lag as useful concept to deal with large FOSS deployments. As real-world systems are increasingly built by assembling large collections of FOSS components, it is evident the need of techniques for managing their complexity. In some areas, such as dependency management or architectural evolution, research has been producing results for many years. But there is little evidence that may help in the system-wide maintenance procedures, including those relatively easy, such as when and what to upgrade. With this paper we propose a new line of research, trying to provide support practitioners in may fields of the industry.

Although we are focused on FOSS compilations, it is interesting to notice that the concept of technical lag can in theory be extended to non-FOSS components. However, in practical terms that may be difficult, except if source code and other related information needed to estimate lag is present. This can be the case in some special cases, such as when a company deploys systems composed by a mix of FOSS and proprietary components, but it has access to all the needed information for proprietary ones.

Acknowledgments and Reproduction Package. The work of Jesus Gonzalez-Barahona and Gregorio Robles has been funded in part by the Spanish Gov. under SobreVision (TIN2014-59400-R), and by the European Commission, under Seneca, H2020 Program (H2020-MSCA-ITN-2014-642954). The research described in this paper was started thanks to a contract funded by Codethink.

All the code and data needed to reproduce the results in this package is available from a GitHub repository (https://github.com/jgbarah/techlag/) (checkout as of December 2016).

References

1. German, D.M.: Using software distributions to understand the relationship among free and open source software projects. In: Proceedings of the Fourth International Workshop on Mining Software Repositories, p. 24. IEEE Computer Society (2007)
2. Michlmayr, M., Fitzgerald, B., Stol, K.: Why and how should open source projects adopt time-based releases? IEEE Softw. **32**(2), 55–63 (2015)
3. González-Barahona, J.M., Robles, G., Michlmayr, M., Amor, J.J., Germán, D.M.: Macro-level software evolution: a case study of a large software compilation. Empir. Softw. Eng. **14**(3), 262–285 (2009)

4. Claes, M., Mens, T., Di Cosmo, R., Vouillon, J.: A historical analysis of Debian package incompatibilities. In: IEEE/ACM 12th Working Conference on Mining Software Repositories (MSR), pp. 212–223. IEEE (2015)
5. Cunningham, W.: The Wycash portfolio management system. In: Addendum to the Proceedings on Object-Oriented Programming Systems, Languages, and Applications (Addendum), OOPSLA 1992, pp. 29–30. ACM, New York (1992)
6. Kerievsky, J.: Refactoring to Patterns. Addison-Wesley Professional, Reading (2004)
7. Mancinelli, F., Boender, J., Cosmo, R.D., Vouillon, J., Durak, B., Leroy, X., Treinen, R.: Managing the complexity of large free and open source package-based software distributions. In: 21st IEEE/ACM International Conference on Automated Software Engineering (ASE 2006), 18–22 September 2006, Tokyo, pp. 199–208. IEEE Computer Society (2006)
8. Wermelinger, M., Yu, Y.: Analyzing the evolution of eclipse plugins. In: Proceedings of the 2008 International Working Conference on Mining Software Repositories, MSR 2008 (Co-located with ICSE), Leipzig, 10–11 May 2008, pp. 133–136 (2008)
9. Bavota, G., Canfora, G., Penta, M.D., Oliveto, R., Panichella, S.: How the apache community upgrades dependencies: an evolutionary study. Empir. Softw. Eng. **20**(5), 1275–1317 (2015)
10. Gala-Pérez, S., Robles, G., González-Barahona, J.M., Herraiz, I.: Intensive metrics for the study of the evolution of open source projects case studies from apache software foundation projects. In: Proceedings of the 10th Working Conference on Mining Software Repositories, MSR 2013, San Francisco, 18-19 May 2013, pp. 159–168 (2013)

Open Access This chapter is licensed under the terms of the Creative Commons Attribution 4.0 International License (http://creativecommons.org/licenses/by/4.0/), which permits use, sharing, adaptation, distribution and reproduction in any medium or format, as long as you give appropriate credit to the original author(s) and the source, provide a link to the Creative Commons license and indicate if changes were made.

The images or other third party material in this chapter are included in the chapter's Creative Commons license, unless indicated otherwise in a credit line to the material. If material is not included in the chapter's Creative Commons license and your intended use is not permitted by statutory regulation or exceeds the permitted use, you will need to obtain permission directly from the copyright holder.

OSSpal: Finding and Evaluating Open Source Software

Anthony I. Wasserman[✉], Xianzheng Guo, Blake McMillian, Kai Qian,
Ming-Yu Wei, and Qian Xu

Carnegie Mellon University, Silicon Valley, Moffett Field, CA 94035, USA
{tonyw,blake.mcmillian,ming.yu.wei,qian.xu}@sv.cmu.edu,
{xianzheg,kaiq}@andrew.cmu.edu

Abstract. This paper describes the OSSpal project, which is aimed at helping companies, government agencies, and other organizations find high quality free and open source software (FOSS) that meets their needs. OSSpal is a successor to the Business Readiness Rating (BRR), combining quantitative and qualitative evaluation measures for software in various categories. Instead of a purely numeric calculated score OSSpal adds curation of high-quality FOSS projects and individual user reviews of these criteria. Unlike the BRR project, for which there was no automated support, OSSpal has an operational, publicly available website where users may search by project name or category, and enter ratings and reviews for projects.

Keywords: Open source software · Software evaluation · Open source forges · Software metrics · FOSS · FLOSS · Software taxonomy

1 Introduction

Free and open source software (FOSS) has flourished in the past decade. GitHub, the leading repository for FOSS projects, now hosts more than 50 million projects (not all FOSS). These projects vary in software quality, project maturity, documentation, and support, and hence in their suitability for widespread use. Projects in their early stages aren't mature enough for use outside the development team and the small band of brave souls who are willing to try almost any piece of software and accept the results.

Over time, some of these projects will thrive, becoming stable and useful software, while other projects will be abandoned, with little or nothing to show for the effort. High quality open source software (FOSS) allows developers to incorporate reliable code in their applications and to focus their efforts on other product functions. FOSS software can also allow users to avoid the costs of proprietary software for use both within their organizations and in their products.

While business decision makers, such as corporate IT managers, have a good understanding of the business models of traditional proprietary software vendors and how to work with them, open source software presents them with a new set of challenges. While some open source software is provided through vendors who offer regular releases, technical support, and professional services, other software may not have an established source of commercial support, even though the software itself is of good quality from a technical perspective.

Evaluating open source software is quite different from evaluating traditional packaged applications and tools. Open source software can be freely used according to the terms of its license (see the Open Source Definition and open source licenses at http://www.opensource.org). Traditional enterprise software vendors often provide pre-purchase support for a trial of the software. While some FOSS projects have commercial sources of training and support, most users of FOSS must seek support from online forums and documentation or, in some cases, from commercially published books. It's still uncommon for industry analysts to include open source software in their product evaluation frameworks.

For organizations without prior experience with open source software, it has, until now, been necessary to rely solely on internal evaluations and "word of mouth" recommendations. Even finding suitable candidate software can be daunting, and the process can prevent managers from trying to do so.

In the remainder of this paper, we review the initial goals and the experience with the Business Readiness Rating (Sect. 2), describe the approach of the OSSpal project (Sect. 3), describe the project status (Sect. 4), and conclude with goals for future work.

2 The Business Readiness Rating

For open source software to be widely accepted and used, it's essential to simplify the evaluation and adoption process and to increase the comfort level of decision makers in choosing and using open source software. Achieving this goal led to the concept of the Business Readiness Rating (BRR) in 2005 [1]. People often rely on reviews from trusted sources, e.g., Consumer Reports in the US, or collected opinions with summary scores, for technical and consumer products, restaurants, films, and automobiles. Some of these ratings are multidimensional, while others are a single combined score reflecting all facets of the reviewed product.

The Business Readiness Rating followed this well-established tradition, giving reviewers a framework to evaluate various characteristics of an open source project as they apply to that reviewer's specific requirements. Golden's Open Source Maturity Model (OSMM) [2] used a matrix of weights and values to calculate a maturity level for open source software. The OSMM, along with QSOS [3], and unpublished work by the consulting firm CapGemini, were all influences on the BRR approach. Subsequently, the OpenBQR project [4], within the Qualipso Project, drew upon all of these to create a new quality evaluation framework, but that effort does not appear to have progressed beyond the initial work reported in 2007.

2.1 Evaluation Categories

From discussions with evaluators, we identified categories that are important for the open source evaluation process. We used those categories, along with those found in standard evaluation process documents (such as ISO/IEC 9126 [5] and ISO/IEC 25010:2011 [6]), and condensed them to seven (initially twelve) areas for evaluation:

- Functionality
  How well will the software meet the average user's requirements?
- Operational Software Characteristics
  How secure is the software? How well does the software perform? How well does the software scale to a large environment? How good is the UI? How easy to use is the software for end-users? How easy is the software to install, configure, deploy, and maintain?
- Support and Service
  How well is the software component supported? Is there commercial and/or community support? Are there people and organizations that can provide training and consulting services?
- Documentation
  Is there adequate tutorial and reference documentation for the software?
- Software Technology Attributes
  How well is the software architected? How modular, portable, flexible, extensible, open, and easy to integrate is it? Are the design, the code, and the tests of high quality? How complete and error-free are they?
- Community and Adoption
  How well is the component adopted by community, market, and industry? How active and lively is the community for the software?
- Development Process
  What is the level of the professionalism of the development process and of the project organization as a whole?

The first four categories are quite similar to those used to evaluate proprietary, i.e., closed source, software. For the latter three topics, it is usually easier to obtain the data for an open source project. In an open source project, the size of the user community is important for assessing the availability of informal support available, and the speed with which a posted question might be answered or a problem in the code might be fixed. Open source projects contain extensive data on the size of the development team and the list of outstanding issues, as well as the number and frequency of releases, data that is difficult, if not impossible, to obtain from closed source products. In this way, the project data can be used in the evaluation process, thus adding a quantitative aspect to what has traditionally been an informal process.

The term "Operational Software Characteristics" refers to those aspects of a software system that can be evaluated without access to the source code. It includes such quality-related areas as reliability, performance, scalability, usability, installability, security, and standards compliance. Evaluating "Software Technology Attributes" involves access to the source code to review software architecture, code quality, and internal documentation.

As additional examples, vendor support, standards compliance, test coverage, and the presence of published books are characteristics that indicate a high degree of readiness for an open source component. Different organizations can and should apply different priorities and weightings to these categories (and perhaps to subcategories), based on the intended use of the software and their risk acceptance profile.

In summary, the BRR was conceived as an open and standard model to assess software to increase the ease and correctness of evaluation, and accelerate the adoption of open source software. Such a model should include the crucial requirements of a good software rating model — that it be complete, simple, adaptable, and consistent.

2.2 Experience and Shortcomings of the BRR

The BRR was used informally for many software evaluations since its initial release in 2005. As a manual process, it failed to gain much traction in the community. We attribute that situation primarily to the absence of automated tools to assist in the calculation, but also because of personal situations affecting team members. In addition, we found that business users of FOSS were rarely willing to take the time and effort to contribute their assessments back to the community, sometimes because they viewed their studies as having proprietary value to their companies. But the problems went well beyond those, and it took us some time to recognize them fully.

First, in most cases, it was easy to estimate which FOSS projects would receive a high BRR score, based on high awareness of the project, along with existing documentation and commercial support. FOSS projects such as MySQL and OpenOffice were mature, well-supported projects, well-suited for organizational adoption.

Next, a numeric score alone fails to reveal necessary details about a FOSS component, particularly how well it works in practice, as well as individual issues that can't be captured in the evaluation subcategories. That's particularly true of the functionality category, where a complex piece of software may be created to perform multiple functions, but may not do all of them satisfactorily for a specific requirement. The BRR didn't have a way to evaluate in detail the functionality of a FOSS product in a specific software category, nor could one easily do an evaluation based on a single key characteristic such as "security".

Third, using the BRR requires finding candidate FOSS software to evaluate. Many organizations lack internal expertise with FOSS software, and thus don't know where to begin, especially when they don't fully understand the concepts of FOSS. Doing a search for "open source content management systems", for example, yields a vast number of results (148 M when one of the authors tried it), that provide very little help to the user. Even if the search led the organization to cmsmatrix.org, which provides comparative information on content management systems (CMS), there are more than 1200 listed CMS's. In short, without previous FOSS experience or the use of external consultants, an organization isn't likely to be successful finding high-quality FOSS candidates this way. It was initially difficult for us to appreciate how challenging it is for someone without FOSS experience and technical knowledge to find FOSS software. For those users, it's easier to rely on opinions provided by IT industry analysts, which are almost exclusively limited to commercial software products and services.

Finally, and most significantly, we found that people rely heavily on the opinions of others, including both peers and "experts". The numeric score from the BRR would help them to form a short list of candidates for their use, but they then wanted to see reviews or experience reports for those candidates.

All of these issues convinced us to take the project in a different direction while remaining focused on the goal of helping people find high-quality FOSS software that they could successfully adopt and use.

3 From BRR to OSSpal

3.1 Overview of Changes to the Model

We changed the project name to OSSpal because we thought that the concept of finding FOSS was broader than just "business" and we wanted a clean break with the BRR approach. But the new name had another nice property, namely the double meaning of "pal". In American and UK English, "pal" is an informal term for a friend, hence OSSpal. But the name was also chosen as a tribute to the late Murugan Pal, a key cofounder of the BRR project.

There are several major differences between OSSpal and the BRR, along with numerous less significant changes. First, we removed the calculated score, based on our previously-noted observation that the single digit result was not valuable to users, particularly because it hid the details of the seven evaluation criteria, which in turn hid the lower level details of such key areas as operational characteristics and functionality. Second, given the difficulty that people have in finding candidate FOSS software, we decided to create short lists for them. In other words, we curated FOSS projects, using some quantitative measures, including the number of commits, the number of forks, and the number of subscribers. Note that these metrics are not specifically correlated to FOSS quality, but rather to the level of project activity. We leave the assessment of quality to the individual reviewers of a project.

Furthermore, we grouped those projects into categories, based on the software taxonomy produced annually by the International Data Corporation (IDC) [7]. This grouping allowed us to define both generic evaluation criteria and category-dependent evaluation criteria. Finally, we built a website, using the open source Drupal content management system (CMS) [8], organizing the projects along the lines of the IDC taxonomy so that users could search by name and category, and allow registered users to enter their own reviews of specific projects.

We explored other sites that provide evaluation of FOSS projects. Of these, the most significant one is OpenHub (formerly Ohloh) [9], managed by BlackDuck Software. OpenHub collects data from open source repositories (forges) such as GitHub. Available information includes the project status, the number of contributors, the programming languages used, the number of contributions made by individual contributors, and metrics of project activity. Site visitors can leave an overall rating and a written review of individual projects, but the rating is simply based on a 1-to-5 star scale, intended to cover all aspects of the project, without the granularity used in OSSpal. Nonetheless, the detailed information provided on OpenHub is extremely valuable, especially for developers looking to join and contribute to a project, and we decided to provide a link between projects on OSSpal and the detailed developer-related data on OpenHub.

The OSSpal approach differs from other evaluation approaches, in that it uses metrics to find qualifying FOSS projects in the various categories, but leaves the assessment of quality and functionality of individual projects to external reviewers, who may also add informal comments to their scores.

3.2 Implementation and the Quick Assessment Tool

Implementation of a site for searching and adding projects, as well as adding user reviews, was a principal goal for the OSSpal project, especially since the absence of automated tools was a major shortcoming of the earlier BRR effort. We chose to build OSSpal on Drupal because using a CMS allowed us to greatly reduce the amount of coding needed and thus devote more effort to creating the content. In retrospect, we are very pleased with this decision. The Drupal core Taxonomy module was particularly helpful, as we were easily able to map software categories from the IDC taxonomy into a Drupal taxonomy, and thus associate FOSS projects with a category in the taxonomy. Furthermore, it's easy to modify the taxonomy as IDC modifies their taxonomy. We also gained the flexibility to modify the implementation taxonomy as needed. While our goal was to stay as close to the IDC taxonomy as possible, we found a few areas, particularly in the area of application development software, where we wanted a finer granularity. Making that change allowed us to refine the functionality for different types of application development languages, environments, and tools.

The quality attributes of FOSS projects can be classified into two general categories, hard metrics and soft metrics. Hard metrics are objective quantifiable measurements, covering most attributes in areas of software technology and development process. They can be collected efficiently through sending API calls to GitHub and Open Hub based on automated scripts. Soft metrics are subjective qualitative measurements, covering most attributes in areas of operational software characteristics as well as service and support.

To make the collection process of the hard metrics more efficient, we developed a web service to gather quantifiable FOSS project information from Open Hub and GitHub to determine if a FOSS project is high quality. Instead of searching for project attributes manually, the relevant attributes are returned to the user after querying the project's name in our web service. A user simply enters the name of a FOSS project into the search bar of the web service, and the script will display the hard metrics for the project after querying Open Hub and GitHub. The project information that is returned to the user includes attributes such as, number of project contributors, number of commits, lines of code, and project activity.

The implementation of the quick assessment tool uses the Flask web microframework, which takes the project name and uses the Open Hub and GitHub APIs to retrieve data which is returned in JSON format and then rendered as a web page. Figure 1 shows the data about project activity returned from a query on Electron. For now, we have used the quick assessment tool to screen 59 additional projects out of 101 candidate projects for inclusion on the site.

Fig. 1. Raw results of quick assessment tool for the electron project

From our work, we were able to extrapolate two key findings pertaining to hard metrics:

(1) Effectiveness of metrics. The most effective hard metrics to find high-quality FOSS projects are the number of contributors, the number of commits, the number of subscribers, the number of forks, and the number of open issues.
(2) Thresholds of metrics. With trial and error, the optimal threshold values for each effective hard metric is identified to meet the quality baseline for including new projects. Such metrics, for example, are the number of commits >1000, the number of forks >100, and the number of subscribers >50.

3.3 A Note About FOSS Quality

We have used, but not defined, the term "high-quality FOSS software". That's intentional, since there are a large number of definitions for "software quality". Miguel et al. [10] reviewed numerous software quality models for evaluating software products (without regard to source code availability). Their comparison of six different basic quality models yielded 29 different characteristics considered by one or more of the models. Ruiz and Robinson [11] published an extensive literature review to identify many different measures of open source quality, grouped by product quality (16 measures), process quality (12 measures), and community quality (11 measures), drawn from more than 20 different relevant articles. Hauge et al. [12] performed an extensive study on adoption of FOSS software in software-intensive organizations. However, their focus was primarily on organizational issues in adoption, rather than on the quality of the software being adopted. The SQO-OSS [13] quality model is interesting because it is specific to FOSS software and focuses on measurable criteria, but our experience from the earlier BRR effort is that some important quality aspects, such as usability, cannot be scored numerically.

Our approach was to include quality characteristics in the list of items that a reviewer could address. Every review of a FOSS component leaves a place for the reviewer to evaluate both generic and specific features of the software. The initial set of generic quality-related features are: installability, usability, robustness, security, and scalability, as well as an overall assessment. Note that it is difficult to find metrics for these five aspects. The set of specific features depends on the category of the software, where the list of features draws from the IDC taxonomy for that category. This aspect of the review allows reviewers to address the important quality issue of how well the software does what it is supposed to do. In summary, a thorough review of a FOSS component could combine quantitative items, as found in SQO-OSS, with an averaged score of community ratings for the generic and category-specific properties.

3.4 Using the OSSpal Site

The user of the OSSpal site can browse by category or can search by category or project name. In that way, the user might find the Electron project, and would then see the information shown in Fig. 2.

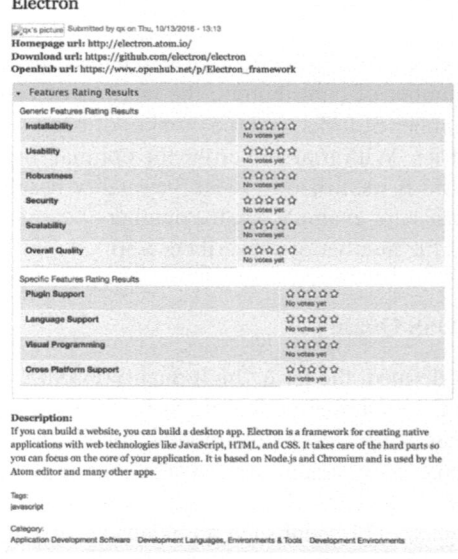

Fig. 2. OSSpal display for electron project

The information presented about Electron shows the user the location for the project home page, the software download page, and the detailed project information on OpenHub. The main section presents an average of the ratings, with the top section addressing generic software product issues and the lower section focused on features specific to its category. In this case, the project is newly listed, so there are no reviews to summarize. Once there are reviews for the project, a user can scroll through them to see the individual ratings and reviewer comments, ten reviews to a web page.

Since the site currently contains a relatively small number of FOSS projects, we wanted to simplify the process for users to propose a new project for inclusion, and included a form on the OSSpal site for that purpose (see Fig. 3). As with traditional open source projects, the average user cannot commit a new project to the directory.

Contribute New Project

Submitted by willQian on Sun, 11/27/2016 - 21:19

Project Name *

Category

Version Number

Homepage or Github URL

Contact Name

Contact Email *

Project Description

Submit

Fig. 3. Form for proposing a new FOSS project for the OSSpal site

Instead, the proposal is scored against the Quick Assessment metrics for possible site inclusion.

4 Status and Future Directions

At the outset, the OSSpal site has more than 300 FOSS projects identified by the OSSpal team, allocated among the 86 IDC categories. Initially, there are no registered users, and hence no reviews of those projects. However, we expect this situation to change quickly once the publicity spreads. We also expect the number of projects to grow significantly, with some projects added by the OSSpal core team but most submitted by the public. As noted, we have developed a tool for quickly assessing candidate projects for inclusion on the OSSpal site, but we believe that further refinement is needed, especially as the number of projects grows and as some FOSS projects become outdated or supplanted by newer projects.

As these numbers increase, the OSSpal site can provide data for analyzing and understanding the process by which people find and evaluate software. We also hope that the IT industry analysts will also draw upon the results of submitted reviews and include FOSS projects, particularly those with commercial support, to their lists of recommended software for their clients.

Another important issue involves handling successive versions of FOSS projects. Of course, the information associated with the FOSS project should be kept up-to-date. Beyond that, though, is the question of how to associate user reviews with software versions, particularly when minor updates are released frequently. Major releases of a software project may have a significant impact on overall quality. It's not unusual for such releases to address a major concern, resulting in greatly improved performance or user interfaces. Thus, it can be valuable to tie evaluations to specific versions of a FOSS project. For example, Drupal 7 was released in early 2011 (after a code freeze in early 2009) and is still being maintained, with Drupal 7.54 being the current version at the time of this writing, even though Drupal 8 was released in November, 2015. On the surface, it seems straightforward to separate reviews of Drupal 7 from Drupal 8, but it's not clear that reviews of Drupal 7.43 should be separated from reviews of Drupal 7.44 (or perhaps anything newer), since the release frequency is approximately once per month. However, the Google Play Store for Android software handles reviews for each release of each app separately. The eventual solution may be to offer multiple options to the user, but that remains a research question.

Finally, there is work to be done with the site functionality and infrastructure. The current OSSpal.org site is hosted on a shared Linux server, which is adequate for light site traffic. As popularity increases, it will become necessary to migrate the site, initially to a dedicated server, and eventually to a dynamically scalable, cloud-based environment. A second issue involves analysis of the site visitors, particularly the source(s) of reviews. The success of OSSpal depends on reliable reviews and the recognition of efforts by people to unfairly influence the overall ratings; this is a problem already faced on a large scale by numerous well-known sites that accept reviews from the public, and we will have to address it in the context of OSSpal so that the results are not skewed.

These projects are just a representative sample of important issues for the OSSpal project. Addressing these issues, among others, will make it possible for the project to help organizations find and adopt FOSS projects.

Acknowledgments. We are grateful to the early sponsors of the Business Readiness Rating project and the lead author's related research: Google, HP, IBM, and Intel. We are pleased to acknowledge the other co-founders of the BRR project: Pete Kronowitt, Nat Torkington, and the late Murugan Pal. Finally, we appreciate the contributions of former Carnegie Mellon University Silicon Valley students (Anirudh Bhargava, Sneha Kedlaya, Poorva Jain, and Pramothini Dhandapany) for their help with the initial version of the OSSpal site and the set of FOSS projects.

References

1. Wasserman, A.I., Pal, M., Chan, C.: Business readiness rating for open source. In: Proceedings of the EFOSS Workshop, Como, Italy (2006)
2. Golden, B.: Succeeding with Open Source. Addison Wesley, Boston (2004)
3. Semeteys, R. et al.: Method for Qualification and Selection of Open Source software (QSOS), version 1.6, Atos Origin (2006). http://www.qsos.org

4. Taibi, D., Lavazza, L., Morasca, S.: OpenBQR: a framework for the assessment of OSS. In: Feller, J., Fitzgerald, B., Scacchi, W., Sillitti, A. (eds.) OSS 2007. ITIFIP, vol. 234, pp. 173–186. Springer, Boston, MA (2007). doi:10.1007/978-0-387-72486-7_14
5. ISO: Software Engineering – Product Quality – Part 1: Quality Model. ISO/IEC 9126-1:2001. International Standards Organization, Geneva (2001)
6. ISO: Systems and Software Engineering – Systems and software Quality Requirements and Evaluation (SQuaRE) – System and Software Quality Models. ISO/IEC 25010: 2011. International Standards Organization, Geneva (2011)
7. International Data Corporation Software Taxonomy 2016. International Data Corporation, Framingham, MA (2016). https://www.idc.com/getdoc.jsp?containerId=US41572216
8. Drupal, 27 February 2017. drupal.org
9. OpenHub, 27 February 2017. openhub.net
10. Miguel, J.P., Mauricio, D., Rodríguez, G.: A review of software quality models for the evaluation of software products. Int. J. Softw. Eng. Appl. **5**(6), 31–53 (2014)
11. Samoladas, I., Gousios, G., Spinellis, D., Stamelos, I.: The SQO-OSS quality model: measurement-based open source software evaluation. In: Russo, B., et al. (eds.) Open Source Development, Communities and Quality. IFIP International Federation for Information Processing, vol. 275, pp. 237–248. Springer, Boston (2008)
12. Hauge, Ø., Ayala, C., Conradi, R.: Adoption of open source software in software-intensive organizations–A systematic literature review. Inf. Softw. Technol. **52**(11), 1133–1154 (2010)
13. Ruiz, C., Robinson, W.: Measuring open source quality: a literature review. Int. J. Open Sour. Softw. Process. **3**(3), 189–206 (2013)

Open Access This chapter is licensed under the terms of the Creative Commons Attribution 4.0 International License (http://creativecommons.org/licenses/by/4.0/), which permits use, sharing, adaptation, distribution and reproduction in any medium or format, as long as you give appropriate credit to the original author(s) and the source, provide a link to the Creative Commons license and indicate if changes were made.

The images or other third party material in this chapter are included in the chapter's Creative Commons license, unless indicated otherwise in a credit line to the material. If material is not included in the chapter's Creative Commons license and your intended use is not permitted by statutory regulation or exceeds the permitted use, you will need to obtain permission directly from the copyright holder.

Longitudinal Analysis of the Run-up to a Decision to Break-up (Fork) in a Community

Amirhosein "Emerson" Azarbakht[✉] and Carlos Jensen

School of Electrical Engineering and Computer Science, Oregon State University,
1148 Kelley Engineering Center, Corvallis, OR 97331, USA
{azarbaka,carlos.jensen}@oregonstate.edu

Abstract. In this paper, we use a developer-oriented statistical approach to understand what causes people in complex software development networks to decide to fork (break away), and what changes a community goes through in the run-up to a decision to break-up. Developing complex software systems is complex. Software developers interact. They may have the same or different goals, communication styles, or values. Interactions can be healthy or troubled. Troubled interactions cause troubled communities, that face failure. Some of these failures manifest themselves as a community split (known as forking). These failures affects many people; developers and users. Can we save troubled projects? We statistically model the longitudinal socio-grams of software developers and present early indicators and warning signs that can be used to predict an imminent break-up decision.

1 Introduction

Social networks are a ubiquitous part of our social lives, and the creation of online social communities has been a natural extension of this phenomena. Social media plays an important role in software engineering, as software developers use them to communicate, learn, collaborate and coordinate with others [31]. Free and Open Source Software (FOSS) development efforts are prime examples of how community can be leveraged in software development, where groups are formed around shared interest, and depend on continued interest and involvement to stay alive [24].

Community splits in free and open source software development are referred to as forks, and are relatively common [27]. Robles et al. [27] define forking as "when a part of a development community (or a third party not related to the project) starts a completely independent line of development based on the source code basis of the project."

Although the bulk of collaboration and communication in FOSS communities occurs online and is publicly accessible for researchers, there are still many open questions about the social dynamics in FOSS communities. Projects may go through a metamorphosis when faced with an influx of new developers or the involvement of an outside organization. Conflicts between developers' divergent visions about the future of the project may lead to forking of the project and dilution of the community. Forking, either as an acrimonious split when there is a conflict, or as a friendly divide when new features are experimentally added, affect the community [8].

Previous research on forking ranges from the study by Robles et al. [27] that identified 220 significant FOSS projects that have forked over the past three decades, and compiled a comprehensive list of the dates and reasons for forking to the study by Baishakhi et al. [7] on post-forking porting of new features or bug fixes from peer projects. It encompasses works of Nyman on developers' opinions about forking [26], developers motivations for performing forks [23], the necessity of code forking as tool for sustainability [25], and Syeed's work on sociotechnical dependencies in the BSD projects family [32].

Most existing research on forking, however, is post-hoc. It looks at the forking events in retrospect and tries to find the outcome of the fork; what happened after the fork happened. The run-up to the forking events are seldom studied. This leaves several questions unanswered: Was it a long-term trend? Was the community polarized, before forking happened? Was there a shift of influence? Did the center of gravity of the community change? What was the tipping point? Was it predictable? Is it ever predictable? We are missing that context.

Additionally, studies of FOSS communities tend to suffer from an important limitation. They treat community as a static structure rather than a dynamic process. Longitudinal studies on open source forking are rare. To better understand and measure the evolution, social dynamics of forked FOSS projects, and integral components to understanding their evolution and direction, we need new and better tools. Before making such new tools, we need to gain a better understanding of the context. With this knowledge and these tools, we could help projects reflect on their actions, and help community leaders make informed decisions about possible changes or interventions. It will also help potential sponsors make informed decisions when investing in a project, and throughout their involvement to ensure a sustainable engagement.

We use an actor-oriented longitudinal statistical model [29] to study the evolution and social dynamics of FOSS communities, and to investigate the driving forces in formation and dissolution of communities. This paper is a part of a larger study aiming to identify better measures for influence, shifts of influence, measures associated with unhealthy group dynamics, for example a simmering conflict, in addition to early indicators of major events in the lifespan of a community. One set of dynamics we are especially interested in, are those that lead FOSS projects to fork.

2 Related Work

The free and open source software development communities have been studied extensively. Researchers have studied the social structure and dynamics of team communications [9,15–17,22], identifying knowledge brokers and associated activities [30], project sustainability [22,25], forking [3–5,24], requirement satisfaction [13], their topology [9], their demographic diversity [19], gender differences in the process of joining them [18], and the role of age and the core team in their communities [1,2,6,12,34]. Most of these studies have tended to look at community as a static structure rather than a dynamic process [11]. This makes it hard to determine cause and effect, or the exact impact of social changes.

Post-forking porting of new features or bug fixes from peer projects happens among forked projects [7]. A case study of the BSD family (i.e., FreeBSD, OpenBSD, and NetBSD, which evolved from the same code base) found that 10–15% of lines in BSD release patches consist of ported edits, and on average 26–58% of active developers take part in porting per release. Additionally, They found that over 50% of ported changes propagate to other projects within three releases [7]. This shows the amount of redundant work developers need to do to synchronize and keep up with development in parallel projects.

Visual exploration of the collaboration networks in FOSS communities was the focus of a study that aimed to observe how key events in the mobile-device industry affected the WebKit collaboration network over its lifetime [33]. They found that *coopetition* (both competition and collaboration) exists in the open source community; moreover, they observed that the "firms that played a more central role in the WebKit project such as Google, Apple and Samsung were by 2013 the leaders of the mobile-devices industry. Whereas more peripheral firms such as RIM and Nokia lost market-share" [33].

The study of communities has grown in popularity in part thanks to advances in social network analysis. From the earliest works by Zachary [35] to the more recent works of Leskovec et al. [20,21], there is a growing body of quantitative research on online communities. The earliest works on communities was done with a focus on information diffusion in a community [35]. The study by Zachary investigated the fission of a community; the process of communities splitting into two or more parts. They found that fission could be predicted by applying the Ford-Fulkerson min-cut algorithm [14] on the group's communication graph; "the unequal flow of sentiments across the ties" and discriminatory sharing of information lead to subcommunities with more internal stability than the community as a whole [35].

3 Research Goals

Social interactions reflect the changes the community goes through, and so, it can be used to describe the context surrounding a forking event. Social interactions in FOSS can happen, for example, in the form of mailing list email correspondence, bug report issue follow-ups, and source code contributions and co-authoring. We consider some forking decisions [27] to be socially related, such that, they should have left traces in the developers' interactions data. Such traces may be identified using longitudinal modeling of the interactions, without digging into the contents of the communications. These three reasons are (1) Personal differences among developer team, (2) The need for more community-driven development, and (3) Technical differences for addition of functionality. In this study, we analyzed, quantified and visualized how a community is structured, how it evolves, and the degree to which community involvement changes over time. Our over-arching research objective was to identify these traces/social patterns associated with different types of undesirable forking

R.G. 1: Do forks leave traces in the collaboration artifacts of open source projects in the period leading up to the fork? To study the properties of possible social patterns, we need to verify their existence. More specifically, we need to check whether the possible social patterns are manifested in the collaboration artifacts of open source projects, e.g., mailing list data, issue tracking systems data, source code data. This is accomplished by statistical modeling of developer interactions as explained in more detail in Sect. 4.

R.G. 2: What are the traces that can explain longitudinal changes in sociograms in run-up to a forking event? What quantitative measure(s) can be used as an early warning sign of an inflection point (fork)? Are there metrics that can be used to monitor the odds of change, (e.g. forking-related patterns) ahead of time? This will be accomplished by statistical modeling of developer interactions as explained in more detail in Sect. 4.

4 Methodology

Detecting change patterns, requires gathering relevant data, cleaning it, and analyzing it. In the following subsections, we describe the proposed process in detail. Figure 1 shows the overview of our methodology.

4.1 Data Collection

The data collected were developer mailing lists, where developers' interact by sending and receiving emails, and source-code repository contribution logs, where developers interact by modifying the code. The sociograms were formed based on interactions among developers in these settings. For the purpose of our larger study, not included in this paper, we gathered data for 13 projects, in three categories of forking, plus a control group. We have included the data for a project that forked in 2010. The name is left out for anonymity, to prevent defaming a project, and to prevent individuals from becoming target of blame, in case our findings may be misused. Mailing list data was cleaned such that the sender and receiver email ID case-sensitivity differences would be taken into account, to prevent duplicity. The Source Code repository version control logs were used to capture the source code activity levels of the developers who had contributed more than a few commits. The set of the developers who had both mailing list activity and source code repository activity formed the basis of the socio-grams we used in our analysis. The time period for which data was collected is one year leading to when the decision to break-up (fork) happened. This should capture the social context of the run-up to the forking event.

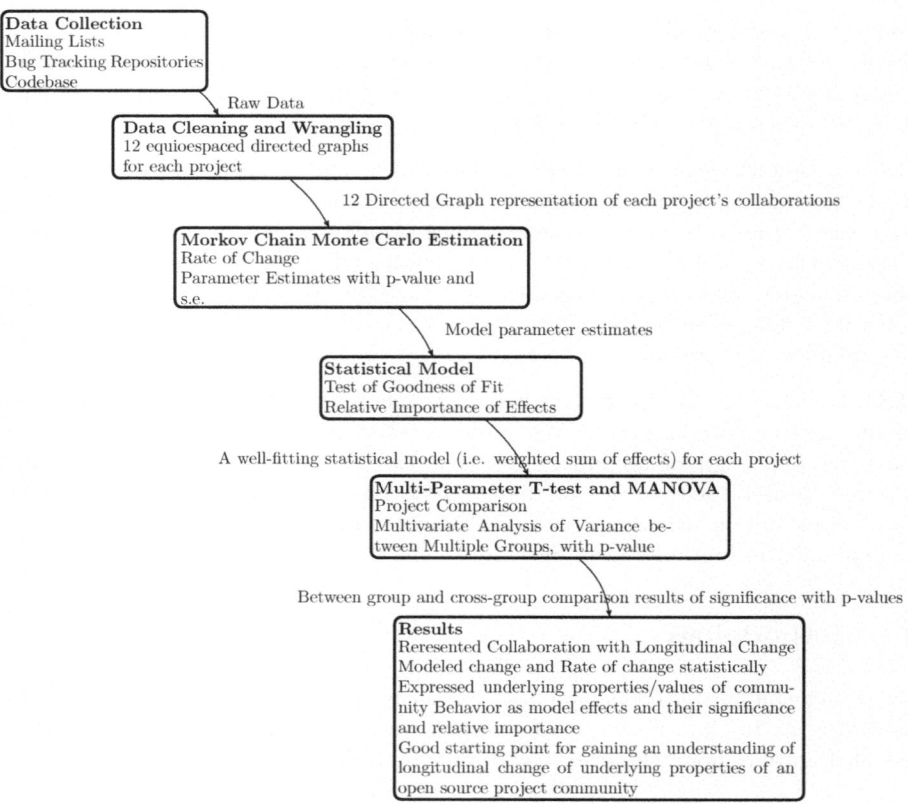

Fig. 1. The methodology in a glance

Social connections and non-connections can be represented as graphs, in which the nodes represent actors (developers) and the edges represent the interaction(s) between actors or lack thereof. Such graphs can be a snapshot of a network – a static sociogram – or a changing network, also called a dynamic sociogram. In this phase, we process interactions data to form a communication sociogram of the community. Two types of analysis can be done on sociograms: Either a *cross-sectional* study, in which only one snapshot of the network is looked at and analyzed; or a *longitudinal* study, in which several consecutive snapshots of the network are looked at and studied. We are interested in patterns in the run-up to forks, therefore, unlike most existing research on forking, we did a longitudinal study. We formed 10 equispaced consecutive time-window snapshots of the socio-grams for the community, using the mailing list interaction data and the source code repository commit activity data. These socio-grams were used to find a well-fitting statistical model that would explain how they changed from time-window t_1 through time-window t_{10}.

4.2 The Statistical Model

Longitudinal evolution of a network data is the result of many small atomic changes occurring between the consecutively observed networks. In our case, software developers are the actors in the networks, and they can form a connection with another developer, break off an existing connection, or maintain their status quo. These are the four possibilities of atomic change within our evolving networks: (1) forming a new tie; (2) breaking off an existing tie; (3) maintaining a non-connection; and (4) maintaining a connection. We assume a continuous-time network evolution, even though our observations are made at two or more discrete time points.

The state-of-the-art in studying longitudinal social networks, is the idea of *actor-oriented models* [29], based on a model of developers changing their outgoing ties as a consequence of a stochastic optimization of an *objective function*. This framework assumes that the observed networks at discrete times, are outcomes of a continuous-time Markov process. In the case of open source developers, the actor-oriented model, can be informally described as OpenSourceDeveloper-oriented model, in which, it is assumed that developers are in charge of their communication and collaboration choices. They choose to have interactions with certain other developers and/or they choose to stop having interactions with another developer. In short, they have autonomy in choosing their connections.

Let the data for our statistical developer-oriented model be M repeated observations on a network with g developers. The M observed networks (at least two) are represented as directed graphs with adjacency matrices $X(t_m) = (X_{ij}(t_m))$ for $m = 1, ..., M$, where i and j range from a to g. The variable X_{ij} shows whether at time t there exists a tie from i to j (value 1) or not (value 0). Be definition, $\forall i, X_{ii} = 0$ (i.e. the diagonal of the adjacency matrices).

In order to model the network evolution from $X(t_1)$ to $X(t_2)$, and so on, it is natural to treat the network dynamics as the result of a series of small atomic changes, and not bound to the observation moment, but rather as a more of less continuous process. In this way, the current network structure is a determinant of the likelihood of the changes that might happen next [10].

For each change, the model focuses on the developer whose tie is changing. We assume that developer i has control over the set of outgoing tie variables $(X_{i1}, ..., X_{ig})$ (i.e. the ith row of the adjacency matrix). The network changes one tie at a time. We call such an atomic change a *ministep*. The moment at which developer i changes one of his ties, and the kind of change that he makes, can depend on attributes represented by observed covariates, and the network structure. The moment is stochastically determined by the *rate function*, and the particular change to make, is determined by the *objective function* and the *gratification function*. We cannot calculate this complex model exactly. Rather than calculating exactly, we estimate it using a Monte Carlo Markov Chain method. The estimated model is used to test hypotheses about the forked FOSS communities.

These above three functions and their definitions taken from [28] are explained in detail the following subsections.

4.2.1 Rate Function

The *rate function* $\lambda_i(x)$ for developer i is the rate at which developer i's outgoing connections changes occur. It models how frequently the developers make ministeps. The rate function is formally defined [28] by

$$\lambda_i(x) = \lim_{dt \to 0} \frac{1}{dt} P(X_{ij}(t+dt) \neq X_{ij}(t) \quad for \quad some \quad j \in \{i, ..., g\} | X(t) = x)). \tag{1}$$

The simplest specification of the rate of change is that all developers have the same rate of change of their ties.

4.2.2 Objective Function

The *objective function* $f_i(s)$ for developer i is the value attached to the network configuration x. The idea is that, given the opportunity to make a change in his outgoing tie variables $(X_{i1}, ..., X_{ig})$, developer i selects the change that gives the greatest increase in the objective function. We assume that if there is difference between developers in their objective functions, these differences can be represented based on the model covariates [28]. For more details, please refer to [28]. The following weighted sum represents the objective function (2):

$$f_i(\beta, x) = \sum_{k=1}^{L} \beta_k s_{ik}(x) \tag{2}$$

Parameters $\beta = (\beta_1, ..., \beta_L)$ is to be estimated. Functions $s_{ik}(x)$ can be the following [28]:

4.2.2.1 Structural Effects
For the structural effects, the following were used in the objective function.

1. The reciprocity effect, which reflects the tendency toward reciprocation of connections. A high value for its model parameter will indicate a high tendency of developers for reciprocated interactions.
2. The closure effects (e.g. in friendship networks, it means, friends of friends tend to become friends) In our case, Transitive triplets effect, which models the tendency toward network closure. It reflects the preference of developers to be connected to developers with similar outgoing ties.
3. Three-cycles, may be interpreted as the tendency toward local hierarchy. It is similar to reciprocity defined for three developers, and is the opposite of hierarchy.
4. Activity, which reflects the tendency of developers with high in-degree/out-degrees to send out more outgoing connections because of their current high in-degree/out-degree.

5. Covariate effects: Developers' covariates may influence the formation or termination of ties. For example: (a) Covariate V-related activity, which reflects the developer i's out-degree multiplied by his covariate V value. (b) Covariate V-related dissimilarity, which reflects the sum of differences in covariate V values' between developer i and all developers to whom developer i is connected. We use the following developer attributes as covariates:
   - (Covariate V1) Developer's level of activity (i.e. mailing list posts per month)
   - (Covariate V1) Developer's level of contribution (i.e. code commits per month) as shown in Table 2
   - (Covariate V4) Developer's seniority as a development community member (i.e. how many total contributions they have had in the lifetime of the project)
6. out-out degree assortativity, which reflects which reflects the tendency of developers with high out-degree to be connected to other developers with high out-degrees.

4.2.3 Markov Chain Transition Rate Matrix

The components of the developers-oriented model, described above, define a continuous-time Markov chain on the space χ of all directed graphs on this set of g developers. This Markov chain is used to estimate the model parameters stochastically, instead of calculating them exactly, which is not possible for us. This Markov chain has a transition rate matrix. The transition rate matrix (also called intensity matrix), for this model is given by expression (3):

$$q_{ij}(x) = \lim_{dt \to 0} \frac{1}{dt} P\big(X(t+dt) = X(i \mapsto j) | X(t) = x\big)$$

$$= \lambda_i(x) p_{ij}(x) \quad (3)$$

Expression (3) shows the rate at which developer i makes ministeps, multiplied by the probability that he changes the arc variable X_{ij}, if he makes a ministep. Our Markov chain can be simulated by following the steps explained in [28].

4.2.4 Markov Chain Monte Carlo (MCMC) Estimation

The described statistical model for longitudinal analysis of open source software development communities is a complex model and cannot be exactly calculated, but it can be stochastically estimated. We can simulate the longitudinal evolution, and estimate the model based on the simulations. Then we can choose an estimated model that has a good fit to the network data. For details of the simulation and estimation procedures please refer to [28]. The desirable outcome for the estimation is the vector parameter $\hat{\beta}$ for which the expected and the observed vectors are the same.

5 Results

The results of parameter estimation are listed in Table 1. The parameter estimates that are statistically significant are marked with an asterisk (*) in Table 1. Recall that the weighted sum in expression (2) represents our objective function, and the effects listed in Table 1 are the parameter estimates of β_k's in expression (2).

The rate parameters represent the rate of change for the period between t_1 to t_2 for developers (i.e. how likely developers were to change ties in that time period). There's a clear trend in the rates 1–9, with a peak of 11.65 for the t_4 to t_5 time period. This suggests a significantly higher "preference" by developers for (a) forming new ties and interacting with previously non-connected developers and (b) terminating a previously connected tie. This peak value dies down as to less than 1, for the t_8 to t_9 time period at 0.79 which can be used as an early warning sign of an imminent change decision.

Table 1. Parameter estimates

Effect	Par.	(s.e.)
Rate 1	1.419	(0.402)
Rate 2	2.633	(0.919)
Rate 3	3.231	(1.222)
Rate 4	11.656	(7.158)
Rate 5	5.238	(1.871)
Rate 6	5.431	(1.901)
Rate 7	1.863	(0.520)
Rate 8	0.791	(0.258)
Rate 9	0.671	(0.206)
outdegree (density)*	−5.389	(0.300)
reciprocity	−6.448	(31.754)
transitive triplets	−0.582	(0.875)
3-cycles	−2.680	(8.084)
out-out degree(1/2) assortativity*	1.123	(0.291)
devScAct alter*	−0.021	(0.009)
devScAct ego*	0.011	(0.003)
devScAct ego x devScAct alter	−0.000	(0.000)
devMlAct alter	0.141	(0.010)
devMlAct ego	−0.037	(0.051)
devMlAct ego x devMlAct alter	0.002	(0.003)
int. devMlAct ego x devScAct ego*	0.003	(0.002)

Table 2. The list of developers source code contributions in the 10 months run-up to the forking event, sorted by total number of commits.

	Developer	t_1	t_2	t_3	t_4	t_5	t_6	t_7	t_8	t_9	t_{10}	Sum $t_1..t_{10}$
1	Anonymized Developer #1	17	54	48	22	86	298	238	154	136	210	1263
2	Anonymized Developer #2	55	100	42	58	74	156	120	16	44	4	669
3	Anonymized Developer #3	7	34	12	70	64	70	8	38	146	118	567
4	Anonymized Developer #4	21	163	54	138	64	46	38	36	0	4	564
5	Anonymized Developer #5	38	190	6	26	40	14	10	30	34	36	424
6	Anonymized Developer #6	21	0	20	58	59	35	48	41	24	80	386
7	Anonymized Developer #7	0	0	0	0	0	36	42	47	143	15	283
8	Anonymized Developer #8	23	22	9	87	72	1	1	0	0	0	215
9	Anonymized Developer #9	8	60	53	55	3	1	0	0	12	0	192
10	Anonymized Developer #10	0	0	3	81	39	12	4	8	2	4	153
11	Anonymized Developer #11	0	0	0	0	8	60	1	6	14	23	112
12	Anonymized Developer #12	2	47	30	1	7	2	0	8	0	0	97
13	Anonymized Developer #13	0	0	3	0	0	0	11	13	1	63	91
14	Anonymized Developer #14	0	0	0	0	0	0	0	8	38	40	86
15	Anonymized Developer #15	3	35	33	1	0	0	0	0	0	0	72
16	Anonymized Developer #16	3	0	0	0	0	0	0	4	17	46	70
17	Anonymized Developer #17	0	3	0	25	40	0	0	0	0	0	68
18	Anonymized Developer #18	0	0	0	55	0	9	0	1	0	1	66
19	Anonymized Developer #19	0	0	0	0	0	0	4	21	17	23	65
20	Anonymized Developer #20	0	0	0	9	15	14	11	2	6	0	57
21	Anonymized Developer #21	13	1	3	3	0	12	17	2	0	0	51
22	Anonymized Developer #22	8	18	12	0	0	0	0	0	3	4	45
23	Anonymized Developer #23	0	0	9	6	0	0	1	3	1	24	44
24	Anonymized Developer #24	0	0	0	0	0	0	13	16	3	4	36
25	Anonymized Developer #25	5	20	10	0	0	0	0	0	0	0	35
26	Anonymized Developer #26	1	0	11	2	14	7	0	0	0	0	35
27	Anonymized Developer #27	0	0	0	0	0	0	4	14	3	13	34
28	Anonymized Developer #28	3	12	4	1	5	0	0	1	1	4	31
29	Anonymized Developer #29	0	0	0	26	1	0	0	0	0	0	27
30	Anonymized Developer #30	0	0	0	0	0	0	0	0	0	26	26
31	Anonymized Developer #31	0	0	0	0	3	8	7	0	0	8	26
32	Anonymized Developer #32	0	0	0	0	10	13	0	1	0	0	24
33	Anonymized Developer #33	0	0	0	0	0	0	19	2	2	0	23
34	Anonymized Developer #34	0	0	0	16	7	0	0	0	0	0	23
35	Anonymized Developer #35	0	0	0	0	0	0	2	19	0	0	21
36	Anonymized Developer #36	0	8	11	0	0	0	0	0	0	0	19
37	Anonymized Developer #37	0	0	0	18	0	0	0	0	0	0	18
38	Anonymized Developer #38	0	0	0	0	0	0	17	0	0	0	17
39	Anonymized Developer #39	0	0	0	11	6	0	0	0	0	0	17
40	Anonymized Developer #40	0	0	0	0	0	0	0	2	0	12	14
41	Anonymized Developer #41	3	0	1	0	0	0	0	0	0	9	13
42	Anonymized Developer #42	0	0	0	0	0	0	7	2	2	2	13
43	Anonymized Developer #43	2	0	0	3	0	1	1	0	1	5	13
44	Anonymized Developer #44	0	0	0	0	0	0	0	0	8	5	13
45	Anonymized Developer #45	1	2	0	5	1	0	0	1	3	0	13
46	Anonymized Developer #46	0	0	0	0	4	5	3	0	1	0	13
47	Anonymized Developer #47	0	0	0	0	0	0	0	0	3	9	12
48	Anonymized Developer #48	0	0	0	0	0	0	10	1	0	0	11
49	Anonymized Developer #49	0	0	0	0	0	0	1	10	0	0	11
50	Anonymized Developer #50	0	6	5	0	0	0	0	0	0	0	11
51	Anonymized Developer #51	0	0	2	1	0	0	0	0	0	8	11
52	Anonymized Developer #52	0	1	0	0	0	0	0	6	2	0	9
53	Anonymized Developer #53	0	0	0	4	4	0	0	0	0	1	9
54	Anonymized Developer #54	0	0	0	0	0	0	0	0	0	9	9
55	Anonymized Developer #55	1	0	0	0	1	6	0	0	0	0	8
56	Anonymized Developer #56	1	6	1	0	0	0	0	0	0	0	8
57	Anonymized Developer #57	1	7	0	0	0	0	0	0	0	0	8
58	Anonymized Developer #58	0	0	0	0	0	0	0	0	0	8	8
59	Anonymized Developer #59	0	0	0	2	4	0	0	0	0	0	6
60	Anonymized Developer #60	0	0	1	1	0	1	1	0	0	1	5

6 Conclusion

In this study, we used a developer-oriented approach to statistically model the changes a FOSS community goes through in the run-up to a fork. The model represented tie formation, breakage, and maintenance between developers. We use 10 snapshots of the graph as observed data to estimate the influence of several effects on formation of the observed networks. We used a stochastic estimation method to estimate several model parameters of the model and used a Wald-type t-test to estimate the significance of these parameters on this longitudinal change.

The results show that the out-out degree assortativity and the outdegree (density) effects are statistically significant, which can be interpreted that developers maintained a "preference" for interacting with developers who had similar outdegree levels. For example, core developers with high levels of mailing list activity responding to messages, were more likely to be connected to other similarly behaving high-outdegree developers. Also, that top answerer/repliers on the mailing list were more likely to contact other top developers, and the community shows a preference for inter-stratum ties.

The developers' source code repository contribution level (devScAct ego) was also statistically significant, which implies developers with higher levels of source code contributions increase their outdegree more rapidly. The developers' source code repository contribution level (devScAct alter) is also statistically significant, which implies developers with higher levels of source code contributions increase their indegree more rapidly.

Perhaps, an interesting observation is the existence of significance for high activity/contribution to the source code repository, however, in contrast, there's a lack of significance for high activity on the mailing list. In summary, high levels of contribution to the source code brings you connections more rapidly, while high levels of contributions to the mailing list is not suggestive of this. This can be interpreted as a sign of meritocracy based on code, rather than talk, which captures a healthy dynamic in this project, that was forked because of addition of functionality, and was classified as a healthy fork.

7 Threats to Validity

The study findings may not be generalized. First, one reason is that the projects is this research study were selected from a pool of candidate projects, based on a filtering criteria that included availability of their data. Given access, a larger number of projects as the sample size could result in a more robust investigation.

Second, we used data from online communications. The assumption that all the communication can be captured by mining repositories is intuitively imperfect, but inevitable. Third, social interactions data is noisy, and our statistical approach might be affected because of this.

Third, the statistical model we use to model the longitudinal evolution of collaboration networks is estimated stochastically, rather than being calculated exactly. The stochastic process might not always arrive at the same results. To counter this issue, we run the algorithm several times to double-check for such irregularities.

References

1. Azarbakht, A., Jensen, C.: Drawing the big picture: temporal visualization of dynamic collaboration graphs of OSS software forks. In: Corral, L., Sillitti, A., Succi, G., Vlasenko, J., Wasserman, A.I. (eds.) OSS 2014. IFIP AICT, vol. 427, pp. 41–50. Springer, Heidelberg (2014)
2. Azarbakht, A., Jensen, C.: Temporal visualization of dynamic collaboration graphs of OSS software forks. In: Proceedings of the International Conference on Network for Social Network Analysis Sunbelt XXXIV (2014)
3. Azarbakht, A.: Drawing the big picture: analyzing FLOSS collaboration with temporal social network analysis. In: Proceedings of the 9th International Symposium on Open Collaboration. ACM (2013)
4. Azarbakht, A., Jensen, C.: Analyzing FOSS collaboration & social dynamics with temporal social networks. In: Proceedings of the 9th International Conference on Open Source Systems Doctoral Consortium (2013)
5. Azarbakht, A.: Temporal Visualization of collaborative software development in FOSS forks. In: Proceedings of the IEEE Symposium on Visual Languages and Human-Centric Computing (2014)
6. Azarbakht, E.A.: Longitudinal analysis of collaboration graphs of forked open source software development projects using an actor-oriented social network analysis. In: Proceedings of the International Network for Social Network Analysis Sunbelt Conference (2016)
7. Baishakhi R., Wiley, C., Kim, M.: REPERTOIRE: a cross-system porting analysis tool for forked software projects. In: Proceedings of the 20th ACM SIGSOFT International Symposium on Foundations of Software Engineering. ACM (2012)
8. Bezrukova, K., Spell, C.S., Perry, J.L.: Violent splits or healthy divides? Coping with injustice through faultlines. Pers. Psychol. **63**(3), 719–751 (2010)
9. Bird, C., Pattison, D., D'Souza, R., Filkov, V., Devanbu, P.: Latent social structure in open source projects. In: Proceedings of the 16th ACM SIGSOFT international Symposium on Foundations of software engineering. ACM (2008)
10. Coleman, J.S.: Introduction to Mathematical Sociology. The Free Press of Glencoe, New York (1964)
11. Crowston, K., Wei, K., Howison, J., Wiggins, A.: Free/Libre open-source software development: what we know and what we do not know. ACM Comput. Surv. **44**(2) (2012). Article 7
12. Davidson, J., Naik, R., Mannan, A., Azarbakht, A., Jensen, C.: On older adults in free/open source software: reflections of contributors and community leaders. In: Proceedings of the IEEE Symposium on Visual Languages and Human-Centric Computing (2014)
13. Ernst, N., Easterbrook, S., Mylopoulos, J.: Code forking in open-source software: a requirements perspective. arXiv preprint arXiv:1004.2889 (2010)
14. Ford, L.R., Folkerson, D.R.: A simple algorithm for finding maximal network flows and an application to the Hitchcock problem. Can. J. Math. **9**, 210–218 (1957)
15. Guzzi, A., Bacchelli, A., Lanza, M., Pinzger, M., van Deursen, A.: Communication in open source software development mailing lists. Proceedings of the 10th Conference on Mining Software Repositories. IEEE Press (2013)

16. Howison, J., Inoue, K., Crowston, K.: Social dynamics of free and open source team communications. In: Damiani, E., Fitzgerald, B., Scacchi, W., Scotto, M., Succi, G. (eds.) OSS 2006. IFIP AICT, vol. 203, pp. 319–330. Springer, Boston (2006)
17. Howison, J., Conklin, M., Crowston, K.: FLOSSmole: a collaborative repository for FLOSS research data and analyses. Int. J. Inf. Technol. Web Eng. **1**(3), 17–26 (2006)
18. Kuechler, V., Gilbertson, C., Jensen, C.: Gender Differences in Early Free and Open Source Software Joining Process. In: Hammouda, I., Lundell, B., Mikkonen, T., Scacchi, W. (eds.) OSS 2012. IFIP AICT, vol. 378, pp. 78–93. Springer, Heidelberg (2012)
19. Kunegis, J., Sizov, S., Schwagereit, F., Fay, D.: Diversity dynamics in online networks. In: Proceedings of the 23rd ACM Conference on Hypertext and Social Media (2012)
20. Leskovec, J., Kleinberg, J., Faloutsos, C.: Graphs over time: densification laws, shrinking diameters and possible explanations. In: Proceedings of the SIGKDD International Conference on Knowledge Discovery and data Mining (2005)
21. Leskovec, J., Lang, K.J., Dasgupta, A., Mahoney, M.W.: Statistical properties of community structure in large social and information networks. In: Proceedings of the 17th International Conference on World Wide Web. ACM (2008)
22. Nakakoji, K., Yamamoto, Y., Nishinaka, Y., Kishida, K., Ye, Y.: Evolution patterns of open-source software systems and communities. In: Proceedings of the international Workshop on Principles of Software Evolution. ACM (2002)
23. Mikkonen, T., Nyman, L.: To fork or not to fork: fork motivations in SourceForge projects. In: Hissam, S.A., Russo, B., de Mendonça Neto, M.G., Kon, F. (eds.) OSS 2011. IFIP AICT, vol. 365, pp. 259–268. Springer, Heidelberg (2011)
24. Nyman, L.: Understanding code forking in open source software. In: Proceedings of the 7th International Conference on Open Source Systems Doctoral Consortium (2011)
25. Nyman, L., Mikkonen, T., Lindman, J., Fougère, M.: Forking: the invisible hand of sustainability in open source software. In: Proceedings of SOS 2011: Towards Sustainable Open Source (2011)
26. Nyman, L.: Hackers on forking. In: Proceedings of the International Symposium on Open Collaboration (2014)
27. Robles, G., Gonzalez-Barahona, J.M.: A comprehensive study of software forks: dates, reasons and outcomes. In: Hammouda, I., Lundell, B., Mikkonen, T., Scacchi, W. (eds.) OSS 2012. IFIP AICT, vol. 378, pp. 1–14. Springer, Heidelberg (2012)
28. Snijders, T.A.B.: Models for longitudinal network data. In: Models and Methods in Social Network Analysis, vol. 1, pp. 215–247 (2005)
29. Snijders, T.A.B., Van de Bunt, G.G., Steglich, C.E.G.: Introduction to stochastic actor-based models for network dynamics. Soc. Netw. **32**(1), 44–60 (2010)
30. Sowe, S., Stamelos, L., Angelis, L.: Identifying knowledge brokers that yield software engineering knowledge in OSS projects. Inf. Softw. Technol. **48**, 1025–1033 (2006)
31. Storey, M., Singer, L., Cleary, B., Figueira Filho, F., Zagalsky, A.: The (R) Evolution of social media in software engineering. In: Proceedings of the on Future of Software Engineering. ACM (2014)
32. Syeed, M.M.: Socio-technical dependencies in forked OSS projects: evidence from the BSD family. J. Softw. **9**(11), 2895–2909 (2014)
33. Teixeira, J., Lin, T.: Collaboration in the open-source arena: the webkit case. In: Proceedings of the 52nd ACM Conference on Computers and People Research (SIGSIM-CPR 2014). ACM (2014)

34. Torres, M.R.M., Toral, S.L., Perales, M., Barrero, F.: Analysis of the core team role in open source communities. In: International Conference on Complex, Intelligent and Software Intensive Systems. IEEE (2011)
35. Zachary, W.: An information flow model for conflict and fission in small groups. J. Anthropol. Res. **33**(4), 452–473 (1977)

Open Access This chapter is licensed under the terms of the Creative Commons Attribution 4.0 International License (http://creativecommons.org/licenses/by/4.0/), which permits use, sharing, adaptation, distribution and reproduction in any medium or format, as long as you give appropriate credit to the original author(s) and the source, provide a link to the Creative Commons license and indicate if changes were made.

The images or other third party material in this chapter are included in the chapter's Creative Commons license, unless indicated otherwise in a credit line to the material. If material is not included in the chapter's Creative Commons license and your intended use is not permitted by statutory regulation or exceeds the permitted use, you will need to obtain permission directly from the copyright holder.

Author Index

Abate, Pietro 139
Andrade, Sandro 34
Avelino, Guilherme 151
Azarbakht, Amirhosein "Emerson" 204

Barany, Gergö 101

Corr, Niklas 60

da Silva Amorim, Simone 89
de Almeida, Eduardo Santana 89
Di Cosmo, Roberto 139

Feist, Jonas 80
Fischer, Thomas 80
Fujibayashi, Daiki 128

Gamalielsson, Jonas 80
German, Daniel M. 69
González Quiroga, Víctor 117
Gonzalez-Barahona, Jesus M. 182
Guo, Xianzheng 193
Gustavsson, Tomas 80

Hammouda, Imed 14, 49
Hora, Andre 151

Ihara, Akinori 128
Inoue, Katsuro 69
Izquierdo, Daniel 182

Jensen, Carlos 204
Johansson, Gert 80

Kilamo, Terhi 23
Krüger, Jacob 60
Kula, Raula Gaikovina 128

Landemoo, Stefan 80
Leich, Thomas 60
Linåker, Johan 55
Lindman, Juho 14, 49
Lönroth, Erik 80
Lundell, Björn 80

Mäenpää, Hanna 23
Manabe, Yuki 69
Männistö, Tomi 23
Matsumoto, Kenichi 128
Mattsson, Anders 80
McGregor, John D. 89
McMillian, Blake 193
Mikkonen, Tommi 23
Mols, Carl-Eric 55

Oppmark, Johan 80

Passos, Leonardo 151

Qian, Kai 193

Raab, Markus 101
Robles, Gregorio 182
Rodung, Bengt 80

Saraiva, Filipe 34
Schröter, Ivonne 60
Sherwood, Paul 182
Squire, Megan 3
Suwa, Hirohiko 128
Syeed, Mahbubul 49

Teixeira, Jose 167
Tengblad, Stefan 80

Valente, Marco Tulio 151
von Flach Garcia Chavez, Christina 89

Wasserman, Anthony I. 193
Wei, Ming-Yu 193
Wnuk, Krzysztof 55
Wolf, Gunnar 117
Wu, Yuhao 69

Xu, Qian 193

Yousefi, Bahram Hooshyar 80

© The Editor(s) (if applicable) and The Author(s) 2017. This book is an open access publication.
Open Access This book is licensed under the terms of the Creative Commons Attribution 4.0 International License (http://creativecommons.org/licenses/by/4.0/), which permits use, sharing, adaptation, distribution and reproduction in any medium or format, as long as you give appropriate credit to the original author(s) and the source, provide a link to the Creative Commons license and indicate if changes were made.

The images or other third party material in this book are included in the book's Creative Commons license, unless indicated otherwise in a credit line to the material. If material is not included in the book's Creative Commons license and your intended use is not permitted by statutory regulation or exceeds the permitted use, you will need to obtain permission directly from the copyright holder.

The manufacturer's authorised representative in the EU is Springer Nature Customer Service Centre GmbH, Europaplatz 3, 69115 Heidelberg, Germany. If you have any concerns regarding our products, please contact ProductSafety@springernature.com

Printed and bound by CPI Group (UK) Ltd, Croydon, CR0 4YY
26/03/2026
02078951-0009